# Beneath
## the
# Apple Blossom

### (Book One of The Hopeful Years)

by

## KATE FROST

*LEMON TREE PRESS*

Paperback Edition 2016

ISBN 978-0-9954780-0-8

Cover design by Jessica Bell.

# Beneath

## the

# Apple Blossom

by

## KATE FROST

LEMON
TREE
PRESS

# CONTENTS

Dedication                          i

Winter                              1

Spring                             59

Summer                             91

Autumn                            139

Second Winter                     192

Second Spring                     261

Second Summer                     294

Acknowledgements                  305

From the Author                   307

# Fertility Treatment Terminology

PUPO – pregnant until proven otherwise

BFP – big fat positive

BFN – big fat negative

TTC – trying to conceive

PCOS – polycystic ovary syndrome

Downregging – use of a nasal spray to suppress production of luteinising hormone

Stimming – stimulation of ovaries via daily injections to produce multiple eggs

2ww – the two week wait between a treatment and a pregnancy test

IVF – in vitro fertilisation

ICSI – intra-cytoplasmic sperm injection (for male infertility)

FET – frozen egg transfer

Blastocyst – an embryo that has developed for five to six days in a laboratory

OHSS – ovarian hyper-stimulation syndrome (ovaries overreact to fertility drugs)

hCG – human chorionic gonadotropin (the hormone produced when implantation takes place)

Ectopic pregnancy – when a foetus develops outside the womb

Braxton Hicks – an infrequent and irregular tightening of uterine muscles

*For Nik and Leo*

# WINTER

## *Pippa*

*15th December blog post:*

### The Hopeful Years

*It starts with sex – a lot of sex. Making babies is good fun in the beginning, but after three years of trying the novelty wears off. Trust me, I know…*

Pippa's hands hovered over the keyboard. Did she really want to open up her life like this? She leant back on the sofa and stared at the flashing cursor willing her to make a decision. She'd always fancied having a blog but never found anything she could write about. Now she finally had and she was getting cold feet because it was so personal. Yet, it was something she felt passionately about, plus she thought it might be helpful, allowing her emotions to flow through her fingers. Cathartic. Anyway, she was only using her first name, wasn't plastering a photo of herself on the Internet, and who was actually going to read it? It was just a diary, except it was online. She took a deep breath and started typing.

*I've always wanted a family and I've never really been career minded. To me a job is just a job, but having a baby would mean everything. I got married three and a half years ago and we started trying on our honeymoon (we stayed at The Sarojin in Khao Lak, Thailand – so amazing!). I thought I'd be pregnant and a mummy before our first anniversary but that wasn't meant to be. It didn't happen by our second*

1

*or third one either. So here I am, three years and eight months later, thirty-four years old, about to embark on IVF. It's daunting, but finally after a year of tests and referrals we're actually being proactive and doing something.*

*So yes, this blog, The Hopeful Years, is going to chart my journey of hope, from infertility to becoming a mummy – at least in a perfect world that's what I dream will happen. Who knows, we might be that lucky.*

Pippa clicked save and logged out of WordPress. She would sleep on it, read it in the morning and then decide if she was brave enough to press 'publish'. After all, it was highly unlikely that anyone would stumble across her blog. At the very least she felt better for getting her thoughts and feelings out.

Tomorrow was a huge step, off to the fertility clinic for their planning appointment. It was the beginning. Pippa finally felt that there was hope, however slim.

Pippa ran her hands down the creases of her stripy skirt and took a deep breath. How had it come to this? All the fun of trying to get pregnant had evaporated once medical intervention and blood tests, scans and sperm samples had become involved. Getting pregnant should be the easy bit, surely? Pippa's friends seemed to have no problems; in fact, a couple of them only had to look at a man and they got knocked up.

'Pippa? Pip, honey? Did you get that?' Clive squeezed her arm.

'Do you want me to show you again?' the nurse asked.

'Yes please, sorry.'

The nurse picked up the little bottle, pierced the top with a needle and drew up the liquid. 'You then take a good pinch of skin on your stomach, plunge the needle in and slowly inject it. Simple.'

'It's the making up of the stuff that worries me,' Pippa said, looking at the bottles of powder and liquid lined up on the desk in front of them.

'You'll be fine,' the nurse said. 'There are instructions with it, and after a couple of goes you'll be a pro. Have you been on the forum? Lots of ladies have said how much it's helped them, going through a treatment cycle with other women. It might be worth taking a look.'

'I'll do that, thanks.'

With the planning appointment over, and how to do the injections floating around Pippa's head, she and Clive thanked the nurse and made their way back along the corridor and through reception to the main doors. There were a few other couples waiting as well as one or two women on their own. Most looked like they were in their mid- to late-thirties. She wondered about their stories and how far along with their treatment they were. Perhaps someone in this room was actually pregnant and waiting for a scan to confirm things.

Pippa shivered as they left the warmth of the fertility clinic and stepped outside. A blast of icy air wrapped itself around them. She tucked her chocolate-coloured snood further into the neckline of her coat and pulled on the matching hat that contrasted with her dark blonde hair. Clive hooked his arm through hers and they set off towards the car park, leaving a trail of frozen breath behind them.

'You're very quiet, Pip,' Clive said once they reached their car. 'How are you feeling about it all?'

Pippa slid on to the passenger seat and buckled up her seatbelt. 'That the situation sucks, but at least we're finally doing something positive.'

Clive turned the ignition and drove out of the fertility clinic car park. 'You never know, in a few months' time, you might be pregnant.'

Pippa bit her lip and looked back towards the hospital as they drove out of the main gate. 'They keep stressing that there's no guarantee of it working,' she said.

'Yeah, but at the same time they've given us a 60% chance of it being successful. That's way better odds than if we just keep trying naturally, which we should still do anyway. As much as possible.'

Pippa smiled and rested her hand on Clive's thigh. 'Maybe we should go see Georgie while we're in Bristol.'

'You feel up to that?' Clive took a left at the traffic lights and headed towards Bradley Stoke instead of home to Bath.

Pippa nodded. 'Yeah. Don't worry, I won't have a meltdown when I see Daisy. I promise. I feel good about things. I mean, I know IVF might not work, but at the same time it feels so positive to finally be doing something. At least now we have a chance of having a family.'

'It's our best shot.'

'It's our only shot.' Pippa hated to sound defeatist but it was the truth. Their consultant had pretty much told them it'd take a miracle to get pregnant naturally, and after more than three years of trying – and they had been trying earnestly, with passion to begin with, followed by more methodical and pressurised ovulation tests – they had nothing to show for it apart from negative pregnancy tests and disappointment. They fell silent; maybe Clive didn't want to open up any old wounds by saying the wrong thing and setting Pippa off. After all, she'd been an emotional wreck for the past couple of years and she'd be the first to admit it.

Pippa's half-sister, Georgie, lived in a detached new-build on the outskirts of Bristol. It had three good-sized bedrooms, a family bathroom, a study-come-playroom, and an open-plan lounge and kitchen-diner, but it was the complete opposite of where Pippa and Clive lived in Bath. Theirs was a two bedroom terraced Edwardian house packed with character and period features. As she rang the doorbell, Pippa thought how she and Georgie had always been the complete opposite of each other anyway, so their taste in houses, decor and indeed men would naturally be different.

'Hey there,' Georgie said as she opened the door and swept the fringe of her bobbed blonde hair away from her eyes. Her daughter Daisy had her little hands clamped tight to Georgie's leg. 'This is a nice surprise. Nathan's not home yet though, Clive.'

'Oh, that's okay,' Pippa said. 'We're not stopping long. Just thought we'd say hi as we were in Bristol.'

Georgie beckoned them through the hallway and into the kitchen with its sleek and shiny dark grey units and pale grey tiled floor.

'How do you keep it so clean with Daisy around?' Pippa ran her hand along the impractically white work surface.

'I rarely cook and I have a cleaner. Daisy, are you going to say hello to Auntie Pippa and Uncle Clive?' Daisy tucked herself even further behind Georgie's legs. 'She's a little shy of st... She's all of a sudden got shy and silly. Typical toddler.'

Strangers. Pippa knew that's what Georgie had been about to say. She hadn't really been an aunt to Daisy since she had been born eighteen months ago, but she was determined to change all that. The start of fertility treatment was the beginning of a new chapter.

'Hey there, Daisy,' Pippa said, holding out her arms. 'You going to give me a cuddle? No? That's okay – next time, eh?'

'Cup of tea?' Georgie asked, prising Daisy's chubby fingers from her thigh. 'Coffee? Daisy, why don't you run and get your toys from the playroom?'

'Coffee would be great, thanks,' Clive said, taking a seat at the breakfast bar at the end of the island.

'Decaf for me, if you have it.' Pippa leant against the end unit and played with the tassel on the zip of her handbag. Georgie raised an eyebrow. 'Because of the treatment – I'm trying to be good, to do anything that might help. No caffeine or alcohol and I'm attempting to cut out sugar.'

'Sounds miserable,' Georgie said, dropping a decaf capsule into the coffee machine.

'Well, I'm willing to do whatever it takes. Considering we only get one go at IVF on the NHS, I want to give us the best chance possible.'

'But do you really think cutting out all the fun things in life is going to up your chances?' Georgie poured frothy milk into a mug and handed it to Pippa. 'I mean, girls get knocked up all the time after drunken one night stands. Maybe you should get pissed.'

'You don't think we've tried that?' Pippa said, trying to control the edge to her voice, pinching the tassel on her handbag and wishing – not for the first time – that it was her half-sister's neck.

Clive cleared his throat and shuffled on the stool. 'I think what Pippa's trying to say is we're out of options. IVF is our only chance of having a family, and she – we – don't want to jeopardise that in any way. Giving up caffeine and alcohol is a small price to pay.'

Georgie laughed. 'Easy for you to say.' She stirred Clive's coffee and handed it to him.

'I'm doing my bit, trust me. Pip's got me dosed up on these vitamins to help boost male fertility.'

Daisy ran back in, pulling a truck loaded with wooden blocks, dolls and teddy bears. 'Waha, waha, waha, waaaaahaaaaa!'

Georgie sighed. 'It's not easy: the sleepless nights, attempting to breastfeed, changing millions of stinking nappies and puked-on vests all the time. And then when they start crawling and walking they're even harder work.'

Daisy flopped down on the middle of the kitchen floor and started pulling wooden blocks out of the truck, sending them flying across the tiles.

'I know it's not going to be easy, Georgie,' Pippa said. 'But I can't wait for all that. I would love to be suffering with morning sickness or be up all night rocking my baby to sleep. I want that more than anything.'

'I'll remind you of that when you get pregnant and are puking your guts up.'

'When – if – that happens then I'll have as much right as any pregnant woman to complain if I want to. I won't be any different then. All I'm asking is for you to not complain in front of me about lack of sleep because of Daisy. Complain away to your friends or to Mum, I just don't want to hear it when I'd do *anything* to be in your position.'

# Georgie

Georgie closed the front door behind them and breathed a sigh of relief. At least Pippa wasn't having a meltdown or being an emotional wreck for once. Even though there was a seven year gap between them they had been close until Pippa started trying for a baby and couldn't get pregnant, while Georgie got pregnant straight away.

Georgie went back into the kitchen and stared in dismay at the toy-strewn floor and Daisy sprawled out on the tiles pretending to be God knows what. Wednesday was her day off, but right now she wished she was back at work with adult conversation and problems more taxing than what to cook for dinner.

'Come on, Daisy,' Georgie said, picking a doll up by its hair from beneath the kitchen table. 'Daddy will be home soon and I want this place tidy before he gets back.'

With Daisy trailing behind her, Georgie carted the truck and toys into the living area. 'Shall we switch the Christmas lights on?'

'Yes!' Daisy screeched as she jumped on the sofa.

Georgie reached down to the switch behind the sofa and twinkling silver lights lit up the Christmas tree that filled the space by the window. Daisy danced around in front of it.

Georgie was beginning to think it had been a bad idea to host Christmas this year.

Georgie had dinner on the table when Nathan got home at 7.30pm. Late again. She'd done all the hard work of making Daisy her tea, getting her a bath and persuading her to put her pyjamas on and have a story. Finally, at just gone 7pm she'd settled down to sleep, all cosy in her sleeping bag and cuddled up to her toy rabbit. All Georgie then had the energy to do was take a shop bought cottage pie out of the freezer and put it in the microwave before boiling some peas.

After watching a bit of mindless TV and telling Nathan about Pippa and Clive popping round, they headed upstairs. Georgie sat at her dressing table and brushed her hair, wondering if she should grow it long again.

Nathan pulled pyjama bottoms and an old T-shirt on. 'We can't put our lives on hold because of your sister's feelings.'

'What?' Georgie asked, putting the brush down. 'What are you talking about?'

'We can't not have another baby because of worrying about upsetting Pippa.'

'Yes, I know that,' Georgie replied. She wiped the make-up off her face and dropped the cotton wool into the wastepaper basket. 'It's just I got pregnant like that.' She clicked her fingers in front of his face. 'And I really don't fancy telling Pippa I'm pregnant again, not until she is too.'

'You do realise that might never happen.'

'Of course. Also, I'm not ready to have another baby. I'm only beginning to feel like I've got back into the swing of work, Daisy is a handful and I'm not ready to lose my body again.'

'Wouldn't it be nice for Daisy to have a brother or sister close in age?'

'Maybe... but you're not the one who has to put their life on hold for the next two years or so while pregnant, giving birth and then dealing with a newborn plus a grumpy toddler. Can't we wait a bit, maybe until later next year, before we start thinking about having another?'

'You'll feel broody once Pippa gets pregnant,' Nathan said, climbing into bed.

'Well, if I do, that'll be fine – at least then I'll know I'm ready to have another baby.'

'You're really not now?' Nathan tucked his hands behind his head and rested back on his pillow.

'I have my hands full with Daisy. I'm forever playing catch-up. It'd be nice to take a breath before launching back into changing ten dirty nappies a day and feeding through the night.'

'We could always bottle feed the next one.'

'That's not what I mean and that's not the answer. I want my life back for a bit. Get stuck into work, further my career, you know.' Georgie slipped into bed next to Nathan and took her Kindle off the bedside table.

'Work will still be there after another baby.'

Georgie's Kindle switched on to the middle of *Fifty Shades of Grey*. She loved her Kindle, knowing that Nathan didn't really have a clue what she was reading.

She turned to him and stroked the greying stubble on his chin. 'Is it because you're older than me that you want another child so soon?' she asked.

'It is a consideration,' he said. 'Now I'm forty I keep thinking the longer we leave it the less time I'll have with them.'

Them? He was talking about more than one child even before they had more than one.

Nathan switched off his bedside lamp and closed his eyes. 'Perhaps you'll feel differently once you turn thirty.'

Georgie sighed and allowed her thoughts to turn to Christian Grey instead.

The Friday before Christmas, and just over a week after Pippa and Clive had popped round, Georgie found herself in the ladies getting changed and doing her make-up with two of her colleagues.

'I wish we weren't having a joint Christmas party with the Cardiff office,' Melinda, the office receptionist, said as she reapplied her lipstick for the third time.

'I quite like the idea.' Georgie looked in the mirror and

smoothed down her little black dress that finished modestly just above her knees but did have a plunging neckline. She turned to the side and sucked in her stomach, feeling glad she was wearing tummy control underwear. 'I am glad we're in Bristol, though, and haven't had to trek over to Cardiff. It'll be good to meet people we speak to all the time in the flesh.'

'I'm with you on that, Georgie,' Sue said. 'Josh from marketing sounds lush.'

'You just like his Welsh accent,' Melinda said, finally tucking her lipstick away in her handbag. 'He's probably ugly as anything in real life. Now Ben and Dave I would quite like to meet.'

'You mean Dave from accounts or Dave from the design team?' Georgie asked.

'Accounts. I know for a fact the other Dave is in his fifties and isn't much of a looker.'

'Oh, and Felix from marketing too,' Sue said, wafting her hand next to her face in a mock 'I'm about to faint' way. 'He has an accent to die for.'

'You two are terrible,' Georgie said, spritzing perfume on her neck. 'You do realise they could be having the same conversation about us?'

'Ooh, let them talk, Georgie,' Melinda said and gave her trademark throaty chuckle. 'At forty-four and divorced, I need all the excitement I can get. You never know, tonight might be my lucky night.'

Georgie put her arm around Melinda as they squeezed out of the door. 'I'm just looking forward to a night away from mummy duties. Oh, and lots of cocktails!'

Sue had been wrong about Josh from accounts looking as lush as he sounded but she was spot on about Felix from marketing – his smooth, deep voice and lilting Welsh accent perfectly matched his six foot frame, dark hair and model looks. It wasn't hard to imagine well-defined muscles beneath his chequered shirt.

'How old do you reckon he is?' Melinda asked, eyeing him up from where the three of them sat at the bar sipping cocktails.

'Late thirties,' Georgie said and laughed. 'Younger than you, my lovely.'

'Too young you think?'

'Not if he likes a slightly older woman…'

'I might have a chance then.' Melinda raised an eyebrow and took a sip of mojito.

'There's always hope,' Georgie said. 'I thought you liked being single.'

'I don't mind it, although I'd prefer to be with someone – always have done, so that's not down to my age. Why do you ask?'

'Ah, no reason,' Georgie replied, casting her eyes towards Felix and another of his male work colleagues from Cardiff. 'I just miss the chase – you know, the excitement of fancying someone and wondering if tonight will be the night you get to kiss them.'

'That's the cocktails talking,' Sue said, knocking her glass against Georgie's. 'You're married to a pretty damn good looking man and have that gorgeous little girl. You wouldn't really want to go back to that period of your life, would you?'

Melinda snorted. 'What would you know, Sue? You've been married for, like, forever.'

'Nah, course not,' Georgie said, taking a sip of her hummingbird cocktail and enjoying the silky smooth sweetness of banana liqueur along with a good splash of rum. 'Although being out this evening reminds me of another time and it's a weird feeling. It's probably because I got married too young.'

'That's always a mistake,' a deep Welsh voice said from behind her.

Georgie swung round on her bar stool and came face to face with Felix.

'You have first-hand knowledge of that, do you?' Melinda

asked.

'Not personally, no,' he said, his smooth Welshness holding their attention. 'I waited to marry my missus to make sure she was the one, but Jeremy here,' he pointed to the colleague he'd been talking to, a guy slightly older than him – closer to Melinda's age, Georgie noted, 'now he stupidly got married in his early twenties, divorced two years later, then married again in his early thirties. Then guess what – that didn't work out either. Married too quickly, see. You need to get to know someone well before committing.' He looked at Georgie. 'Not that I'm saying you did that… just pointing out that Jeremy is single and available.'

Georgie wiggled her wedding ring finger in the air. 'Well, as you know, I'm taken and so is Sue as she's been married for, like, forever, but Melinda…' Georgie raised her eyebrows and nudged her friend, ignoring the fact that even in the dimmed lights of the bar Melinda's cheeks had flushed.

Jeremy shook Melinda's hand then Georgie's and Sue's. 'Nice to meet you all – and I apologise for Felix painting me in such a bad light. I'm a good guy really.'

'I believe you,' Melinda said and beamed at him.

'So, you married too young?' Felix asked, perching on the empty stool next to Georgie.

'Well, I'm twenty-nine and I've been married for five years, was engaged for two before that and have an eighteen-month-old daughter, so yeah, you could say that. I sometimes think I did the marriage and kids bit too early and should have concentrated on my career.'

How easily that all slipped out, Georgie thought, and to a complete stranger too, albeit a handsome one.

'There's always time for a career,' Felix said, playing with a beer mat. 'Some people regret leaving it too late to start a family.'

'I guess so,' Georgie said. 'I know my sister feels like that now she's in her mid-thirties and is having trouble getting pregnant. She's never really been career minded and didn't meet the right guy early enough. Life's like that, I guess – not always fair.' She realised she was sharing way too much, and yet the evening continued with Georgie talking to Felix as easily as if she'd known him her whole life while the cocktails and lager flowed and the Bristol and Cardiff offices happily mingled.

'I'll find you on Facebook,' Felix said, kissing Georgie's cheek as the night ended. He lingered and she shivered as his stubble grazed her skin.

'I'm on there as Georgina,' she called after him, sighing as the Cardiff lot trailed out of the bar. She didn't want the evening to end and she certainly hadn't wanted her conversation with Felix to finish and for him to go. When she got home it'd be back to mummy and wife duties. She'd had too much fun tonight – a reminder of her pre-marriage and baby days.

# *Pippa*

It had only been just over three weeks since the planning appointment, although it felt longer with Christmas and New Year in between. Christmas had lost its magic for Pippa, which was all down to being childless and struggling through the fourth festive season since they'd started trying for a baby. Even Daisy getting excited about her new toys and wearing a cute Santa hat while they sat down for their turkey dinner failed to inject any happiness into the festivities. All Daisy, Georgie and Nathan did were remind Pippa about what she didn't have. Christmas was a time for children; it was about the excitement and expectation of waiting for Father Christmas on Christmas Eve, and then the sheer joy of Christmas morning with a full stocking at the end of the bed. Pippa longed to share those moments with a child of her own and yet another Christmas had gone by.

Once New Year's Day was over and done with, Pippa kissed goodbye to the pretence of being happy. Finally she could focus on the countdown to the start of treatment.

Receiving the box of medication was an oddly exciting event, a bit like another Christmas present despite it being filled with needles, syringes, nasal spray and a sharps box rather than chocolates and toiletries. With everything stacked neatly away in an empty kitchen cupboard, Pippa went online and logged on to the fertility centre's forum, set up a user name of Hope and added her first post to the January 'starters' thread.

*Hello, I'm starting our first cycle of IVF in two days' time after nearly four years of trying unsuccessfully to get pregnant. As far as we know it's only me with an issue as I have PCOS, so hopefully IVF will be what helps us to get our much longed for baby. I'm looking forward to getting to know you all and sharing this journey with you. The box of meds arrived today so it finally feels real now! Roll on 4th January!*

*Hope xx*

Pippa ringed the date in her diary and added two stars for good measure. Although anxious at how she'd feel and cope with the medication and invasive procedures, she was beyond excited that the potential outcome could be a baby. She closed her diary and laptop, sank on to the sofa and didn't attempt to hold back her tears.

Two hours later Pippa slicked on a rust-red lipstick that complemented the oranges and reds in her White Stuff dress. She pulled on her tan boots, her coat and added a scarf for good measure. It seemed like she hadn't been out for ages – months in fact – mainly because she hadn't felt like socialising, even with her best friend. Pippa was conscious that she was always moaning or breaking down in tears every time she saw or spoke to Sienna. Their relationship hadn't always been like this; they used to have fun, but over the past three or four years their lives had gone in drastically different directions. Tonight, however, was cause for celebration. She was feeling happy, optimistic and in the mood for celebrating the future.

Sienna, as usual, looked effortlessly cool, dressed in skintight black jeans, grey boots, and layered grey and white tops. Her long black hair was loose and fell in perfect waves, framing her tanned face. It wasn't the first time, and it wouldn't be the last, that Pippa wished she had Sienna's bone structure and Italian heritage.

Sienna leapt up from her seat at a corner table of the bar and put her arms around Pippa. 'It's so good to see you. You've taken the plunge then?'

'Just two days to go until we start treatment.'

'Nervous?'

'Of course, but excited too.'

Sienna handed her a glass of rosé.

'I can't,' Pippa said. 'I've given it up, while doing IVF.'

'Make it your last then.' Sienna clinked her glass against Pippa's as they sat down.

'You always were a bad influence.'

Sienna grinned. 'I try my hardest. Anyway, you might as well enjoy yourself before you get pregnant.'

'You do realise that IVF might not work?'

'I know, but I've got a good feeling about it. After all, you were born to be a mother.'

Pippa bit her lip and swirled the wine around her glass. She took a sip and savoured its fruitiness on her tongue. 'Maybe I'll have a lemonade instead. Start as I mean to go on. I'm sorry for being a party pooper.'

'Party pooper?' Sienna said, taking the wine away from her. 'What are you, eight?'

'Believe it or not I've really been looking forward to tonight even if I'm not drinking. I miss you, you know. How was the shoot?'

'Freezing but great fun,' Sienna said with a sigh. 'Iceland is beautiful. The crew were a class act and the actors were all pretty friendly. I miss it, you know, when I come home – that way of life, the camaraderie.'

'Well, I'm not surprised. You're around the same people day in, day out for a couple of months at a time, so it must feel strange when that all comes to an end. A bit like when we were in plays at school – minus the million-dollar budgets and famous actors.'

'Ha, yes, just like school.' Sienna winked.

'What's next?'

'I've only got these next two weeks at home and then I'm off to Croatia to scout locations for this movie about the rise of the Roman Empire being filmed later this year.'

'Why don't you and Ashton have a holiday then? I mean, I

know you travel all over the place with work, but you never just go away and relax. Do nothing. Lie on a beach for a week. I'd do that if I could.'

'It's tempting… I guess I do get restless when I'm home.'

'Does Ashton have any time off?'

'Amazingly, yes, week after next.'

'There you go, sorted. Get a last minute deal somewhere hot and exotic. It might give Ashton the perfect opportunity to propose.'

Sienna coughed and nearly spat out her mouthful of wine. 'What? Are you crazy?'

'You don't think he wants to propose?'

'I'm so not marriage material.'

'To him you are.'

Sienna raised a neatly shaped eyebrow. 'Well, I hope he's not thinking about it.' She brushed her fringe away from her eyes. 'Enough about me. How about you – are you feeling ready to start IVF?'

'Way to go changing the subject.' Pippa smiled and nodded. 'I think so, yes. It finally feels like we're doing something positive.'

The first thing Pippa did after getting home and saying hello to Clive was to log on to the forum and read her first couple of welcome messages.

*Welcome Hope! It's my first cycle too and my story is similar to yours in that we've been ttc unsuccessfully for three years as well. The difference with us is that we're having to do ICSI because it's my husband with the fertility issues (low sperm count and mobility). They can't seem to find anything wrong with me so I'm hoping that's a positive and with treatment it'll mean I can get pregnant. We start a day after you so we really will be going through it together.*

*All the luck in the world!*

*Zanzi x*

*Hellooo there Hope! Another January starter! Welcome and the very best of luck. This is my third cycle of IVF (so any questions just ask!) Hoping it's third time lucky...*

*Clover xxxx*

It was good to know that she wasn't alone. After spending the last couple of years being surrounded by friends and family getting pregnant and giving birth, she found it a refreshing thought, despite the fact it meant there were others suffering the same fate as her. She'd be going through the treatment with other women and that definitely made it less daunting. Poor Clover on cycle number three – Pippa really hoped it wouldn't come to that for them.

She closed her laptop, slid across the sofa to where Clive was watching TV, and edged her hand across his thigh. 'Fancy having another shot at making a baby the natural way?'

Clive immediately switched off the TV. 'I thought you'd never ask.' He kissed her and ran his hand across her lower back. Pippa took his other hand, pulled him off the sofa and led him up the stairs to their bedroom. It was possible, she thought as her dress crumpled to the floor, still to get pregnant like normal couples did. They'd give it a damned good try at least.

# *Sienna*

The pink cocktail topped with cherries, pineapple and an umbrella was just within arm's reach on the low table beneath the sunshade. Sienna stretched out on the sun lounger and rested her book on her bare stomach. She pushed her sunglasses up into her hair, wiggled her tanned toes and looked down the gentle slope of the white sand beach to where it reached the emerald green shallows of the Indian Ocean. A snorkel bobbed along a little further out where Ashton was exploring the house reef of the Maldivian island they were staying on.

She had to admit that Pippa had been right about her needing a holiday. However much she loved her job, she'd been getting seriously close to burn out. This was exactly what she needed: sunshine, peace, relaxation and delicious food and drink. She reached for her cocktail and took a sip – surprisingly alcoholic and it was only the middle of the day too. At least she thought it was. It was easy to lose track of time on the island – it would be down to her rumbling stomach to let her know when it was lunch or dinner. After a long flight and a seaplane transfer from the airport on Malé it was their first full day on the island and she intended to do nothing but chill out. A bit of sunbathing, a seafood lunch, a little swim, maybe lazy afternoon sex with the breeze blowing through the open windows of their beach villa.

Ashton emerged from the ocean like someone out of a Bond movie, all glistening tanned flesh, although his shorts were more substantial than the ones she remembered Daniel Craig wearing. Shame. Sienna stuck two fingers in her mouth and wolf-whistled.

Ashton grinned and did a slow motion *Baywatch* run up the bit of beach they had to themselves.

'You're starting on the cocktails early then?' He flopped down on the sun lounger alongside Sienna's and sent a spray of water and sand in her direction.

She brushed grains of sand off her stomach. 'I'm on holiday, I deserve this.'

'I totally agree.' He rubbed the beads of water off his arms and chest with a towel and put his sunglasses on. 'I might head to the bar and get a beer. Do you want another?'

'Someone will come round soon enough and take a drinks order for you.'

'Nah, it's alright, I fancy a wander.' He leant over and kissed her on the lips. He smelt of saltwater, suntan lotion and his Jasper Conran aftershave – a totally intoxicating smell. Maybe lazy afternoon sex should be moved to a lunchtime quickie…

'I'll be here,' Sienna said, stretching out her long, tanned legs. 'Reading my book and drinking my cocktail.' She blew him a kiss as he sauntered across their stretch of beach towards the restaurant and bar. Her typically Italian mum thought he was perfect marriage material and couldn't understand why they weren't engaged yet, let alone not living together, but Sienna wasn't willing to give up her independence or her beautiful house in Bath. She'd worked ridiculously hard for that, plus she liked her space and it kept their relationship spicy.

Sienna smiled. Spicy was definitely the right word. How many of her married friends still had a spark in their relationship? Pippa was only shagging Clive so much because she was desperate to get pregnant. That was Pippa's motivation, while hers was lust. Plain and simple.

She drained the rest of her cocktail, pulled her sunglasses back down from where they wedged her hair off her face, and closed her eyes. Heat enveloped her along with the sound of waves rhythmically lapping the beach and the occasional squawk of a bird flying overhead.

Flaming torches wedged into the sand surrounded a table next to the ocean, sending flickering light dancing across the water. Now the sun had gone down the sand was a pleasant temperature on bare feet, and hand in hand, Sienna and Ashton strolled down the beach to the table. A waiter pulled back Sienna's chair and she sat down.

'A-maz-ing,' she said, squeezing Ashton's hand and giving him a massive grin across the candlelit table.

'It's pretty special, isn't it?' Ashton's linen shirt was open halfway down his chest revealing smooth tanned skin. She knew they looked good together: quite a power couple, both successful, both attractive, so why then did she have a funny feeling in the pit of her stomach? Her conversation with Pippa before she'd booked their last minute holiday flitted into her head. Was she really blind to what Pippa saw their relationship as? Sienna absorbed the setting: the candles, the gentle swoosh of the surf, the silky soft sand between her toes, champagne in glasses, their own waiter bringing their starters...

Despite the heat Sienna shivered with the realisation of where this was leading. She barely tasted the platter of lobster and prawns, and their conversation about what they planned to do for the rest of the week washed over her. By the time their dessert of mango sorbet and an exotic fruit salad was placed in front of them and their waiter topped up their glasses with champagne, Sienna had noticed beads of sweat on Ashton's forehead.

Sienna took a mouthful of sorbet. Ashton reached into the pocket of his shorts. He slid off his chair and got down on one knee.

'Ashton, don't.' Sienna shook her head and grabbed at his arm to pull him back up. 'Don't do this.'

'You're kidding me, right?'

Sienna dropped her spoon into her bowl of sorbet. 'You

know I don't want this – a romantic proposal, marriage. It's not for me and it's never going to be. You know this.'

Ashton shook his head. 'You're seriously not going to let me do this?'

Sienna bit her lip. 'I'm sorry.'

Ashton tucked the small box back in the pocket of his shorts and sat down.

'We can still be together and try and spend more time with each other – do stuff like this more often,' Sienna said.

'I couldn't agree with you more, it's just you're working all the time.'

'Is that a dig?'

'Only if you think it is or that you really are working too hard.'

'I love my job.' Sienna scrunched her toes in the sand and relished the feeling of the cool grains as she dug deeper.

'I know.'

'You work crazy hours too.'

'That's why it doesn't work with us both working crazy hours,' Ashton said.

'Drop some of yours then.'

'You know I can't.'

'And you know I can't either.' Sienna folded her arms and looked at him. In the warmth of light from the torches he was as handsome as she'd ever seen him with the flickering flames accentuating his high cheekbones. He was sexy as hell but could infuriate her so badly at times. 'It's the nature of being a location manager – long hours, away from home, lots of travel, and I'm not willing to give that up or even slow down at the moment.'

'Is that why you don't want to marry me?'

'You know I'm not marriage material.'

'Maybe so, but you're thirty-five this year. What about starting a family?'

'Are you basically saying I'm not getting any younger?'

'No, not exactly, but how long are we going to wait?'

'We're not waiting, we're just not having kids. Seriously, Ashton, you've known that ever since we got together.'

'Seeing my brother and his wife have my niece makes me want kids more. I thought your biological clock would have kicked in by now.'

'Yours obviously has.' Sienna stared out at the perfectly calm moonlit ocean. She reached for her champagne and took a sip, then gestured around her. 'You'd seriously want to give this up?'

'We could do this with kids.'

'Yeah, right,' Sienna snorted. 'When have your brother and family been to the Maldives or anywhere abroad without a kids' club and crappy family entertainment?'

'We don't have to be like my brother or your sisters; we can still travel, go on adventures. We'd just have to plan things a bit more.'

'You're out of your mind.' Sienna put her hand to her ear. 'Hear that?'

'Hear what?'

'Exactly. Peace and quiet, no babies crying or children screaming. I want to relax, forget about work and life back home, and I certainly don't want to be thinking about having a baby who will take over our life – it'll be a whirlwind of dirty nappies, no sleep, vomit. I don't want to end up like my mum, losing out on having a career because she was raising a family. Do you want me to go on?'

Ashton leant forwards, rested his elbows on the table and rubbed his forehead like he did when he had a migraine. 'I thought I could change you.'

'You know I'm happy – really happy – with us as we are. I don't need a piece of paper to prove otherwise. Me and you, how we're living at the moment – I love it. It feels right. I don't want to get comfortable and be married and boring.'

'Oh come on, Sienna, getting married doesn't make people boring. It wouldn't make us boring. It's just a way of me showing how much I love you.'

'You can show that in other ways, you know.'


'You were right about Ashton proposing.' Sienna had been home for less than an hour before she phoned Pippa.

'And you said?'

'No, of course.'

'What?' Sienna could hear the disappointment in her best friend's voice. 'I really thought you'd change your mind once he actually popped the question, given the setting and all.'

'Oh, I give him that – the setting was beyond beautiful: a private dinner on the beach by the Indian Ocean. I mean, wow. It's just I don't want to get married. I'm not even sure I'd want to live with him.'

'But you love him, right?'

'Yes.' There was silence from Pippa down the other end of the phone. 'I know you don't get it – I don't expect you to. No one gets it, least of all my mum. I'm happy being me and living by myself.'

'You can still be yourself even if you're living with and married to someone, Sienna. Plus you don't have to change your name if you don't want to.'

'It's not just about losing my identity, it's more the case of me liking my own space – you know that. Things are so perfect at the moment with work, financially, Ashton, and we've had an incredible holiday. I really don't want to spoil all that. I know I'm a freak saying this but the thought of marriage makes me feel claustrophobic. I think it would hurt our relationship rather than make it stronger.'

'I know you've never wanted marriage or kids,' Pippa said. 'I guess I shouldn't have expected you to change your mind.'

'That's exactly what Ashton was hoping – that I had changed my mind.' Sienna pulled the kitchen blinds closed and popped a Waitrose chicken korma in the microwave. 'He also brought up the subject of kids.'

'Oh, really?'

'For fuck's sake, it should be me who's broody, not a

career-minded rugby-playing still very much 'a lad' thirty-eight-year-old graphic designer.' Sienna poured herself a large glass of red wine and sat down at the kitchen table. 'Talking of which, how're things with you?'

'Well, I'm nearly two weeks into treatment.'

'How are you feeling?'

'Pretty good. I mean, the aftertaste of the nasal spray is pretty rank and I've set alarms on my mobile to remind me to sniff every four hours because I'm worried I'll forget, but yes, apart from a few headaches and feeling a bit emotional, it's all good so far. Another few days and I'll be injecting into my stomach – now that I'm not looking forward to.'

'You're sounding positive about it though.' Sienna took a large sip of her wine and swilled it around her mouth, wishing it was a mojito and she was back on the little stretch of Maldivian heaven.

'Yes, really positive. I joined the fertility centre's forum and there's another girl roughly the same age with a similar story who started a day after me, so we'll be going through it together. I think that's really going to help.'

'You know you're so brave doing this. I can't even commit to a man I actually love, and here you are putting yourself through hell so you can have a family. That takes strength. I wish I had your guts.'

'All that sun's gone to your head, crazy lady. You have tonnes of guts – I'd never be able to do your job or travel all over the place on my own like you do. We want different things, that's all.'

The microwave pinged and Sienna got up and took her curry out. 'I guess you're right. Always the sensible one.' Using one hand she managed to pull back the plastic cover without burning her fingers. She shivered and wrapped her cardigan tighter around her. 'It's so fucking cold. I'm missing sunshine and forty-degree heat. And not having to do anything if I don't want to. I really could be back on that beach right now with cocktails being brought to me.'

Pippa laughed. 'That's the life! I fancy that too. But there we go – it's January and England so no chance.'

'Instead, I'm drinking wine and about to eat a microwave curry on my own.'

'Ashton went home?'

'Uh-huh.' Sienna tipped the korma and rice into a bowl and sat back down at the table.

'Was he upset that you said no?'

'Of course, male pride and all that. I turned him down essentially. He was bummed for a couple of days afterwards and then thawed out. Getting him drunk and having sex pretty much did the trick.' Sienna spooned a mouthful of korma and rice and washed it down with a gulp of wine.

'But have you talked about it since?' Pippa asked. 'About where you go from here?'

'We're the same as we've always been.'

'You may feel the same but I bet Ashton doesn't. If he wants marriage and kids and you don't, that's kind of a problem, isn't it?'

Sienna placed her spoon back in the bowl, her appetite suddenly deserting her. How naïve was she not to have thought about what her saying no would do to Ashton? Of course it was easy for her to continue as they'd always done, but if he didn't think there was any chance of tying the knot and starting a family, why would he even stay with her?

# Pippa

Pippa's hands shook as she carefully made up the first injection. She'd watched the video that came with the kit three or four times before getting the nerve to draw up the liquid and release it into one of the little pots of powder.

'Are you sure you don't want me to do it?' Clive asked from where he sat at the kitchen table.

Pippa sat opposite, leaning back in her chair with a big pinch of stomach between her fingers and the needle poised ready to stab her skin.

'No, I'll be fine, thanks.' She took a deep breath and pushed the needle in slowly before steadily injecting the liquid. There was a slight stinging sensation, nothing really bad and just a droplet of blood when she pulled the needle out. She breathed out at the realisation that she could do this and injection number one was over and done with.

Pippa sat on the sofa with a hot water bottle hugged to her stomach and her feet up, flicking through the channels: the news; *Keeping Up With the Kardashians*; *One Born Every Minute*... she wasn't ready to start watching *that* quite yet. She continued to flick and settled on *QI*, keeping the hot water bottle on her stomach with her hands clasped over it and marvelling at the bubbling sensation low down in her belly. That had to be good, surely?

Over the next few days Pippa went through the motions at work, keeping her head down and concentrating as much as her body would allow. Being an administrator for a large architect practice in Bath at least meant she spent most of the day sitting in front of her computer or answering the phone.

She managed to take the nasal spray discreetly either by nipping to the ladies or, if no one was looking, ducking behind her computer and doing the sniffs. At least the injection could be done in the evening in the privacy and comfort of home. Although she'd told most of her friends that she was going through IVF, she didn't want the whole office knowing the ins and outs of her life.

'Bit early for hay fever, isn't it?'

'I'm sorry?' Pippa tucked the nasal spray back in her bag and looked across the divide that separated her from her colleague, Sita.

'The nasal spray. I don't usually get hay fever until at least April.'

Pippa's heart skipped a beat. 'Oh that, yeah – it's not for hay fever.' She glanced around to check that no one else was in earshot. 'It's part of the medication for IVF.'

Sita opened her mouth to say something, then closed it again. 'Oh hun, I'm so sorry, I assumed too much – there you go, me putting my foot right in it. I had no idea.'

Pippa shook her head and waved her hands. 'Don't be silly. I'm quite open about it. I've kept it quiet at work because it's nice to have somewhere to come and get on with normal life.'

'I totally understand. I won't say a word.' Sita leant forwards as one of the architects walked by. 'My cousin had IVF a few years ago and she's got a gorgeous little girl now, so it'll be worth it.'

'I hope so.'

\* \* \*

*29th January blog post:*

### Scans and Injections

*Sorry for the radio silence but it's been quite a week. After ten days of injections I'm quite the pro now at stabbing myself in the stomach and I don't even flinch any longer. I felt more and more bloated as the week*

*went on, which I took to be a good sign that the stimming was working
and I was growing lots of follicles.*

*The first scan on Wednesday was, for the want of better words,
THE MOMENT OF TRUTH – had all those injections done their
job? Was I bursting with loads of lovely follies? The simple answer was
yes. Hubby came with me and held my hand while the deed was done.
Unfortunately I'm getting used to dropping my kecks and spreading my
legs for a nurse with the tool of choice – a dildo-shaped scanner complete
with a condom and lubricant. The technicalities aside, on the screen we
could see a mass of follicles on both sides, some of which – according to the
nurse doing the scan – were a decent size. The outcome – a couple more
days of stimming injections and then we're back tomorrow to see if any of
those follicles are the right size (between 17 and 22mm, in case you're
interested). Fingers crossed we'll then be booked in for the egg collection
operation. It's all happening, and now it's crunch time it feels very real...*

After a positive second scan Pippa took the following Monday
off work and was back at the clinic early in the morning for
the egg collection operation. She spent the rest of the day at
home being looked after by Clive and then it was back to
waiting, this time for a daily phone call from one of the
embryologists updating her on how their embryos were doing.
Despite them starting off with twelve eggs, only seven
fertilised, and by the second day only four had continued to
divide and grow. On day three the embryologist called her
into the clinic to have the two best embryos transferred back.

She felt exposed in a hospital gown, perched with her legs
spread to aching proportions in a chair that looked like a
contraption from a sci-fi film. The room was white and sterile.
The nurse doing the procedure was friendly yet efficient. After
the last checks were made, the embryologist brought the two
embryos into the room in what was effectively a large syringe
and the nurse transferred them into Pippa via the catheter-
type thing lodged uncomfortably between her legs. This was
not how Pippa had imagined she'd get pregnant. And yet
there was a question mark over whether that would even
happen as she had another two weeks to wait to find out if the

procedure had worked.

*    *    *

*14th February blog post:*

### The Two Week Wait, aka Hell

*I've never known anything like it. The two week wait. Sounds harmless enough, doesn't it? No horrible nasal spray to be sniffing, no injections to be done – in fact, apart from the unpleasantness of having to insert a daily pessary, it should be the easiest part of the whole treatment. Trust me, it's not. The two week wait messes with your head. After all the physical upheaval of downregging then stimming, going under a general anaesthetic for the egg collection op before having those little embies put back a few days later, the two week wait toys with your emotions like nothing else I've known. I'm questioning every tiny twinge and second guessing every goddam symptom. Only three more days until our official test day and I have no clue whether it's worked or not.*

Pippa woke before her alarm went off on the 17th February. Darkness still enveloped their bedroom. Test day. She glanced at the clock on her bedside table: 05.37, then rolled on to her back and slid her hands across her stomach. Did she feel pregnant? Would she know deep down if she was? Please, please, please let this have worked, she thought.

'Clive,' Pippa whispered, gently shaking her snoring husband. 'Clive,' she said louder.

'Huh?'

'I'm going to do the pregnancy test. You coming?'

'What time is it?'

'Nearly quarter to six.'

'Be there in a minute.'

Pippa swung her legs out of bed and slipped her feet into her fluffy slippers. How could he not be jumping out of bed, desperate to know the fate of eight weeks of medication and procedures; to know if they were going to be a family? Or not. Shivering, Pippa wrapped her dressing gown around herself and padded along the landing to the bathroom.

She studied her face in the mirror: pale skin, blue eyes with a bit of mascara still around them, neat eyebrows. She didn't look any different to how she had eight weeks ago. What was she expecting, a pregnancy glow already?

Pippa opened the cupboard above the sink and pulled out the First Response pregnancy test. Her heart thudded and her stomach churned; the slight bubbly feeling of discomfort she'd felt on and off all week returned to her lower abdomen – surely a good sign? Carefully, she unwrapped the test from the cellophane wrapper and placed it on the side of the sink. All she had to do was pee on a stick and await the verdict.

She traipsed back along the hallway to find Clive snoring. She turned on the light, leant across the bed and nudged him.

'I'm doing the test now.'

'Um, okay,' he replied, stretching and yawning. He sat up and pulled on a sweater.

Back in the bathroom Pippa did the test and, with trembling hands, placed it on the shelf.

'You've done the deed already?' Clive asked as he came into the bathroom.

Pippa nodded, fighting back tears.

'What do you think it's going to say?'

'I honestly don't know. Every symptom I've had I've hoped is a positive thing but they could just mean my period's about to start.'

'Your body's gone through so much. You can't analyse symptoms one way or another. They could be down to anything.'

'I'm worried, that's all,' she said, unable to contain her tears any longer.

'Oh Pippa, I know.' He pulled her close and wrapped his arms around her where they stood in the middle of the bathroom. 'How long does it take?'

'A couple of minutes; it should be nearly ready.' Pippa held on to Clive tighter. 'It's crazy to think our future is going to be decided in the next minute or two.'

'You do realise even if it doesn't work out now, it's not all over. We can try again.'

Pippa nodded, nausea creeping from her stomach up towards her throat. She took a deep breath and pulled away from Clive. Stepping over to the shelf where the test lay, she saw that their fate was sealed and her heart skipped. With a shaky hand she picked up the test and let tears stream down her face as she showed it to Clive.

# *Georgie*

'What are you doing this weekend?'

Georgie looked up from her computer to where Melinda was sorting out paperwork on her desk opposite.

'Having a family lunch for my mum's birthday tomorrow.'

'Nice.'

'What about you? You seeing Jeremy?'

'I just might be,' she said and winked. 'Another trip to Cardiff for a bit of shopping, dinner out, the cinema, then back to his place...'

'Yeah, yeah, I know the rest, no need to elaborate.' Georgie turned back to the annual leave spreadsheet and glanced at her watch – only fifty minutes left to get everything finished. Her mobile pinged. She finished what she was doing and glanced down, drew in a breath, looked around and checked that Melinda was talking to another colleague.

Georgie clicked on the private Facebook message from Felix.

*Felix: Hey there, not heard from you in a while. How's tricks? All OK?*

Georgie paused. There was a reason that she hadn't messaged Felix recently and it was purely out of guilt. Ever since they'd met at the Christmas party two months earlier, she seemed to have had more meaningful conversations with him – albeit via Facebook – than with her own husband. Deep down she knew she should ignore his message or suggest they kept their communication on a professional level only.

Her thumb hovered over her smartphone. She enjoyed receiving his messages... no, in fact, she *loved* getting them. Without a doubt they brightened up her day.

*Georgie: Sorry Felix, just been busy with work and at home too. Need a holiday.*

Almost immediately he messaged back.

*Felix: Know the feeling. Working in Bristol next week, you going to be in?*

Her heart skipped a beat. So much for attempting not to communicate again.

*Georgie: Yes, in all week apart from Wednesday.*

*Felix: Great. Planning on going for drinks after work on Friday so make sure you're free.*

A night out. With work. With Felix. Just what she needed. She tapped her manicured fingernails on the desk and started to think about what to wear.

'Are you going to be home on time next Friday?' Georgie asked Nathan the moment he stepped through the door, late again.

'By on time you mean...'

'By 6pm. We've got a bit of a work do going on so I can get Mum to babysit Daisy until you get home, but I don't want her to have to be here all evening.'

Nathan dumped his briefcase on the hall floor. 'Another night out?'

'Excuse me?' Georgie put her hands on her hips. 'The last time I went out with work was the Christmas do.'

'You've been out with Melinda a few times.'

'She's a friend outside of work too. Plus, I don't consider the cinema twice to really be "a few times".'

'It's fine, honestly.'

Doesn't sound like it, Georgie thought. She sighed and resigned herself to a large glass of white wine and Friday night telly. She always found the weekends trying with Nathan and Daisy at home all day, and added to the mix this weekend was a family get-together. Pippa must be close to finishing treatment by now. Georgie had let her get on with it and hadn't talked to her for a couple of weeks, not wanting to intrude or ask too much. She'd had a couple of updates from their mum around the time Pippa had gone in for the egg collection bit but that was about it.

Georgie took a gulp of wine – maybe she should have made more effort to support her, but Pippa's emotions over the past year or so had been so difficult to judge. Georgie had always taken the easier option of avoiding her.

She flicked through the channels while Nathan pottered about in the kitchen, heating up his dinner. She missed her older sister and the way they used to talk, but she couldn't quite see how they'd get their relationship back on track unless Pippa got pregnant. Boy, did she hope that would happen soon – maybe Pippa would have good news to share with them on Sunday.

Georgie settled on *The Graham Norton Show* and topped up her wine. Nathan sat down on the sofa and tucked into his plate of leftover spaghetti bolognese and salad, his fork clattering against the plate while he slurped spaghetti into his mouth. Georgie turned up the volume, letting Graham, Sean Penn and Celia Imrie drown out the sound of her husband. What she needed was a girlie weekend away to a spa hotel. Some serious pampering would help lift her spirits… at least she had Friday night to look forward to.

'It's not good news,' Georgie's mum, Bridget, mouthed as soon as she opened the door.

Georgie frowned.

'Pippa,' she whispered, motioning down the hallway. 'She's in the kitchen putting on a brave face but she did a pregnancy test on Tuesday and it was negative.'

Georgie's heart sank. Nathan grunted as he kissed Bridget on the cheek and brushed past her with Daisy.

'Maybe just don't bring the subject up,' Bridget said as she hugged Georgie.

'I can't not say anything, Mum.'

Bridget sighed. 'It's going to be one of those days.'

'Well, happy birthday anyway.'

Bridget closed the door behind her daughter and led the way through to the living room. All Georgie wanted to do was leg it right back out the front door. It wasn't just Pippa's hopes riding on her getting pregnant, although at least Georgie would have a reason to hold off trying for a baby for a bit longer.

'Hi, Dad.'

'Hello, love.' Alan sat in his armchair by the window with his feet up, the sports channel on and a mug of tea on the coffee table next to him.

'You alright?' Georgie asked.

'Feels a bit tense in here today.' He nodded in the direction of the kitchen.

'Cup of tea, Nathan? Georgie?' Bridget asked, picking up an empty glass from the fire surround.

'Andma, Andma, Andma!' Daisy pulled at Bridget's trouser leg.

'What is it, love?'

Georgie took the glass from her mum. 'I'll sort the drinks out, you sit down and play with Daisy.' She took a deep breath and walked back out of the living room and down the hall to the kitchen. Pushing open the door she was met with a delicious smell of meat and spices and the sight of Pippa pulling jacket potatoes out of the oven.

'I didn't know you were doing lunch.'

'It's only chilli and jacket potatoes. Easy stuff.'

'Where's Clive?'

'He went into work. Apparently a film crew are filming at the Roman Baths today and he wanted to be there to oversee everything,' Pippa replied, and shrugged. 'In truth he didn't want to come and be sociable and I didn't have the energy to argue with him.'

Georgie took another deep breath, placed the dirty glass next to the sink then went over and put her arms around Pippa.

'I'm sorry, Pip. Mum said it was a negative test.'

Pippa didn't hug her back. Instead Georgie felt her pull away, and then she busied herself putting the potatoes in a dish.

'Are you okay?' Georgie asked.

'We knew from the beginning that there was a very high chance this would be the outcome. It's just I had hope, you know?' Pippa turned back to the cooker and stirred the chilli con carne.

'You can try again though, can't you?'

'Yes, and we will, but we're going to have to pay for it next time.'

'I thought it was on the NHS.'

'Only one cycle is, so if we want to try again we have to do it privately.'

'Ouch. I had no idea.'

'Why would you?'

Georgie bit her lip and wondered if that was a dig about the fact she hadn't really been involved in Pippa's life for a while or asked about the treatment.

'When do you think you'll try again?'

Pippa switched off the gas burner and swung round to face her sister.

'Georgie, I only got the negative test three days ago, and for the last eight or so weeks I've been pumping myself full of hormones, feeling like shit, made to have an horrendous period, had various blood tests, a general anaesthetic and undergone a procedure where I had to sit with my legs spread in a chair that looked like something out of a horror movie. I don't want to think about going through all that again quite yet. Trust me, it's not as much fun as trying to get pregnant the natural way.'

Georgie forced herself not to snap back at Pippa. She

took a glass and filled it with water from the tap.

'I'm sorry,' Pippa said. She took a large dish from the cupboard next to the cooker and spooned the chilli into it. 'I'm just not in the mood to be playing happy families today.'

'You didn't have to come, we would have understood.'

'I need to keep busy and carry on as normal, otherwise I'll go demented thinking about what could have been. It's not like we see you all very often, and I'm sorry that we've not seen much of you over the past year or two – it's been hard, you know, seeing you and Nathan with Daisy, and Mum and Alan as grandparents.'

'I know,' Georgie said. 'And there's no need to apologise. I should have made more effort involving you but I wasn't sure that's what you wanted.'

'Yes, it is, but it's so much easier if it comes from you. I love spending time with Daisy; it's just I feel so down for a few days afterwards realising what I'm missing out on – I often don't want to put myself in that position because I know it's hard.' Pippa handed Georgie a large bowl of salad and picked up the bowls of chilli and potatoes. 'If Mum's able to babysit on Friday evening, how about you and Nathan come over to ours for dinner and we can talk properly?'

'This coming Friday? I can't, I'm sorry. There's a work thing that I'm going to. But another evening, definitely. We'd love to.'

'Great,' Pippa said, kissing Georgie on the cheek. 'I've missed you. Now, hold the door open so we can eat before it gets cold.'

# *Sienna*

'Your place or mine?' Sienna asked.

'How about we stop having this silly decision to make all the time and have *our* place instead? We have clothes and wash things at each other's – wouldn't it be easier to simply live together instead of this crazy set up? We've been together three years.'

It was Saturday night and Sienna and Ashton sat opposite each other in The Herd Restaurant in the centre of Bath. The remains of their late night steak dinner were in front of them, along with a second bottle of red wine. Sienna wiped the corners of her mouth with a napkin and topped up their glasses.

'You know I don't want to sell my house,' she said.

'Then I'll sell my flat and move in with you.'

Sienna took a large sip of wine and didn't say anything.

'Or,' Ashton continued, 'we both sell our houses, pool our resources and imagine what we could buy together.'

'A family house?' The wine had begun to taste a little sour.

'Well yes, actually.'

Sienna sighed. 'We were having a lovely evening and you had to spoil it by bringing this whole subject up again.'

'I'm sorry,' Ashton said, leaning back in his chair. 'Should I have waited until we were sat at home one evening watching TV? Oh wait, we don't do that because we don't live together, plus I have to take the opportunity to talk to you about these things when I do actually get to see you. You've been in Croatia for the past few weeks and you're off to Yorkshire on

Tuesday. Our relationship is little more than friends with benefits.'

'And you're complaining? Most men would think that's perfect.'

'Maybe in their twenties or early thirties, but not every man wants a relationship based purely on sex.'

'That's not what I meant and it's not like our relationship is just that. We do other stuff too – we talk, a lot, about everything: politics, music, theatre, film, art, travel, the world. We go out, we enjoy ourselves, live life to the full.'

'We're not committed though.'

'You're not going to pull that ring out again, are you?'

Ashton threw his napkin on the table. 'You're unbelievable.' He downed the last of his wine, stood up and took his coat from the back of his chair. 'You can pay the bill. After all, it is your turn as you have to be so anal about maintaining your independence from me.'

Sienna watched him weave his way past the remaining diners and out of the restaurant door. He managed to irritate her and yet she found him incredibly sexy at the same time. Was she really messing with him, trying to maintain some kind of relationship when she had no real intention of moving it on to the next level?

'Can I have the bill, please?' Sienna caught the attention of a waiter. Bollocks to it all, she hadn't led Ashton on at any point – she'd made it clear from the very beginning that she didn't want the marriage and kids thing, but maybe he had a point about the moving in together part. Why didn't she want to? Deep down she knew it was more than not wanting to sell her house.

The waiter returned and she paid the bill before finishing her wine, pulling on her coat, doing up the buttons and heading outside. The street was quiet with only a couple of lads walking across Pulteney Bridge and a handful of cars passing, headlights blazing. Ashton was nowhere to be seen. Sienna sighed: Saturday night and it looked like she was heading home alone.

Sod that, she wasn't going to end the night with the conversation half finished. She had to admit it was good to wake up on the weekends with Ashton next to her before enjoying a lazy breakfast in bed – there would be plenty of perks to living together. She started walking in the direction of his flat.

Ashton's flat occupied the second floor of a large Georgian terraced villa. With two bedrooms, it was larger than Sienna's ground floor flat in the house she owned, minus a garden. She rang the buzzer to his apartment and stood back, looking up towards his living room window and shivering – the 22nd February and it was cold, particularly this late at night. She rang the buzzer again. Still no answer.

Taking her phone from her bag, she rang him.

'What?' Ashton answered.

'Are you going to let me in? I know you're home already, your living room light's on. It's freezing out here.'

The front door buzzed and clicked and she pushed it open, relieved to get inside. She took the stairs two at a time and found Ashton holding his front door open for her.

'I'm sorry,' she said, brushing past him and gently kissing his cheek. 'It was out of order what I said – I didn't mean to make a joke about you proposing again.'

Ashton closed the door and she followed him through to the living room. He slumped down on the sofa by the window and she sat on the sofa opposite and wriggled out of her coat.

'I think we want different things from life,' Sienna said slowly, the wine she'd drunk making her thoughts fuzzy.

'You're breaking up with me?' His handsome face pinched into a frown.

'No,' she said, moving across the room to sit next to him. 'We just need to work some things out, compromise a bit.'

'Sienna, I'm up for that but you have to compromise too. It can't all come from me.'

'I know, I just need some time to think things through.

42

Our life isn't bad, even if it's not exactly what you want at the moment. Pippa did a pregnancy test earlier in the week and it was negative, and that was after eight weeks of fertility treatment and nearly four years of trying. We have nothing to complain about.'

'There will always be someone worse off than us, but it doesn't mean we can't talk about our own problems or take them seriously.'

'But we don't really have any problems, we just don't have a solution to us both wanting different things from life.'

'And that's the problem.'

'I'm trying to be positive here.'

'And I'm being realistic.' Ashton turned to her. 'You can forget about me wanting to marry you – I promise I will never propose to you again. I can live without us getting hitched, that's my compromise, but I'm not going to continue our relationship as it is with us living separate lives and only seeing each other for what seems like occasional dates and fucking. Moving in together has to be your compromise.'

She stroked the side of his face and stubble grazed the back of her hand. She now had an ultimatum – move in together or part ways. 'Okay, that's fine, I'll seriously think about it.'

'I can't believe you have to think about it.' He pushed her hand away and went to stand up. Sienna grabbed his arm.

'I'm drunk and it's late, so not the time to be making life changing decisions. But I do love you.' She pulled off her tunic top revealing a black vest top and the hint of a lacy bra beneath. 'You want to continue arguing or get down to the fucking part of our relationship?'

'You're impossible,' Ashton said, but he didn't protest when Sienna tugged at his belt and undid his jeans.

'You don't enjoy our life, the freedom, the excitement, the unpredictability of it?' She pushed him back on to the sofa and pulled his jeans off so he was just in his pants. 'You're obviously excited...'

Ashton pulled her towards him until she straddled him. 'I do enjoy our life – I love it and I love you, but I want more…'

'Shush,' Sienna whispered, kissing the side of his face. 'That's enough talking for one night.'

There was an awkwardness the next morning that wasn't usually there: a heavy weight of expectation from Ashton for her to make her decision there and then, with a hangover. She didn't. Instead, she had the luxury of being able to say goodbye and escape back to her own house – the irony being this was exactly what Ashton was asking her to give up.

Her flat was only a fifteen minute walk away: a spacious ground floor apartment in a two storey plus attic terraced Victorian house that she owned. It had been in a state when she'd bought it – hadn't been touched since the seventies and had retained all its original features. To make it work and have any chance of paying back the mortgage, she'd always rented out the top flat. She closed the front door to her flat behind her and leant against it. This was what she enjoyed – space of her own, a place to retreat to, be quiet in, walk through naked if she chose to. A place to call home. She had similar taste to Ashton with the rooms painted various shades of grey, although the palette was warmer than at his with hints of rose and aubergine. There was also a worldly feel with various trinkets and art from her travels abroad.

She unzipped her boots and kicked them off before hanging up her coat and walking through to the kitchen. The irony wasn't lost on her that she needed to talk to someone about her dilemma with Ashton and yet she chose to live alone. She thought about phoning Pippa but decided against it, considering how upset Pippa had been when she'd phoned to tell Sienna about the negative pregnancy test. Pippa might be her best friend but Sienna wasn't about to dump the trivialities of her relationship woes on top of what she was already going through.

Grabbing a packet of Jaffa Cakes from the cupboard,

Sienna knocked on the door of the upstairs flat. It took a while before the door opened and a young, skinny woman with a shock of messy blonde hair appeared.

'Hey, Amy,' Sienna said, clocking the fact that she was wearing an oversized T-shirt and had bare legs. 'Do you have company?'

'Nope.' Amy rubbed her eyes. 'Just a late night.'

'Tell me about it.' Sienna waggled the biscuits in front of her. 'Fancy coffee and a chat?'

Amy yawned. 'As long as it's at your place and we can have proper coffee instead of my crappy instant.'

'Deal.'

'I'll be there in five.'

Sienna headed back to her flat and turned the coffee machine on. She popped a capsule in, put the milk on and made Amy a latte before making an espresso for herself. Tipping half the biscuits on to a plate, she took everything into the living room and collapsed back on to the sofa, tucking her legs beneath her and flicked through her emails on her phone.

'Door's open!' Sienna called when Amy knocked.

'Ah, lush.' Amy grabbed a Jaffa Cake and her latte and sat next to Sienna on the sofa. 'What's up then?'

'Nothing and everything.'

'As clear as mud, Sienna.'

'Ashton kind of gave me an ultimatum last night.'

'Oh really?' Amy leant forwards and took a sip of her coffee.

'Move in with him or move on.'

'Well, you have been together a while now.'

'Three years.'

'I've got friends who've moved in with their boyfriend after a few months.'

'That's just stupid.'

'Not if you know they're the one.' Amy munched round the edge of the Jaffa Cake. 'Is he? The one?'

'By "the one" you mean someone I can see myself spending the rest of my life with?'

'Er, yes – someone you want to get married to, have kids with and grow old together.'

Sienna shivered. 'See, this is the problem. I don't want the marriage and kids bit and I don't think being with Ashton, or anyone else for that matter, would change my mind. I do love him, though. I miss him when I'm working away and love the time we spend together. And the sex is unbelievable – I mean great, really great. He sort of accused me of only wanting him for his body…'

Amy winked. 'It is a great body – I mean, from what I can tell.'

'Yeah, but there is more to our relationship. It's not just about sex.'

'I'm only saying that's the way it can look.'

'I know it can.'

'Wouldn't you be better off single?'

'I'm not into one night stands.'

'But then you don't seem to be into a relationship either.'

'I am, just not in the traditional sense.'

'I'm enjoying being single,' Amy said.

'Yeah, but you're younger than me. Everyone thinks I should grow up.'

'Like who?'

'Like my parents, Ashton, Pippa…'

'Pippa's not been round for ages, how is she?'

'Wading through the shit that is fertility treatment.'

'Oh really? That sucks.' Amy dunked what was left of her Jaffa Cake into her latte and popped the soggy bit into her mouth before it dropped off. 'Have you talked to her about how you feel about Ashton?'

'I have done but she's got more than enough to deal with at the moment. Plus, I know what she's going to say – she thinks I'm crazy for not wanting to marry him, let alone move in with him. She's wanted the whole marriage and kids thing since we were teenagers and I've always been the complete opposite.'

'Then why don't you move in with Ashton for a couple of weeks, no strings attached, and do a trial run? You wouldn't have to move all your stuff in or anything, just be based in his flat the whole time and not come back here. You never know, you might like it.'

'Amy, that is actually a brilliant idea.'

'That, my friend, is why I'm a lawyer – I'm brilliant at solving problems. Other people's at least. Go talk to him today before you go off to Yorkshire. You'll feel so much better for it.'

# Pippa

It had been an incredibly difficult week for Pippa, going through the motions of trying to hold things together – seeing everyone on her mum's birthday, then facing five long days at work with no one, not even Sita, aware of the turmoil she was going through inside. On Friday afternoon she went home sick, faking a migraine but easily fooling her boss as she looked like death warmed up and about to burst into tears. Back home she changed into leggings and an oversized jumper and sat on the sofa with her laptop, a box of tissues next to her and a mug of hot chocolate on the coffee table. She didn't have the energy or heart to write a new blog post, so she read back over the forum messages, starting with the one she'd written the week before.

*Posted 17th February:*

*We got a BFN. Absolutely gutted. The further along treatment we got, the more positive I became and I really thought it was going to be first time lucky for us. How wrong I was. Don't know what to think or feel, except I can't stop crying. All that effort, all those crappy symptoms, all for nothing. It feels so unfair. Zanzi, I'll be praying so hard that you get a BFP when you test tomorrow.*

*Without hope at the moment. Xx*

*Posted 20th February:*

*Oh Hope, I'm gutted for you too and unfortunately I've got bad news as*

48

*well as I was naughty and tested 2 days early as I was way too impatient to wait and it was a BFN. I'm with you on everything we put ourselves through being all for nothing. This 2ww has nearly killed me, questioning every tiny twinge, cramp and symptom. Evidently it's just my period about to start. Zanzi x*

*Posted 20th February:*

*Ladies, I'm so very sorry it's not worked out for you guys this time, but Zanzi, don't give up hope. You tested early so there might not be enough hCG in your system. Def try again on your actual test date as you never know. I've still got another week to go and dreading having to do that test! Much love to you both, Clover xxxxx*

*Posted 20th February:*

*Zanzi, Clover's right, don't give up, there's still hope. I'll PM you. H x*

Pippa had been in tears when she'd typed the private message to Zanzi. She'd connected with her – maybe it was the fact that they'd been going through treatment at the same time or simply that she felt they'd get along in real life too. Whatever it was, she'd wanted it to work for Zanzi, even though it hadn't worked out for her. It seemed different somehow – when friends told her they were pregnant she was happy for them, but she'd be *really* happy for Zanzi knowing what she'd gone through to get to this point.

*Posted 20th February:*

*Hi Zanzi, it's Hope, although my real name is Pippa. I'm really struggling with this negative test and hate the fact that you're in the same position (although like I said in my post do try again) – I'll be sending you positive vibes. Do you fancy meeting up? I've found infertility to be such a lonely thing, I could really do with a coffee and chat with someone who understands. Let me know if you'd be up for that. I'm in Bath but depending on where you are I'd be happy to meet in Bristol or wherever's easiest.*

*Pippa xx*

Pippa had been worried all week that she hadn't heard anything back from Zanzi and hoped that she was okay – like her, Zanzi had been pinning so much hope on the first cycle of treatment being a success. She breathed a sigh of relief when she realised that Zanzi had replied that morning.

*Posted 27th February:*

*Hey there, Pippa, I'm Connie – nice to find out your real name! Sorry for disappearing – I didn't much feel like going on the forum the past few days. As you've probably guessed from not hearing from me, I got another BFN, so it really is all over. Deep down I knew that was going to be the outcome as it never felt right all the way through, but there you are, that's the way things go. It sucks big time.*

*Yes, yes, yes! I'd love to meet up with you. I've got plenty of friends but I haven't wanted to tell anyone about having treatment and I'm fed up with friends and family (and even strangers!) asking when I'm going to have a baby. I live in Cardiff so could meet you in Bath or Bristol. Let's arrange something soon.*

*Take care,*

*Connie x*

Sienna was working on location up in Yorkshire for the next five weeks, too far for Pippa to jump in the car to go and see her for a chat and a shoulder to cry on, but Pippa needed to talk.

'Hey, hun,' Sienna said when she finally answered her mobile. 'How are you?'

Pippa took a deep breath at the sound of her best friend's voice, willing herself not to burst into tears immediately. 'Are you sure you can talk at the moment?'

'Yeah, it's fine, I've nipped somewhere quiet. Jude Law is rather distracting when trying to listen and hold a conversation.'

'Lucky you.'

'Trust me, it's not as glamorous as it sounds but you know that. I've been freezing my arse off all day, so I'm glad of the distraction and to be inside in the warm. Anyway, I'm blathering on. How are you, my lovely?'

'It's been a pretty shit week to be honest.'

'Oh Pip, I'm sorry, but it was bound to be, wasn't it? I mean, everything you've been through over the past few years and with the treatment came down to one fucking stupid pregnancy test, and it wasn't the result you wanted. That would get anyone down.'

'I guess I was hoping for a miracle. Our consultant warned us this could well be the outcome, but at least we got all the way through treatment, and everything else up until doing the test went perfectly. One poor girl got over stimulated and ended up with ovarian hyperstimulation syndrome so couldn't continue the treatment, and another girl, whose first try it was, only managed to get one egg collected and it didn't fertilise.'

'Shit, that sucks.'

'I had no idea how many things could go wrong at all the different stages, so to make it to test day was more than some poor women did.'

'I think you're amazing. I can't even contemplate what you're putting yourself through.'

'You'll have to read my blog then.'

'Your blog?'

'Don't laugh, but I'm writing a blog about my experience of going through fertility treatment.'

'Why on earth would you think I'd laugh at that? It's a great idea, channelling your energy and emotions into something creative.'

'I am finding it quite cathartic to write my feelings down and get them out into the open, even if no one reads it.'

'I'll read it – you should have told me before,' Sienna said.

'What's it called?'

'*The Hopeful Years.*'

'Oh Pippa, you're going to make me cry. That's so sad but so perfect too.'

'Don't be soft.' She heard Sienna tapping away. 'Are you looking at it now?'

'Yep, in front of my laptop. Ah, it looks great, Pip.' There was more typing. 'There you go, just tweeted about it.'

Sienna had thousands of Twitter followers. Pippa had a sudden rush of fear at the thought of strangers reading what she'd written as it was so personal, but then if it helped someone else suffering with infertility or thinking about undergoing fertility treatment then that could only be a good thing.

'Thanks, Sienna.'

'It's nothing. Now at least I can keep up with how it's all going.'

'Like we don't text each other a million times a week?' Pippa smoothed down her skirt and realised her grey nail varnish was chipped. 'How are you doing?'

'Oh, don't worry about me. I'm fine, keeping busy as always.'

'What's wrong?'

'Nothing, really. You've got enough going on without me adding to it.'

There was silence on the other end of the phone and Pippa wondered if Sienna was crying.

'It's just you were right,' Sienna eventually said. 'About Ashton not being okay and able to move on after I said no to him proposing.'

'Oh Sienna, I'm sorry.'

'Don't be; it's my own doing, and I shouldn't have been so naïve as to think he'd be fine with being turned down and having his pride dented.'

'You're still together though?'

'As much as we always have been – still seeing each other

and having sex. I'm such a fucking teenager still.'

'Yeah, one with their own house and high-flying job.'

'I'm going to move in with Ashton – before you get excited it's only temporary for two weeks once I get back from Yorkshire, just to see how things go. It was Amy's idea.'

'What does Ashton think?'

'He's happy. Although I think he was hoping I would decide to move in permanently, he's pleased it's a start. Anyway, my troubles are nothing and something only I can solve. It's you I'm worried about.'

Pippa curled her feet beneath her on the sofa. 'I'll be okay. It felt like a lot was riding on this treatment – well, there was a lot riding on it and maybe I was being too hopeful that it would work first time. I talked to Clive last night and we decided we're going to try again as soon as we can, so I'm going to phone the clinic on Monday and see if there's anything we need to do first or if we can get the ball rolling as soon as my next period arrives.'

'Seriously, Pip, I've no idea how you're doing this.'

'This is our only chance to have a baby of our own and I'll do anything to make that happen.'

'Oh hun, I'd do anything for that to happen for you too.'

# *Georgie*

Georgie had barely seen Felix all week, let alone had a chance to talk to him. He'd recently been promoted to Senior Account Manager and so was in meetings most of the week – plus, he had no reason to talk to her about work related matters. The times he did appear in the open-plan office where Georgie worked she couldn't take her eyes off him, particularly when he took off his suit jacket revealing deliciously snug-fitting grey trousers and a white shirt. She noticed that she wasn't the only one looking.

By 5pm on Friday afternoon she'd had a text from her mum letting her know she'd collected Daisy from nursery, and there was nothing from Nathan to say he was going to be late home. Georgie shut down her computer, took a pocket mirror out of her handbag and refreshed her lipstick. She'd worn clothes she was happy to go out in – boot-cut black trousers with heels that made her look taller than her 5ft 3inches and a silky patterned blouse that clung in all the right places.

'You look good,' Melinda said, perching on the edge of Georgie's desk.

'Thanks. It's not often I get to go out on a Friday for drinks.'

'Is Sue coming out?'

Georgie shook her head. 'Something about her husband cooking her a special meal for their anniversary.'

'Just you and me, then, out on the town.'

'Except you'll have your lips permanently attached to Jeremy.' Georgie nudged her friend.

'Can you blame me?'

It was like the Christmas party all over again except with fewer people and a more sedate sit down meal before the drinking took place. Full of chicken passanda and naan bread, Georgie was confident that she would stay reasonably sober this time when they arrived at Horts in the centre of Bristol.

'Who's up for tequila slammers?' the Bristol office manager asked when they reached the bar.

Oh lord, Georgie thought, it was going to be one of those nights. So much for remaining sober – she'd not done tequila slammers since her early twenties when she was single, carefree and it didn't matter if she had a hangover or not.

'A glass of wine for me,' she said, deciding a hangover and a twenty-month-old to look after really didn't mix.

'I'll join you,' Felix said, leaning on the bar next to her. 'I can't stand tequila – got very ill on it in my teens and the stuff now makes me retch. Even seeing a slice of lime makes me a little queasy.'

'What are you two like?' Jeremy said, putting his arm round Melinda who smiled and couldn't hide her joy as her cheeks flushed.

'Sensible, I'm afraid,' Georgie said, immediately wishing she wasn't.

'Well,' Jeremy replied, squeezing Melinda's shoulder, 'I ate enough curry to dampen the effects of a caseload of tequila, so bring it on!'

They were a small enough group to be able to sit round a large table where the banter flowed as easily as the tequila and wine. As the night wore on people began to drift away: some home, others to sit by the bar; a few, like Georgie, Melinda, Felix and Jeremy, outside. By 10.30pm even Georgie was feeling like she'd drunk a bit too much, and she shivered despite the warmth from the outdoor heater.

'We're going back to Melinda's,' Jeremy announced, his words slurring into themselves. He had his arm slung around

Melinda's shoulders, his hand resting on her right breast.

'Yeah, you two look like you need to get a room,' Felix said and winked.

'You going to be okay?' Melinda asked Georgie as Jeremy began leading her away.

'I'll make sure she gets home safely,' Felix said, waving them off.

'I'm going to get a taxi back,' Georgie said. 'My hubby is babysitting and I live too far to be catching a bus.'

'Ah, but there's no rush, the night is yet young,' Felix said, perching on the edge of the table next to her. 'My hotel's just round the corner — how about a drink back there then I can call you a taxi?'

Georgie's head screamed, 'Bad idea', but she decided she could listen to his lilting Welsh voice forever, plus the way his arm gently brushed against hers made her tingle and long for him to touch her properly.

'That sounds like a great idea.' The words were out before she had time to censor them or think them through. No one would see them leave together as everyone had either already gone home or were off their faces somewhere inside. She downed the rest of her wine and left the glass on the table before walking arm in arm with Felix to his hotel.

When Felix had suggested a drink she'd pictured a cocktail in the hotel bar rather than a bottle of Corona in his hotel room. She knew she was walking a dangerous line but so far it was simply an innocent drink.

Felix tapped the neck of his Corona bottle against hers. 'Have a seat.'

There was one chair by the window and a huge queen-sized bed. She opted for the edge of the bed and took a swig of Corona.

Felix sat down on the bed next to her making the top of her chest flush hot up to her neck and her palms sweaty.

'I've enjoyed working in Bristol this week,' he said. 'Shame I didn't get to see you much.'

'Well, that was to be expected, with the HR team and marketing not having much to do with each other. Are you going to be working in Bristol again?'

'Yep. It'll be an occasional thing but I should be back in a couple of months.'

Georgie bit her lip, acknowledging the fact she wouldn't get to see him for weeks. 'I've enjoyed seeing you about the office. It's a shame Bristol's a bit too far for you to commute.'

Felix's hand found hers on the duvet next to him. It was warm, his touch firm and she imagined that firmness travelling up her arm and across her body. It was a long time since she'd felt this excited by someone other than a fictional character.

'You make me feel so good, Georgie.'

Oh God, Georgie thought, don't say anything – walk away and go home to your husband and daughter.

'You make me feel good, too. I mean, really good.'

Keeping his hand on hers, he leant towards her and kissed her neck, sending shivers through her body. Every part of her ached for him and she was so tempted to let her hands loose on his belt – not just tempted, she felt desperate. His lips reached her mouth and she kissed him back, allowing his hands to travel up towards the buttons of her blouse. He tasted of red wine, Corona and mints, and smelt lovely, spicy, different to Nathan.

Nathan…

Georgie ran her hands up Felix's taut back into his hair. Felix kissed her harder before gently pushing her back down on the bed until she was lying flat and he was above her, caressing her skin with one hand and undoing her buttons with the other. As her hands travelled down his back she began to imagine what he was about to do to her.

Her eyes flicked open – she'd been reading way too much erotica.

Georgie pulled away, wriggling out from beneath him, realising she'd put on her laciest bra in case this moment happened.

'We're both married.'

'I know,' he replied, but didn't try to pull her back. 'There's something about you... I haven't stopped thinking about you since the Christmas party.'

'I need to go home. Nathan will be wondering where I am. Daisy will be awake at some ridiculous time in the morning...' Her words hung heavily in the room. Her blouse was open, revealing her cleavage; his shirt was unbuttoned, revealing a toned chest that was crying out to be touched and kissed. Georgie shook her head, willing her thoughts to leave Felix and go back to Nathan and Daisy. 'I need to go home.'

He nodded and his hands slipped away from her skin. 'I'll call you a taxi.'

# SPRING

## *Pippa*

Pippa scanned the coffee shop on George Street in Bath until her eyes rested on a woman with long dark-brown hair wearing zigzag-patterned leggings, a long grey tunic and beautiful chunky silver jewellery. The woman met her eyes and smiled. Pippa wound her way past the crowded tables.

'Connie?' she asked.

Connie stood up and wrapped her arms around Pippa. 'Hello. It's so good to finally meet you and see the person behind "Hope"!'

Pippa hugged her back, surprised by the instant familiarity and connection they had. 'It's so good to meet you too. I've been longing to talk to someone who completely understands what I'm going through.'

'Me too,' Connie said, sitting back down.

Pippa took off her coat and hung it on the back of her chair. 'My family and friends – none of them understand the impact this treatment is having on us like my new forum friends do.'

'I know. It's not like we can simply try again next month – we're talking thousands of pounds and weeks of physical and emotional upheaval, all potentially for nothing.'

'It's pretty depressing, isn't it?' Pippa said as the waitress came over. 'What would you like, Connie?'

'Ooh, um, a decaf latte and a piece of carrot cake, please.'

'And for you?' The waitress turned to Pippa.

'I'll have a decaf latte too and the chocolate fudge cake. Thanks.'

'Nice,' Connie said.

'I was being good but since the negative test I've thought, what's the point?'

'A treat now and again won't matter anyway.'

Connie wasn't exactly how Pippa had imagined her to be. She looked younger than thirty-six and more bohemian compared to the polished fashionista Pippa had thought she'd be. Her jewellery wasn't flashy – just beautiful, understated pieces that were eye-catching in an un-obvious way.

'Mine's self-explanatory, but where did your forum name come from?'

'Zanzi?' Connie said and smiled. 'My aunt, who I've always been close to, lives in Tanzania – well, splits her time between Tanzania and Zanzibar. She's lived there for decades, and the best time I've ever had was when I stayed with her for a couple of summers during uni when she was living on Zanzibar. So Zanzi – it reminds me of a happy time. I thought it was an appropriate name.'

'Wow, that sounds incredible.'

'Have you ever been to Tanzania?'

'No, never been to Africa at all, not even North Africa, although we've always talked about going to Morocco.'

The waitress came back and placed two creamy topped lattes and two generous slices of cake in front of them.

Pippa emptied a packet of sweetener into her latte and stirred it. 'When was the last time you saw your aunt?'

'Quite a while ago. Her and my dad had a massive falling out a few years ago so she's not been over here, and there have been less and less opportunities and time for me to go and visit her. I've been focused on my business – I make jewellery,' she said, jangling the silver bracelets on her wrists. 'Getting married and buying a house all took up time, and of course more recently the fact that trying for a baby means I can't take malaria tablets.'

'Oh, of course – that's why we went somewhere on our honeymoon that was malaria free.'

'You started trying straight away then?'

'Yep,' Pippa said, taking a bite of her chocolate fudge cake. 'Oh my God, that's good.' She finished her mouthful. 'I've wanted a baby for as long as I can remember, it just took a little while to meet the right man.'

'Ha, I know what you mean about the meeting the right man bit. I didn't ever not want to have kids but I wasn't really broody until I turned thirty, and then boom! It was like a switch had been flicked inside me and I went all giddy if I saw a baby, felt so desperate to have a little one of my own. It's a funny thing, our biological clock. Sometimes I wish I didn't feel so strongly about having a baby and I could simply walk away from all this crap and come to terms with being childless. But I can't.'

'I absolutely know what you mean. I see friends of mine getting pregnant so easily and it kills me. I mean, I am happy for them, like truly happy, but I'm so heartbroken for us. I want to feel that joy and have something so amazing to look forward to, and yet all we keep getting is knock backs and disappointment. And then another friend announces that they're pregnant, or even worse, pregnant with their second child in the time Clive and I have been trying for our first, and it makes things even harder.'

'I've got an older brother who has a family and that's been tough, seeing my sister-in-law getting pregnant and having babies. Plus my mum never helps by banging on about me and Felix hurrying up and having kids before I get too old – little does she know the struggle we're going through.'

'You haven't told your parents about doing fertility treatment?'

Connie shook her head. 'No, we're not that close.'

'My best friend's parents are like that – well, her mum is at least. They're Italian and are always going on at Sienna about when she's going to settle down and have a family like her sisters. Sienna is the least maternal person I know and has never wanted children and never will, however much her mum has a go at her about it.'

'You never know, she might get broody one day.'

'She's married to her job and it's one that isn't exactly family friendly so I can't see that ever happening.' Pippa took a sip of her latte. 'You know what, though, it's really lovely having a friend who isn't interested in babies and doesn't have kids of her own. It's refreshing being able to talk about other stuff; I mean, we do talk about my fertility treatment but not all the time.'

'How did you find it, the first cycle?' Connie asked.

'Harder than I thought I would. I mean, I knew it was going to be tough but I wasn't prepared for just how physically and emotionally demanding it would be. In fact, I think the physical side of things like the headaches and tiredness was easier to deal with than the emotional side. I remember one day, like about a week or so into the treatment, when I just couldn't stop crying – I was totally overcome with this feeling of hopelessness and cried at anything and everything.'

'I had a few days like that where I felt really moody, although that got better once I started the injections.'

'The forum was a lifesaver, though – being able to let off steam to you and the other girls. I'm so pleased it worked for Clover,' Pippa said. 'Third time of trying, can you imagine?'

'Have you been following her over on the first trimester thread?'

'Yeah, I cried when I read they saw a healthy baby at the twelve-week scan. If only, eh?'

'That'll be us one day.'

# Connie

Connie decided she liked Pippa. It wasn't often that she clicked with someone so easily, but she felt as if she'd known Pippa for years rather than just a few weeks, and via a faceless forum at that. That was the power of having something in common, particularly on such an emotional level. Funny how similar their experiences already were – obviously sad, yet comforting at the same time.

'So,' Connie asked, popping the last piece of carrot cake into her mouth, 'talking about treatment, how's cycle number two going?'

'It's weird. I feel calmer about this cycle despite the negative outcome of the first one.'

'It's probably because you know what to expect this time.'

Pippa nodded. 'I had a couple of sessions of acupuncture after you and so many others on the forum swore by it and I find it really relaxing, so I think that's helping.'

'How are you feeling? Still getting headaches?'

'Yep, and I'm feeling pretty tired but hopefully once I start stimming it'll be a bit better. I think I've been less emotional this time – I guess I'm looking at it realistically whereas last time I was so optimistic – too optimistic. I think I was really stressed the whole way through.'

'Ah, it's good. You sound really calm about it and being less stressed can only be a good thing. I think you're brave starting treatment again so soon.'

'You don't feel ready?'

'I'm not sure I'll ever feel truly ready to put myself through all that again. I think I need time to concentrate on something else for a while – maybe only another couple of months and then I'll feel ready. I know my husband isn't in any rush for us to try again. He's recently been promoted at work and is under a lot of pressure, plus I've got my jewellery business and some art fairs coming up this spring and summer and I don't particularly want to be a hormonal mess – well, more than I normally am – sniffing and injecting while busy spending time with potential customers.'

It felt really good for Connie to talk, knowing she wasn't boring someone who didn't understand the implications of what she was going through. They chatted a bit more about their jobs before swapping mobile numbers and agreeing to stay in contact.

'Thanks for meeting me in Bath,' Pippa said as they paid the bill. 'I can always come to Cardiff next time.'

'Oh, it's no problem.' Connie pulled on her cardigan and draped her scarf around her neck. 'I love Bath, so any excuse to come here is fine by me, plus I'm going to visit my parents in Cheltenham this afternoon.'

'You said you didn't get on.'

'We don't particularly, but we all try and make the effort from time to time. My brother and his family are there from London, staying with my parents for a few days, and I've not met my new nephew yet, so that's why I'm going.' Connie pushed open the cafe door and let Pippa through before stepping out into the warmth of the spring sunshine.

'That's going to be hard, isn't it?'

'Yes, but I can't be doing with all the comments if I make up an excuse for not going.'

'Your brother and his wife don't know you're going through fertility treatment either?'

'Nope, and I have no intention of telling them. They wouldn't understand and I don't want any prying questions.' They stood on the pavement outside the cafe, out of the way of the throng of people passing by. 'I feel bad too because it's actually my husband who's infertile, which is why we're doing

ICSI – they haven't found anything wrong with me.'

'That's good then,' Pippa said, 'in the sense that there might be a decent chance of you getting pregnant the next time you try.'

'I hope so.'

'How's your husband dealing with it all?'

'He's not.' Connie shrugged. 'I mean, he doesn't want to talk about it – about the fact that he's infertile. I know it was really tough on him, watching me go through all the ups and downs of treatment. I really hope he doesn't blame himself, because I certainly don't blame him.'

'See, for me it's different: Clive is fine and I'm the one with the problem.'

'I wish it was me with the issue. At least that way I could deal with it and wouldn't have to worry about Felix and how he's coping. He's the main reason why I haven't told anyone, particularly my family. He made it really clear about that, and we haven't told any of our friends – even friends of mine who Felix doesn't know.'

'God, that's tough, not having anyone you can offload on.'

'I've got you now,' Connie said and laughed.

'Absolutely! Anytime you need a chat or a shoulder to cry on, I'm here.'

'The same goes for you.'


The drive to her parents' house in Cheltenham took over an hour and a half because Connie opted for the longer yet scenic route past Westonbirt Arboretum and through Tetbury rather than along the M4 and straight up the M5. She liked having the time to think and what better place to be alone with her thoughts than on a drive through beautiful countryside. It was good to have met someone going through the same thing; however much she didn't wish her misery on anyone else, it was refreshing to have someone who understood the uncontrollable feelings of jealousy, resentment and even rage – all feelings she needed to get under control before walking through the front door of her parents' house. The thought of seeing her brother with his new baby erased the optimism she'd felt talking to Pippa, and so before reaching Cheltenham and facing her family, she decided to stop at the arboretum.

Dappled sunlight filtered through leafy branches and cast comforting warmth on the twig and leaf-strewn ground. It was too beautiful a day to be having negative thoughts, yet even the sight of a forest of acers in a blaze of deep red, fresh green and buttercup yellow did little to lift her spirits. She trudged on, forcing one foot in front of the other, determined to pound away the melancholy gripping her like a vice.

It was peaceful and she was glad there weren't many people about – fewer and fewer the further she walked away from the cafe and shop. She pulled a bottle of water from her bag and immediately wished it was spiked with vodka – anything to numb the pain. She'd been good for too long, drinking decaf tea and coffee, abstaining from alcohol, taking pre-pregnancy vitamins, and all for what? Nothing she'd done had actually helped her to have a baby. How many young women got knocked up after an alcohol or even a drug-fuelled evening out? Maybe a night of drunken sex with Felix was exactly what was needed. Everything had become so clinical and all the fun of trying to get pregnant had disappeared a long time ago – as soon as needles, scans and low mobility had been mentioned.

Connie stopped and looked around. She had wandered a little way off the path and was in a small grassy clearing surrounded by trees heavy with spring leaves and blossom. Not in the mood for making small talk with a stranger, she chose a spot in semi-shade out of sight of the path, leant back against the slender tree trunk and closed her eyes. A slight breeze caressed her face and every so often she got the wonderful sensation of sunlight on her. She took a deep breath and drank in the scent of damp grass and spring flowers – fresh, sweet and alive – then opened her eyes to a canopy of white against the blue sky. The apple tree was bursting with blossom like masses of white teardrops.

She had everything to live for even if it didn't feel like it right now. Life was a journey, and the best journeys were the ones that couldn't be predicted before setting off, or that weren't an easy ride to reach the destination. Right then, on a perfect spring day beneath the apple blossom, she made a pact with herself to keep loving life whatever was thrown at her. She may have suffered yet more disappointment but she could still see beauty in the world and feel at peace, enjoy the simple things in life: sunshine, the English countryside, a good book, a glass of wine...

Connie smiled as she took a sip of her water and picked up a fallen apple blossom. Sod it, she'd open a bottle of red tonight and have a glass or three. Onwards and upwards, that's what her aunt would tell her. In fact, she'd phone her aunt when she got back home; it had been a while since they'd spoken, with Connie being too wrapped up in her own life. She and Felix would move on from this failed cycle and try again, see if they'd have more luck the second time.

She felt somehow lighter on the walk back to the car, and although her eyes were tight and puffy from crying, she focused on the way the warmth of the sun hugged her shoulders and how the light filtered and danced through the lush green leaves overhead.

Her childhood home was an elegant Georgian house in a leafy and exclusive part of Cheltenham – so very different from where she lived with Felix in a modern two bed apartment on Cardiff's regenerated waterfront. The house reminded her of blazing rows with her parents over everything from her tomboyish nature when she was younger to her choice of clothes and career as she neared adulthood. Hate was too strong a word, but Connie never relished the thought of returning to her childhood home. She'd moved on and left behind the strained relationship she had with her parents and that was how she liked it. She wasn't even close to her older brother, Alexander, and the thought of playing happy families with him, her sister-in-law, her two-year-old niece and her new nephew made her feel physically sick.

With a deep breath, Connie thumped the door knocker and stood back, waiting for her father to open the blue Farrow and Ball painted front door.

'Constance, we expected you earlier.'

'I'm sorry, I said I was meeting someone and wouldn't be here until after lunch.'

Her father grunted. 'Well don't just stand there, come on in.'

Connie had always felt like the odd one out, not living up to the seriousness of her full name. Connie suited her better, more in keeping with her artistic and creative spirit. She followed her father through the spacious yet dark hallway and out to the formal dining room. It opened on to a large conservatory overlooking the perfectly manicured garden, her mother's pride and joy. Her father sat back down at the head of the table while her mother cleared away, kissing Connie on the cheek as she went past holding a pile of plates. Connie's brother sat between his daughter Francesca and his wife, Rachel, who held three-week-old Tobin in her arms.

'He's beautiful,' Connie said, unsure what to do with herself. 'No, no, don't get up.'

Too late – Alexander was already round her side of the table and Rachel was on her feet, Tobin snuggled against her, with his eyes closed, rosebud lips pouting.

Alexander hugged her. 'It's good to see you. We don't get to see you often enough.'

'Well, we all have busy lives.'

Rachel leant towards her and kissed her cheek. Up close, Tobin was even more gorgeous, his little hands tightly curled, his cheeks ridiculously squashable.

'Would you like a drink, Constance?' Her mother reappeared in the doorway. She looked tired – her hair greyer, the lines around her eyes more defined than the last time

Connie had seen her.

'Only if you're all having something.'

'I'm making a pot of Earl Grey.'

'Then yes, please.'

Connie turned back to her brother. 'Here, a little something for Tobin.' She handed Alexander a new baby boy bag and he passed it to Rachel who oohed and aahed as she reached in and pulled out four tiny outfits. It had been a bittersweet experience for Connie, walking into Next, the whole time wondering whether that was the only way she'd get to buy baby clothes – for someone else's baby. She'd allowed herself to dream for a minute that she was choosing them for her own baby, for a non-existent baby bump.

'It'll be you next,' Rachel said, as if reading her thoughts.

'Excuse me?'

'It'll be you and Felix, having a baby next, a little cousin for Francesca and Tobin.'

Connie felt her cheeks flush. She forced herself to smile. 'Hopefully one day.'

'Don't leave it too long – it'll be so nice if there's not too big a gap between the cousins. I always thought you'd have a baby first seeing as you got married before us.'

'Connie's been too busy with her work to worry about having kids,' Alexander said.

Connie nodded, doubtful she'd be able to contain her emotions if she tried to speak. If only they knew the truth.

'I'm just going to freshen up,' she managed to say, excusing herself from the room. She took the stairs two at a time to the bathroom on the first floor, locked the door behind her and leant against it. She shouldn't have come today, it was just too hard. All that positivity she'd felt after meeting and talking to Pippa had disappeared the moment she'd laid eyes on Tobin. She slumped down on the bathroom floor and sobbed. Her duty was done: she'd met Tobin, congratulated his parents, handed over a present. Now all she had to endure was a cup of tea and small talk before making her excuses and heading home to Cardiff.

# *Sienna*

It had been four days and nine hours, give or take a few minutes, since Sienna had temporarily moved in with Ashton and she was already going insane. To his credit Ashton was trying really hard – maybe a bit too hard – to make her feel at home and give her enough space, but Sienna's idea of space was quality alone time, not just half an hour with a book in the living room while Ashton disappeared into his bedroom.

His bedroom. Yes, over the past three years she had spent a lot of time in there, but it was still his room, and she quite liked that arrangement – along with the excitement of whether to stay over or not, or invite him back to her place. Not living together and staying over meant having sex, but Sienna had discovered that living together meant going to bed and not always having sex – reading instead, or only one of them going to bed early while the other watched a film. Four days and nine hours and she already felt like they'd been married for years.

Being between jobs, Sienna had the week off and escaped back to her flat when Ashton was at work. Living with Ashton meant she felt obliged to cook dinner for when he got home instead of ordering their usual takeaway or sticking a ready meal in the microwave. Another week and a half to go and she could go back home, yet she knew if she did their relationship was as good as over. If she didn't want to marry him, move in or have kids with him, what was the point? Best he move on and find someone who wanted all of those things. Maybe it'd be better next week when she had work to focus on and a couple of days in London. She would give it everything to make it work. After all, she did love him, she was certain of that – she'd never felt so strongly about anyone, and there were plenty of ex-boyfriends.

It had only been four days so Sienna needed to hold her tongue. Be positive and make the best of it – that's what both Pippa and Amy had advised her to do. She would go with the flow and happily snuggle on the sofa with Ashton in the evening watching *Britain's Got Talent*. The cuddling, at least, was nice.

Sienna groaned; nice was a word she so didn't want their relationship to be described as, but it seemed to be turning out that way – so very domesticated. Her mum would tell her that at thirty-four it was about time she grew up, acted her age and settled down with someone, preferably Ashton. Even her parents approved of him, and that was a first. It must be something to do with his good yet clean-cut look, his fantastic job and impeccable manners. What the fuck was wrong with her?

She took a sip of coffee and scrolled through her emails, stopping on one from Tulip, a good friend and a first assistant director she'd worked with numerous times.

*Tulip: I hear you're in London for a couple of days next week. How about crashing at mine hun so we can catch up? X*

Ashton was so not going to like that idea as he was expecting her to 'live' with him for the full two weeks. It was, however, crazy to commute between Bath and London for three days when she could stay with Tulip and save so much time and effort.

*Sienna: You're a star, Tulip! Would love to crash at yours, it'll be for two nights if that's okay, and obviously not going to get to you until later in the evening. Xx*

Done. Too late to change her mind, she'd just have to talk to Ashton when he got home. Sienna sighed; date nights and sex were so much easier than this living together bullshit.

\*     \*     \*

'So, you couldn't even last the full two weeks?' Ashton let his knife and fork clatter on to his plate.

Sienna had made an effort; after replying to a few emails, she'd cooked steak with a homemade peppercorn sauce, potato wedges and asparagus. Over dinner they'd talked about Ashton's day at work and Sienna's day off, which had been pretty uneventful, then after a couple of glasses of wine, she'd plucked up the courage to broach the subject of her staying with Tulip.

'It's practical,' Sienna replied.

'Maybe, but this is important.'

'I can't put my life on hold, Ashton, to play "house" with you.'

'Oh, you're unbelievable.'

'I can't help the fact that I'm working in London next week – you knew that when we organised these two weeks. It was now or wait until after the summer when I'm not on location any longer.' Sienna stuck her fork in a piece of steak and played around with it on her plate. 'If I commute I probably won't even get back here until after you've gone to bed, so what difference does it make?'

'It's fine, Sienna,' Ashton said. 'You don't need to keep making excuses. We might as well be honest: us living together is never going to work. Your heart's not in it.'

'What are you saying?'

'Why don't you just go back home?'

'I am trying, Ashton. This is me trying.'

'I'd hate to see what you'd be like not trying.'

Sienna looked across the table at Ashton with his arms folded and a frown etched across his face. She hadn't seen him laugh or even smile for a long time, probably not since the Maldives. He was deadly serious, no messing about – this time she'd really pissed him off.

'Just tell me one thing,' he said quietly. 'Is there someone else?'

'What? No. *No*. Of course there isn't. You really need to

ask that?'

'Yes, I do. I'm trying to understand what the problem with us is.'

'I'm the problem. Just me, not you, and there's not anyone else either.'

'Okay, I believe you.' He scraped back his chair and began clearing away the plates. 'Instead of temporarily living together, why don't we take a break from this.' He gestured towards her.

'You mean break up?'

'Yeah – temporarily, unless you want to end things.'

'No, I don't, I've never wanted that.'

'Fine. Let's give it four weeks where we don't see or speak to each other. I need space and you sure as hell do.'

'Starting when?'

'No better time than the present.' Still holding the plates, he kissed Sienna on the cheek before leaving her alone in the living room.

'We're on a break,' Sienna said. 'God, I sound like Ross from *Friends*.' She curled her legs beneath her and sank back into Tulip's huge sofa.

Tulip handed her a large glass of wine and sat down next to her. 'I thought you guys were going to get hitched at some point – I so did not see this coming.'

'No one seems to, except me.' Sienna took a large gulp of wine, immediately thinking she was drinking way too much. Relationships were stressful. Her job was stressful too but in a different way. She at least felt in control at work. With Ashton, she was out of her depth, playing at being a grown-up when she still felt and acted as if she was in her early twenties.

'What does Pippa think?'

'I can't burden Pippa with my fucked up life. She has enough to deal with, and anyway, I know what she'll say – she thinks I'm crazy for not jumping at the chance of moving in with Ashton and finally settling down, but that's because all she's wanted her whole life is a husband and a family. At least on the husband front she's found a keeper.'

'At least you've got work.' Tulip clinked her glass against Sienna's.

'Yeah, that's true. I think I need to be free to know that I can take on any job and be away from home for days or even weeks at a time. I don't want to have to turn down an opportunity because I'm living with someone.' Sienna played with the hem of her top. 'That's so fucking selfish of me, isn't it?'

'Maybe. Okay, yes, but it's kinda the way I feel about my job too. I don't want to turn down the chance of working on an amazing film because I'm worried about what my boyfriend thinks, but for me it's fine because my boyfriend works in our industry and so totally understands. He's away filming a lot of the time anyway so we both get to do what we love and don't resent each other.'

'So, what you're saying is I need to find some assistant director or sexy producer or crazy good-looking sparks guy to go out with instead of Ashton.'

'I'm not saying that but it would make life a little easier for you.'

That it would, thought Sienna. There was only one problem and that was she loved Ashton so wasn't sure she could give him up. She had a long day ahead of her and Tulip's comfy spare bed was calling.

She snuggled down beneath the duvet with her iPad and went on to Pippa's blog to read the latest post.

*4th May blog post:*

### *It Only Takes One*

*Yesterday I went to the clinic for my second egg collection operation under general anaesthetic. I never wanted us to be in the position of having to go through treatment for a second time, but on the plus side it's so much easier knowing what to expect at each stage having done it all before.*

*Clive did his bit – a private room, a collection tube and some dirty magazines seems so unfair compared to an operating theatre, a general anaesthetic and a ruddy great long needle being inserted into a place that a needle should never be inserted. The upside to undergoing a general was being knocked out and unaware of all the prodding and poking. The downside was coming round in the recovery room when a horrible grogginess, an ache in my lower abdomen and groin, along with slight queasiness took over. It was all worth it though when the doctor told us they'd collected fourteen eggs. Fourteen! Two more than last time. Does that bode well? I know it's quality over quantity, but even so, a couple more eggs to play with – as it were – can be no bad thing.*

*Now I'm back home and off work for a couple of days with Clive looking after me and it's the waiting game again, this time for the embryologist to ring the day after next with the details of how many eggs have fertilised. We only got seven last time so this time we're hoping for more. Although, as everyone on the forum keeps saying, 'It only takes one'. True enough, but a few will be less nerve-wracking than pinning all our hopes on just one little embie.*

*Until I have more news I'll sign off and get some rest. Fingers crossed. x*

Sienna took out her mobile and replied to the text Pippa had sent earlier in the day.

*Sienna: Sorry Pip, didn't have enough time to phone but been thinking about you loads. I've just read your blog post – loving your humour and I'm going to say again how brave you are. Had to read most of it with my legs crossed though – ouch! So pleased it all went well and you got that many eggs :-) Will def have to catch up when I'm back in Bath. Virtual hugs to you. Xx*

Sienna shut down her iPad and hugged the pillow. She had an early start in the morning but her head was buzzing and wouldn't let her switch off and sleep. She kept thinking about Pippa, hoping that the success of the treatment would translate into a pregnancy, until her head flooded with thoughts of Ashton back in Bath and how she was going to get out of the mess they found themselves in. Relationships sucked; she'd never been any good at them and her disastrous temporary move in with Ashton had proved that.

She closed her eyes and willed sleep to take over and erase the image of Ashton imprinted on her mind.

# Pippa

It was good news, actually brilliant news the embryologist rang her with two days after the egg collection operation. Out of the fourteen eggs collected, twelve of them had fertilised. Such a good number didn't stop her feeling nervous about the daily call from the embryologist updating her with how the embryos were progressing, but by day four, six embryos were still going strong and she was booked in for the egg transfer procedure the next day. On a high, and before even texting Sienna, Pippa emailed Connie.

*Hi Connie,*

*So happy! We have six embryos that have made it to the blastocyst stage and the embryologist is going to phone again in the morning with another update but the bottom line is we're going in tomorrow to have one transferred. Everything feels more positive this time round and I don't know whether it's simply my attitude or if I'm more relaxed because I've done this all before. I have pre and post transfer sessions of acupuncture booked so we're all set. It sounds like we might get some blastocysts left over to freeze too. Amazing!*

*How are you? It was so lovely to meet you in person the other week and we should definitely do it again soon.*

*Hugs to you,*

*Pippa x*

*Hey Pippa,*

*I agree about meeting up again and I loved being able to talk to you about everything. I'm totally made up you've had such a success with this cycle and I have a good feeling about what lies ahead for your two week* wait. The acupuncture will help too so enjoy those couple of hours of relaxation and think positive, welcoming thoughts to that little blastocyst!

As for me, I phoned the clinic only a couple of days after meeting you. Seeing my brother with his wife, daughter and new baby made me feel unbelievably crap about everything, despite feeling so optimistic after seeing you. I figured having my work to concentrate on while going through another cycle of treatment might actually be a good thing, to have something else positive going on, so after discussing it with Felix – who is happy as long as I'm happy – we're going to start treatment again. In fact really soon as I spoke to one of the nurses at the clinic and we're booked in to start on the 9th of May. Not going to be too far behind you now! Excited and scared at the same time. Can you imagine if we end up pregnant together? Okay, so I'm getting ahead of myself, but like you I feel really positive at the moment. Long may that last. The very best of luck for tomorrow – I have everything crossed that your little blasto gets sticky, and if you need a distraction or a shoulder to cry on during the dreaded two week wait you know where I am.

Love Connie xx

Pippa re-read Connie's reply and couldn't believe she'd only known her a few months and met her for the first time a couple of weeks before. It felt as if they'd known each other for years, they'd been so comfortable with each other from the moment they met. She quickly typed a reply and thought how wonderful it really would be if they ended up pregnant at the same time.

That's amazing news, Connie! So excited you're starting again – here's hoping it'll be happy news for us both this time. Think I will definitely need distracting during the next couple of weeks so I may well take you up on your offer :-)

Pippa x

A busy time at work did little to take her mind off the two week wait. With every twinge and symptom Pippa couldn't help but allow her mind to wander to the what ifs – what if she was pregnant? That would mean in a few months' time she could go on maternity leave and kiss her job goodbye for a year at least. When she wasn't working she spent as much time as possible outside, making the most of the spring sunshine: weeding the garden, wandering through Bath and even treating herself to a swim at the Thermae Bath Spa.

It was a beautiful early evening when she left the spa, and instead of heading straight home, she decided to go via Ashton's to surprise Sienna.

'Pippa, hi,' Ashton said, answering the intercom.

'Hey, Ashton, is Sienna home?'

'Nope.'

'I thought she was back from London.'

'She is,' he said. 'But she's at her house.'

'Oh, I thought she'd moved in with you. Temporarily at least.'

'It was so temporary it could only be described as staying over. She's back at hers, I presume – we've not seen or spoken to each other since she went to London. She didn't tell you we've split up?'

'What? No.'

'Well, we're taking a break at least.'

'I've kinda been wrapped up in my own stuff. I'm so sorry, Ashton.'

'Thanks, and if you see her you might want to try talking some sense into her.'

Ashton said goodbye and disconnected and Pippa leant back on the front garden wall. Had she really been so consumed by her own life and fertility treatment she did not see what was going on with Sienna? With a heavy heart she walked the fifteen minutes to Sienna's place and rang the doorbell.

'Hey, Pippa,' Sienna said and flung her arms around her friend. Pippa hugged her back.

'I've just been to Ashton's because I thought you'd be there.'

'Oh.'

'Why on earth didn't you tell me you'd split up?' Pippa asked, following Sienna through the living room and into the kitchen.

'Honestly, Pip, I didn't want to burden you with my worries.'

'You're my best friend, Sienna, you can talk to me about anything. I know fertility treatment is taking over my life but I'd be glad of a distraction and talking about something else.'

'Come and sit outside.' Sienna handed her a Magnum from the freezer. 'I need ice cream and I'm not eating one on my own.'

Sienna's garden was smaller than Pippa's and simply shingled with a few shrubs dotted along the edges. There was a BBQ area against the far wall, table and chairs outside the kitchen's bi-fold doors and a small water feature trickling over pebbles shadowed by the dusky red leaves of an acer in the centre.

Pippa sat down on one of the chairs that faced the garden. 'Tell me what happened, then.'

'It's as simple as I moved in with him, suggested I stayed with Tulip when I worked in London, and he wasn't happy about that so suggested we take a break, which we're doing.'

'What does your mum think about all this?'

'I haven't told her because she'll think I'm a fool, like you do.'

'I don't think you're a fool, you know that; it's just I wish you'd see how good you are together.'

'I don't know what the answer is. I can't see it working if I try and move back in with him and if I don't then it's pretty much over anyway.'

'So you're avoiding making a decision.'

'That's about right.' Sienna took a bite of her ice cream. 'You know me too well.'

'You can't bury your head in the sand over this.'

'And you're in the middle of your two week wait?'

'Nice change of subject, Sienna.'

'I'm a master at avoiding difficult questions, and now, it seems, you are too.'

Pippa laughed. 'We should see each other more often, you make me laugh. Yes, I'm about halfway through the two week wait and so could be pregnant or not. I have no idea. I test in six days' time, if I can bear to wait that long.'

'And you really have no idea?'

'I've had twinges, a bit of period type pain, a weird bubbly feeling but it could mean something positive or it could be that my period's about to start. I'm trying not to analyse it but it's hard, and I don't know what I'll do if we get another negative.'

'You won't, though.'

'Sienna, there's every chance we will.'

Sienna reached out and squeezed Pippa's hand. 'I know, my lovely, but I'm going to be overly optimistic because I know you won't be. I've taken on a last minute job so I'm going to be away but make sure you text me as soon as you know. Just six more days then.'

'Yep, six very long days.'

\*     \*     \*

*19th May blog post:*

## Test Day Number Two

*Why is it always the way when you want something so badly it seems to be constantly paraded in your face? Whenever I go anywhere all I see are ladies with lovely pregnant bumps and mums with their babies having coffee and cuddles in our local cafe. On TV every programme seems to feature someone being surprised to find out that they're pregnant (because it's that easy). Grand Designs makes me laugh because you can guarantee the young couple building their dream (family) house will reveal halfway through the programme that they are expecting and need to get the build finished before the baby arrives. And as for the TV programme One Born Every Minute that so many people are raving about, well, I can't even bear to watch that. Is there a baby boom or is it the simple fact that I'm so wrapped up in having a baby that I'm suddenly noticing all these things?*

*Well, today I have real hope that I'll be joining those lovely mammas drinking coffee and breastfeeding their little ones in our local cafe. I've never known a feeling like it – after the disappointment and upset of the first cycle's negative when I did the pregnancy test, I couldn't look this time. My nerves were so bad I was shaking and felt physically sick – how I would have coped seeing another negative I don't know, but not well. I had to get Clive to look I was such a mess and, unbelievably, it was a positive! So, that feeling I've never felt before, it was a combination of sheer relief and utter joy. I cried and laughed at the same time, we hugged and cried some more, then we phoned my parents and then Clive's and we all laughed and cried a lot more.*

*I know there's a long way to go and I'm only four weeks and two days pregnant, but life is good. Life is finally very good. I called this blog The Hopeful Years and today that hope has turned into reality.*

*It goes to show that the downs of life make the ups all the sweeter.*

*I don't have work today, which is just as well because I don't think anyone would be able to drag me down from cloud nine to do anything the least bit productive. Instead, I'm going to celebrate and enjoy today. After four years, one month and seventeen days since we started trying, I am pregnant. I am actually pregnant!*

Pippa logged out of WordPress and realised she couldn't stop grinning. What a day – what a year. It was the craziest feeling in the world, knowing she was pregnant – that after all those weeks of treatment and procedures, a tiny life was growing inside her.

The first thing Sienna had said to her when she phoned to share the good news was, 'I told you so.'

All day Pippa was conscious that she was pregnant – she went for a walk through the centre of Bath and browsed the shops, allowing herself a brief sneaky peek at the baby clothes section of Next and H&M before getting a takeaway latte and drinking it in the peace of Henrietta Gardens. Silently she talked to her little embie about how she would take him or her to play in the park when he or she was older. Four weeks and two days old and she already had a part of her embie's future planned.

She logged on to the forum on her phone and started writing.

*Posted 19th May:*

*Ladies, I didn't dare hope but this morning I got a BFP! I still can't believe it! Everything went right this cycle and I'm praying that will continue. Stay sticky, little embie. I have everything crossed that all of you lovely ladies get good news too when it's your turn to test. Fingers crossed I'll see you all over on the first trimester thread.*

*Hope Xx*

# *Georgie*

'When can I see you again?'

'It's not that simple, Felix,' Georgie said, tucking her feet beneath her on the sofa. The baby monitor was on the coffee table and Nathan wasn't home yet. 'It's Daisy's second birthday tomorrow, plus Nathan has been working late a lot recently. Planning an evening out takes some doing. Are you not working in Bristol again anytime soon?'

'No plans to for a while as there's lots to do in Cardiff and the team needs me here. If you can manage to get a free evening, then I'll be able to make an excuse to come to Bristol.'

An excuse for his wife. It didn't sit comfortably with her, the thought of cheating with a married man, but she was doing exactly the same to Nathan. It bothered her that she felt guiltier about Felix's wife than her own husband. Georgie didn't know anything about her – who she was, what she looked like, how old she was, what she did, even her name – the same as Felix didn't really know much about Nathan. She figured it was better this way to keep the guilt at bay – not having to think about what they were doing behind their other half's backs.

'I want to see you,' Felix said.

'Where's your wife?'

'At yoga. Why?'

'I wondered how long we've got.'

'She won't be back until half nine.' There was a pause and Georgie held her breath wondering what he was about to say.

'I keep thinking about that night. I wish we hadn't stopped.'

Georgie bit her lip and smoothed out a crease in her black linen trousers with the back of her hand. 'I wish we hadn't either but we were both drunk and I had to get home. It would have been rushed and the last thing I want is to regret something.'

'But you do want *something*?'

All she needed to say was no and it would put an end to it. She had Nathan and Daisy, a good job and a beautiful home – why would she want to risk all of that?

'Yes, if you do?'

'You know I do.'

'I'll work on trying to get a babysitter for an evening, even if it can't be Nathan. Maybe Daisy can stay at my mum's.'

'Or even better a weekend.'

Georgie snorted. 'I'm not a miracle worker…' A key turned in the front door. 'I'll see you at work on Monday, then, and we can talk about it more.' Nathan came into the living room and dumped his briefcase on the sideboard. 'But a spa weekend sounds like a fabulous idea, Melinda. I'll have a word with Nathan.'

'Clever girl,' Felix said. 'Talk to you soon.'

'Bye.' Georgie pressed end call and tucked her mobile in her trouser pocket. 'Hey there. Long day?'

Nathan nodded and slumped in the armchair closest to the TV. 'What's that about a spa weekend?'

'Oh nothing, just something Melinda from work was suggesting. She thought I could do with some relaxation but to be honest I think it's her excuse to get a bit of R&R.' Georgie shocked herself with how easily the lies tumbled from her mouth. 'I sounded interested for Melinda's sake, but I know a weekend away is asking too much, so don't worry.'

'When are you thinking of going?'

'Oh, um, Melinda suggested sometime soon.'

'As long as it's not the last weekend in July when I've got this conference in Manchester, then go ahead and organise it.'

Nathan picked up the remote. 'Do you mind if I watch the news?'

'Go for it.'

How easy was that? Georgie sank back into the cushions and realised she'd done it now. Committed to her deceit, she texted Felix on his work mobile to let him know the good news.

Georgie's mind was still firmly on Felix the next morning, which made her worry that she'd said something during the night like mentioned his name. She glanced at the bedside clock and groaned when she saw it was only 6.14.

'Why is it when Daisy sleeps in I end up waking early?'

Nathan was already sitting up in bed typing on his laptop. Georgie sighed, sank back on to her pillow and closed her eyes.

'I'm surprised too – thought she'd be dying to open her presents.'

Georgie's eyes flew open. Daisy's birthday. Oh God, how had she managed to forget about that and be thinking about Felix instead after all the preparations she'd done yesterday?

'Your body clock has adjusted to early mornings, that's why you wake up early,' Nathan said, looking at her over the top of his glasses like a teacher at parents' evening.

'Well, I wish it would adjust back again.'

'I'm sure it will when she's a teenager and doesn't want to get out of bed.'

'Mummy!' A little voice called out on the monitor. 'Mummy!'

'There you go,' Nathan said and smiled. 'Lie-ins never last long.' He closed his laptop and put it on his bedside table.

'Mummy!' There was a thump which sounded like Daisy sliding out of bed and landing on the floor before tiny feet thudded across her bedroom. She opened her door, crossed the landing and came crashing into their room.

'Happy birthday, sweetie,' Nathan said as Daisy launched

herself on him. He picked her up and cuddled her until she was sprawled in the middle of the bed between them. Georgie leant down and kissed Daisy on the forehead and stroked her strawberry blonde hair.

'Happy birthday, baby girl.'

The house was packed with family and friends taking over the open-plan kitchen and living area and spilling out into the garden. Daisy's first birthday had been a quiet affair, but this was a proper celebration and Daisy was loving every second of it, particularly all the attention. Presents were piled high on the coffee table, the birthday cake was a tower of pastel-coloured fairy cakes that Georgie had picked up the day before, and Daisy's toddler friends were careering around the living room, chasing each other and throwing themselves on to the sofa, the armchairs and anyone foolish enough to sit down.

The only people that seemed to be missing so far were Pippa and Clive who were coming along with Sienna. Their lateness made Georgie wonder what was going on. She knew that Pippa and Clive had had a successful second round of fertility treatment, but she hadn't heard anything since they'd had the seven-week scan the day before. Pippa's mood could change the whole tone of the party – maybe they wouldn't come if it had been bad news. Georgie didn't think she could deal with an emotional fallout from Pippa today of all days. She knew it was horrible to think like that but to hell with it. She wanted a simple, uncomplicated relationship again with her sister. That wasn't too much to ask, surely?

Georgie grabbed a jug of elderflower for the grown-ups and one of squash for the kids and started walking around the room, topping up drinks and talking to friends as she went, minding out for screeching two-year-olds as they darted around legs and furniture.

The doorbell rang. 'Nathan, can you get that?' Georgie called across the room. When he didn't answer she looked round to find him deep in conversation with one of the dads from her antenatal group. She set the jugs down on the table, left the chatter behind in the living room and went to the front door.

'Pippa! I wasn't sure if you were coming.'

Pippa leant forwards and gave her a hug and a kiss on the cheek. 'Sorry we're late.'

'My fault,' Sienna said, planting a kiss on both cheeks. 'I got the train back from London this morning and it was delayed.'

'Hi, Clive,' Georgie said as he gave her a hug, then she turned back to Pippa. 'Well? You're pregnant, and?'

'And the scan was amazing, like incredible. There was a heartbeat, an actual heartbeat. This tiny jellybean shaped thing is alive with a little thumping heartbeat.'

Georgie pulled her in for a hug. 'You look like you've been crying.'

Pippa nodded. 'Happy tears. And Clive too. We couldn't believe it. To wait all this time and then to see that – it was beyond a miracle.'

'So what's next?'

'Well, we've officially been signed off from the clinic and it can be treated like a normal pregnancy now, so I need to make a midwife appointment and then wait for the twelve-week scan.'

'Oh Pippa, that's fantastic news.' Georgie hugged her sister again. 'Come on through, all of you. Daisy's around somewhere.'

Georgie led them through to the living area, bit her lip and glanced across the room to where Nathan was still deep in conversation. Gone was her excuse for delaying having another baby. She was happy that Pippa was finally pregnant but she hadn't thought it would happen anytime soon for her and Clive, even with fertility treatment. Pippa was always saying it was a gamble and how slim their chances were.

Daisy was lying in the middle of the floor, screaming and thumping her fists on the carpet while Nathan's mum tried to calm her down. Why did Pippa want this when she had a perfectly lovely life that involved plenty of sleep, spur of the moment trips to the cinema and meals out in restaurants without a kid's menu?

Georgie took a deep breath and crossed the room, knelt down and placed her hand on Daisy's back. 'She's tired and has had too much cake,' she said to her mother-in-law. 'Daisy, why don't we go upstairs so you can have a little sleep?'

'No!' Daisy shrieked, flinging Georgie's hand away and throwing herself back down on the floor.

You have all this to look forward to, Georgie thought as she struggled past Pippa with a screaming Daisy under her arm in a rugby ball hold.

# SUMMER

## *Connie*

Test day was officially Sunday 21st June but by Friday morning Connie couldn't wait any longer. With no specific symptoms telling her deep down that the treatment had worked, she had to know one way or another.

She woke up early with her stomach churning. What if it was negative? Would it be better to wait one more day and have another twenty-four hours of being blissfully PUPO? But it might be positive and then she could relax. Swinging her legs out of bed, she made her mind up, told Felix and went into the bathroom. With shaky hands and a thudding heart, she did the test and placed it on the shelf above the sink. Now for the agonising wait for the digital test to show 'pregnant' or 'not pregnant'.

Connie was about to go and ask Felix to come into the bathroom when she noticed that the flashing timer symbol on the test had stopped and the result was already showing.

'Pregnant 2–3 weeks'.

That was quick.

She checked it again. Oh. My. God.

Connie padded down the hallway to the bedroom.

'Felix, it's positive.'

'You've done it already?' He slid out of bed and followed her along the hallway to the bathroom.

'It came up straight away. I thought it was going to take ages.'

How very different it was this time. Last time she'd been convinced that the treatment had worked only to be bitterly disappointed by a negative test result. So she'd been right to test early. Had she known deep down that she was pregnant? Whatever it was, it was the most incredible feeling. She pinched herself, actually pinched herself to make sure she was awake.

Felix pulled her to him and hugged her tight before nuzzling his face in her hair and kissing the top of her head.

'Babe, I'm so happy,' he said.

How cute would it be if their baby ended up having a Welsh accent as gorgeous as Felix's? Slow down, Connie, she thought, resting her face against Felix's chest and breathing him in. It was a positive, yet there was a very long way to go, and somehow she needed to contain her emotions.

To hell with that. 'Could you not phone in sick today so we can celebrate together?'

'Haven't you got work to do?'

'Yes, but nothing that can't be put off until tomorrow. It's not every day you find out you're pregnant.'

'I'd love to, babe, but I've got a big client meeting this afternoon and then I've got to prepare for working in Bristol next weekend. We can celebrate together this evening, go out for a meal. How does that sound?'

'That sounds fine.' Connie made a pouty face and then smiled. 'I know you're married to your job as well as me. You'll just have to promise to make more time when we have this baby.'

'Jumping a bit ahead there, Connie.'

'I know, I just never really imagined this day would actually happen.'

'Pippa, I'm pregnant!' Connie shrieked down the phone.

'Oh my God, that's amazing!'

'I can't believe we're pregnant together and there's only about a month between us.'

'Oh Connie, do you know how happy that's made me? I was praying that you'd tell me good news. I seriously couldn't stand the thought of being pregnant and it not working out for you.'

'How are you feeling? Still nauseous?'

'Yeah, really nauseous and I've been sick a couple of times. I feel really fat too and look like I'm pregnant already but I think that's down to the treatment: the boosting follicles stage just leaves me really bloated, but I can't wait to have a bump – ah, it'll be so amazing. I bet Felix is over the moon.'

'I think so. He had to shoot off to work this morning so we didn't have much time to talk. We're going to go out this evening to celebrate.'

'Nice. It's such a special moment, isn't it, realising that all those weeks of treatment and years of trying for a baby have finally resulted in being pregnant?'

'Have you got your twelve-week scan booked yet?'

'Yep, 15th July.'

'Are you nervous?'

'It's weird – it's only been a week since the first scan but it seems forever until the next one. I just hope everything is fine with the baby and it's developing normally. It was a tiny jellybean shaped thing last week, but by twelve weeks it should actually look like a little baby. I can't get my head around it really.'

'Well, roll on the seven-week scan for us – that'll be the next hurdle.'

The restaurant Connie and Felix went to that evening was one that they'd wanted to go to for ages. If ever there was a reason to go, then today was the day. Dressed in a floaty maxi skirt with a couple of layered cotton tops, Connie felt as if she was walking on air. Felix met her straight from work but he'd taken off his grey suit jacket and unbuttoned the top two buttons of his white shirt to reveal a hint of his tanned and toned chest. Connie almost had to pinch herself that this was real – not only was she married to the most gorgeous man in the world, but she was actually pregnant with his child.

'I still can't believe it,' Connie said, clinking her glass of pineapple juice against Felix's wine glass. They were seated on plush velvet-covered chairs at a table on the mezzanine level which overlooked the rest of the restaurant and the impressive chapel arches and tiled walls.

'To be honest, I didn't think it was going to work,' Felix said, taking hold of Connie's hand across the table. 'Not after the first time.'

'Same here, but it did. Are you ready for this?'

'Is anyone ever ready?'

'I guess not.'

'Are you going to tell anyone?' Felix asked. 'Like your parents?'

Connie shook her head. 'No, I don't think we should until after the twelve-week scan. It's not like anyone knows we've been having fertility treatment anyway. I have told Pippa, though.'

'Pippa?'

'You know, the friend I told you about.' When Felix still looked blank, Connie continued, 'We met via the fertility centre's forum.' Felix frowned. 'Her and her husband have been trying for a baby for the same length of time we have, and she's actually eight weeks pregnant now after their second cycle worked too.'

'Ah okay, Pippa, I remember now. That's pretty cool, you both being pregnant at the same time.'

'That's what we said when we spoke earlier.'

Connie's stomach was rumbling by the time her slow roasted belly pork arrived along with potato and parsnip mash, spring greens and a redcurrant jus. They ate in silence for a while, and all Connie could think about was that she was feeding her baby and helping it grow.

'I'm just going to pop to the loo,' Felix said, putting his napkin on his plate and smoothing down the front of his shirt as he stood up. 'Wine's going straight through me.'

'Rub it in, why don't you, that you have a whole bottle to yourself.'

He kissed her on the forehead and walked away.

Connie got her mobile out of her bag and scrolled through her contacts. It was strange not being able to tell anyone the greatest news she'd ever had. She placed her mobile on the table and sighed. How sweet would it be after the scan in eight weeks' time when she could tell the world.

Buzz, buzz, buzz...

It wasn't her mobile. She glanced across to where Felix had left his on the table, but it wasn't that one either. It sounded like it was coming from his jacket pocket. Connie leant across and pulled out an iPhone. It must be Felix's work mobile, she thought. 'Georgie' the name on the screen said, above which was an image of a smiling and rather pretty blonde woman. Connie toyed with the idea of answering it but let it go to voicemail. Georgie didn't leave a message.

Connie popped the iPhone back in the jacket pocket and sat down. She rested her hands across her stomach and smiled – grow, little embie, grow big and strong.

'Do you fancy pudding?' Felix asked as he rejoined her.

'No thanks, I'm stuffed. I could manage a coffee, though. By the way, your phone was ringing.'

'Did you answer it?'

Connie shook her head. 'It was the one in your jacket pocket.'

Felix coughed. 'My work phone? I thought I'd switched it off.'

'Someone called Georgie.'

'Oh right, yes, that, um, that must have been about the meeting in Bristol.' Felix picked up his wine and took a couple of sips. 'Whatever it was it can wait until tomorrow as I'm out celebrating with my wife. I do love you, Connie.'

'I love you too.'

# *Georgie*

'I really appreciate you letting me have a weekend away.' Georgie kissed Nathan on the cheek.

'You do realise you don't need permission from me to go away.'

'I know, but I'm leaving you with Daisy for a whole weekend while I go and get pampered.'

Nathan stroked Georgie's cheek. 'Hey, it's no hardship spending time with Daisy. I'm looking forward to it.'

'That's good, and Daisy will love having some alone time with you. She's such a Daddy's girl.' Georgie put her overnight bag into the car and closed the passenger door with a thud. 'Give her another kiss from me when she wakes up.'

'Of course.' Nathan kissed her before opening the car door. 'Have fun.'

'I will, thank you.' Georgie popped on her sunglasses, climbed into the car, started the engine and pulled out of their drive before she had a chance to change her mind. Nathan kept waving until she rounded the corner at the end of their cul-de-sac.

Nathan loved her, there was no doubt about that, and he was besotted with Daisy – she was too, but she needed some time away. Time away from them both. The sensible thing would have been actually to go for a spa weekend with Melinda rather than hooking up with Felix, but she couldn't resist him any longer. She needed to know whether it was some very early midlife crisis she was going through and she simply needed to get it out of her system, or if she really had fallen for Felix and out of love with Nathan.

She turned the radio on and increased the volume as she joined the M4 in the direction of Wales. It was the first weekend in July, the sun was shining, music blared and she fought back any feelings of regret or worry, willing herself to enjoy the moment. She had a nearly three hour journey ahead of her – plenty of time to calm her nerves and quash any lingering worries.

Georgie almost believed she was arriving at a spa retreat, the place was so secluded. A single track wound its way through a forest of trees and dappled sunlight danced on to the lane through the leafy canopy. The cottage was less cottagey and more log cabin than she'd imagined, yet it had a stunning position on the edge of a lake miles from anyone or anything. Georgie's heart skipped a beat when she realised Felix's car was already parked outside. Was it total madness that she was effectively meeting a stranger in the middle of nowhere and no one knew where she actually was? No one. Two evenings out along with a handful of phone calls, emails and texts did not constitute really knowing someone.

Felix appeared in the doorway of the cabin wearing jeans and a fitted T-shirt and clutching two bottles of beer. Georgie's hand hovered over the ignition before her heart won over her head – she wanted to feel his hands on her again, plus she was dying for an ice cold beer in the sunshine. She turned off the ignition, took her overnight bag off the passenger seat and stepped out of the car.

She'd dressed in a black and white strapless maxi dress that showed off her tanned shoulders, hint of cleavage and skimmed her stomach. Her blonde hair was down and fell in loose waves against her neck.

'You found it okay, then,' Felix called out as she walked towards him. She could sense him looking her up and down inch by inch. He reached down to take her bag and handed her one of the beers before brushing her cheek with a stubbly kiss. Georgie breathed a sigh of relief that he hadn't tried to kiss her properly straight away. However much she thought he was sexy – and he was, very – she wanted to be eased in gently and with quite a bit of alcohol inside her before anything else…

Georgie felt herself blush at the thought. It was like she was a teenager again, about to sleep with someone for the first time, except it was so much more romantic than any liaisons she'd had before meeting Nathan.

'How did you find this place? It's gorgeous,' Georgie said, taking a large swig of lager and following Felix inside.

'One of my mates from the gym brought his girlfriend here last year and I thought it sounded perfect.'

'It is.'

'Nice and secluded – there's not even mobile reception. My kind of relaxation.'

Inside was open-plan with a sleek modern kitchen and contemporary living space complete with comfy sofa, flat screen TV and a wood burner.

'It must be really cosy in winter.'

'But in summer there's the added advantage of a deck with a hot tub that overlooks the lake.'

Georgie peered past the dining table to open bi-fold doors that led on to a deck. She wandered over, took another swig of lager and gazed down towards the shimmering lake with a picnic table on its shore.

And just one bedroom, Georgie noted. She swallowed – she was going to have sex tonight with someone other than her husband.

'I hope you brought plenty of beer.'

'Yes, and wine. What do you like? Red, white or rosé?'

'A glass of white out on that deck sounds perfect to me.'

With the wine flowing, Georgie began to relax, and after a couple of glasses and small talk about work, Wales and the cottage, she swapped her sandals for a pair of canvas trainers and they took a walk around the lake. It was only towards the end of the walk when the cottage was in sight that Felix took hold of her hand and pointed to a squirrel scampering across the path and up the nearest tree. Then he kissed her, a long, lingering kiss that made Georgie forget all her worries and sent tingles coursing through her body.

Felix had told her not to worry about food and for dinner he produced stir-fried prawns with noodles and pak choi along with more wine. They ate at dusk by the lake on the picnic table lit by candlelight. Lanterns hung above the deck so they could find their way back once it got fully dark.

'I haven't been this relaxed for a very long time,' Georgie said, putting her fork on her empty plate and picking up her wine glass. Holidays since Daisy had been born had been hectic and not exactly restful, and before that they'd tended to go on city breaks or somewhere further afield where there was plenty of culture as Nathan wasn't keen on just lying on a beach. Georgie had enjoyed seeing all the places they'd been to, but she hated the way her feet always ached at the end of the day. Felix seemed to be the kind of person who simply enjoyed kicking back and relaxing, and Georgie wasn't going to argue with that. In fact, it felt pretty much like heaven right that minute.

'You certainly know how to look after a girl. That was seriously delicious.' Georgie patted her stomach. His wife was one lucky lady – the thought slipped into her head before she could censor it. She shrugged it off; she had to stop thinking about his wife and about Nathan and Daisy. Selfish as it was, this weekend was for her and about her. It would be the only way that she'd be able to decide about her relationship and her future. She knew Pippa and her friends would have suggested marriage counselling as the sensible option but she was fed up with being sensible.

'Fancy a soak in the hot tub?' Felix asked.

'I didn't bring a swimsuit.'

'What's wrong with bra and knickers?'

Georgie blushed. 'Um, I'm kinda not wearing a bra.'

Felix's smile looked wicked in the flickering candlelight.

'Nothing wrong with just knickers then.'

Felix took another bottle of white that had been chilling in a cool box and sauntered over to the hot tub on the deck. Georgie downed the dregs of her wine and followed him, aware her head was slightly fuzzy and she definitely couldn't walk in a straight line. By the time she reached the tub, Felix already had his T-shirt off, had kicked off his trainers and was unbuttoning his jeans. To hell with it, Georgie thought, this was what this weekend was all about.

She slipped off her shoes, and without a second thought wriggled her dress up and over her head, leaving it pooled on the decking. Felix was just in his pants. He held out his hand to help her into the hot tub, all the while his eyes feasting on her nakedness, then climbed in after her. Before she could say a word he'd wrapped his arms around her. His hands found her breasts as he pulled her close and kissed her neck. Georgie leant back into him, rested her head in the crook of his shoulder and looked up to the canopy of trees above and the black sky beyond pitted with silver stars. When Felix's hands began to tug down her knickers, she closed her eyes and emptied her mind.

# Connie

Connie woke late on Saturday morning, yawned and stretched out across the king-sized bed. Not only did she have the bed to herself, she had the whole weekend stretching ahead with no work planned. Felix had left early and was working away in Bristol for the rest of the weekend, so she was going to use the time to do things for herself, starting with a lazy breakfast followed by lunch with friends, a takeaway for dinner and a film that Felix wouldn't be interested in.

She tucked her hands behind her head and rested back on the pillows. She wasn't alone, though; she kept having to remind herself that she was pregnant. Five weeks and five days to be exact. Inside, her tiny baby was growing each day, and the nausea, which had started the day after she took the pregnancy test, was a constant reminder – except this morning she wasn't feeling sick, she realised.

She made herself scrambled eggs on toast and sat outside on their balcony overlooking Cardiff Bay. Born in a large Georgian terraced house packed with original features in Cheltenham, Connie had been surprised by how much she'd fallen in love with a modern open-plan apartment in Cardiff when she and Felix had bought the place three years ago. It felt good not only being independent from her parents but in a place that was so far removed from what they liked and valued – like their opinion of Felix. They thought he was too flashy. Connie knew they'd have preferred for her to settle down with a doctor or an accountant rather than the account executive of a large advertising company. But then again, she was fully aware that they didn't approve of her own career.

Despite her showing initiative and building up a successful business, it was far too creative for their taste.

After breakfast and a leisurely shower, Connie dressed in multi-coloured palazzo trousers and a black vest top before retrieving her car from the underground car park. The drive to Cheltenham was familiar and weirdly comforting despite her never thinking of Cheltenham as home. In fact, she always dreaded visiting her parents but this time it was different. She was meeting friends and her parents had no clue she would even be there.

Connie met Tilda and Charlotte in a coffee shop in the centre of Cheltenham. Friends since school, both had kids, with Charlotte a stay at home mum of two and Tilda a busy full-time working mum of one. Connie hadn't seen them in a long time, mainly because hearing about their kids had all been too much. Until now. Now, with the knowledge she was pregnant, she was looking forward to catching up. Despite them all being another year or two older with busy lives, she liked the way they slotted back together and their conversations seemed to continue from where they'd last left off.

'How was Menorca?' Connie asked Charlotte once they'd ordered food, got their coffees and settled down at a table towards the back of the cafe.

'Amazing, and believe it or not, actually more relaxing than I thought it would be with a toddler and an eleven-month-old.'

'That's because you went all-inclusive,' Tilda said, taking a sip of her cappuccino. 'I've never liked all-inclusive but we're thinking of doing that when we go to Greece in September.'

'It's totally worth it, so easy,' Charlotte said.

Tilda turned to Connie. 'So, when are you and Felix going to have a baby, then?'

Connie had been waiting for this question, inevitable ever since she'd turned thirty and got married. It was a question she dreaded but at the grand old age of thirty-six it was one that people seemed to ask her frequently.

'We're working on it.'

'Well, that is the fun part. It all goes downhill once you're pregnant and you've actually had the baby.'

Connie smiled and took a sip of her lemonade. All she wanted to do was shout 'I am pregnant!' at them, but she didn't want to jinx anything before she reached the magical twelve week mark.

'I found both my pregnancies so hard,' Charlotte said. 'Sickness day and night for three months, then awful heartburn once I got to the last trimester, and as for the tiredness...'

It was second nature for Connie to tune out of pregnancy and baby talk – in the past it had been too hard to listen and pretend to be okay while desperately longing to suffer with morning sickness, heartburn and stretch marks. She took a bite of her feta and sweet potato panini and shifted positions, realising there was a dull ache in her lower abdomen – probably her little embryo digging in deeper or general pregnancy aches, she thought.

Connie was buzzing by the time she hugged her friends goodbye with the promise of seeing them again soon. She almost told them her pregnancy news but the nagging thought that she'd somehow mess things up made her stop. She'd be able to tell them in a few weeks anyway, and then they'd have a good laugh about how she'd actually been pregnant when they'd last seen her.

The journey back to Cardiff was slow, and Connie had painful twinges in her lower abdomen that made her thankful to get home. She was beginning to understand Charlotte's pregnancy complaints. As soon as she got in the apartment, she switched the kettle on, then nipped to the toilet and gasped. There was blood – not a lot but definitely some. With her heart thumping, she went back out to the living area, sat on the sofa and took deep breaths. The ache in her lower stomach was still there and now this.

She texted Pippa.

*Connie: I've just had some spotting – completely freaked me out x*

Within a minute, Pippa replied.

*Pippa: Is it just spotting? No bright red blood or lots of blood?*

*Connie: Just spotting but my lower abdo hurts. I've just got this horrible feeling. X*

*Pippa: Oh my lovely, I'm sure everything's ok. Lots of women have bleeding in early pregnancy and it all turns out fine. You can always phone the clinic if you're worried.*

*Connie: I'll see how things go. I think I'm just worrying more with Felix away with work. I'm going to put my feet up this afternoon, watch a film and go to bed early. Thanks for putting my mind at rest. x*

*Pippa: You're welcome. Sending you a virtual hug and you know I'm here – call me anytime if you need to. Xx*

*Connie: Thanks Pippa. Xx All ok with you? Xx*

*Pippa: All good thanks. Morning sickness is beginning to ease off at last and in fact I didn't feel sick at all this morning. Nearly eleven weeks now and scan is only week and a half away – exciting but nerve-wracking at the same time! Let me know how things go and remember I'm here. Xxxx*

Connie knew something was wrong the moment she woke up. The ache she'd had the day before was now a full on searing pain across her lower stomach and back. But something else felt very wrong. She flung the duvet back, swung her legs out of bed and shakily stood up. Blood dripped down her leg from beneath her shorts. The cream sheet was stained red, and the pain intensified now she was standing.

'No, no, no,' Connie sobbed, still in a daze from sleep. Feeling as if she was in the middle of a nightmare, she staggered along the hallway to the bathroom.

There was too much blood. Way too much blood and pain for everything to be okay. This was no longer spotting – she couldn't kid herself any more that everything would be fine. In a haze of tears she cleaned herself up, pulled on yoga pants, stripped the bed, found her mobile and called Felix. It went straight to answerphone. She pressed end call and redialled but got his voicemail again.

'Felix, when you get this, please call.' She took a deep breath and fought back fresh tears. 'I think I'm having a miscarriage. There's so much blood. I really need you here.'

He would be home by early evening but it was nine in the morning, too many hours to wait. Unable to get hold of Felix, she took Pippa's advice from the day before and phoned the fertility clinic, but had an agonising twenty minute wait until one of the nurses was able to phone her back.

'Hello, Connie, it's Kathryn. You left a message to say you've had some bleeding?'

Connie somehow managed to find her voice. 'A lot of bleeding and pain.'

'Where's the pain?' Kathryn asked.

'My lower abdomen and back.'

'Is the pain on one side of your abdomen or all the way across?'

'All the way across. I'm pretty certain I'm miscarrying.'

'That is a possibility,' Kathryn said. 'But there may be other reasons too for the bleeding. Any shoulder pain?'

'No.'

'How many weeks are you?'

'I'll be six weeks tomorrow.'

'And when did the bleeding start?'

'This morning, although I had some spotting yesterday.'

'Have you done a pregnancy test?'

'No, I didn't think about that.'

'That's no problem. Once we've finished talking, if you're able to get a pregnancy test it might give us an idea of what's going on.' Kathryn paused and Connie could hear muffled voices in the background. 'There are likely to be three scenarios. The first is that you are unfortunately having an early miscarriage and a pregnancy test will show up as negative. The second possibility is that you're losing one of the embryos that were transferred and you're still pregnant with the other one. And thirdly, which is why I asked if the pain was on one side or your shoulder, you're suffering an ectopic pregnancy, in which case a pregnancy test would come back as positive.'

'Okay,' Connie managed to say despite feeling numb.

'Is there anyone with you?'

'No, my husband's away with work and I can't get hold of him.'

'Is there anyone else you can call?'

'Yes, there's someone.'

'Okay, good. So, give us a call back once you've got the test result and then we'll see where we go from there. And if you have any other worries just call, particularly if your pain and bleeding worsen.'

'Thank you so much.'

'You're welcome. Take care.'

Perched on the edge of the sofa, Connie gripped her mobile tight and sobbed. Three possibilities and only two were realistic – the two that she didn't want. Deep down, Connie knew the truth without having to do another pregnancy test, but she did one all the same.

Nearly two weeks before she'd celebrated with Felix when the test had almost immediately stated 'pregnant 2–3 weeks'. This time she was alone and after an agonising wait it simply said 'negative'. She wasn't pregnant any longer. Her hopes and dreams for their future had literally been flushed away. It all made sense now, the reason why the nausea had stopped and the start of the dull period-type pain.

She'd had two weeks to dream and plan and feel wonderfully alive and pregnant. And now nothing, only emptiness.

'Felix, I presume you haven't heard my earlier message yet or you've been unable to phone me. It is definitely a miscarriage. I've lost our baby.'

What she needed was Felix to hold her tight in his arms and tell her that it would all be okay, that he loved her and one day they would have their much longed for family. One day. After all, it was what she and Felix wanted more than anything in the world.

# *Sienna*

'I know we're on a break but I've come over to talk.'

Sienna was fully aware that it was early on a Sunday morning and Ashton wasn't one for getting up when he didn't have to, but she'd had stuff on her mind for days, plus a big work decision to make. The radio silence with Ashton had to stop.

There was a pause over the intercom before Ashton said, 'Come on up.'

Sienna took the stairs two at a time and found Ashton with sticky-up hair, wearing boxer shorts and a T-shirt, holding the door open for her. She really had got him out of bed.

'Hey,' she said as she brushed past him.

'Hey.' He closed the door behind her.

'I know it's early,' she said, following him into the kitchen, 'but I've got things I need to discuss with you.'

Ashton picked up a mug of coffee from the worktop. 'Is this personal stuff or work related?'

'Work related but that makes it personal too because it'll potentially have an impact on us.'

'There is no us at the moment.'

Sienna took a step back.

'Oh, well I thought we were on a break not actually splitting up, but if that's how you feel about things, maybe there's no need for me to be having this conversation with you after all.'

'Sienna, I'm sorry. I'm angry, that's all. It's been nearly

two months since we last saw each other, so let's talk.' He motioned towards the living room. 'Do you want a coffee?'

'No thanks.' Sienna walked into the next room. 'You do realise I'm trying to do the grown-up relationshippy type thing here by discussing my life with you?'

Ashton followed her in with his coffee and sat next to her on the sofa. 'Yes, I realise. So shoot, what is it?'

'I've been offered a job working on a series that's tipped to be the next *Game of Thrones* and I really want to do it, but...'

'But?'

'It's a huge commitment, potentially over a number of years if it gets the green light, and I'm likely to be away from home a lot.'

'So no different from how things already are?'

'Except this could be an ongoing project and a series takes up a lot more time than a film.'

Ashton took a sip of his coffee, put it down on the coffee table and turned to Sienna. 'If you're wanting me to give you my blessing then that's not going to happen. You know how I feel about things and what I want from our relationship. Marriage and kids pretty much sound like they're off the table if you're contemplating taking on a job like this.'

Sienna bit her lip.

'You've already made up your mind, haven't you?'

'It's an opportunity I can't say no to.'

'Then you've just made a mockery of saying this is a conversation about us, because it blatantly isn't if you're going to say yes to the job. You know our relationship won't survive something like this.'

'I know, but I hoped it would.'

He downed the rest of his coffee and slammed the mug on to the table. 'Then you're naïve as well as selfish.'

Sienna couldn't argue with that. It hurt, but it was true – she was hoping for the impossible; for Ashton to change what he wanted from life without her having to budge one bit. The decision between working on a fantasy adventure series like she'd been offered compared to having kids and settling down was an easy one. The decision to give up Ashton was a lot harder, and that was what hurt.

'How can I love and hate you so much at the same time?' Ashton said.

'I can't begin to tell you how sorry I am that I make you feel that way, and yes, it's probably down to me being selfish, but I can't give up my career.'

'I'm not asking you to give up your career, just make different choices so we can actually function as a normal couple.'

'Like work on *Casualty*?'

'I didn't say that.'

'You do realise that any film or interesting series is likely to take me away from home; that's the nature of my job and you've known that ever since we got together.'

'Then the reality is we've grown apart.'

Sienna pulled him to her until their foreheads touched. 'So, this is it?'

'I can't see how we can continue with us both wanting such different things, and I'm not prepared to do the long distance thing any longer.'

Sienna kissed the top of his head. 'It may not seem like it but I do love you.'

Ashton gave a hollow laugh. 'Yeah, you're right about that – it doesn't seem like it.'

She pulled slightly away and looked at him. He leant forwards and kissed her, this time on the lips. Without thinking she ran her hand beneath his T-shirt and up his smooth back, feeling his muscles tense as she did. He kissed her harder and pushed her back on the sofa. The last thing she'd expected to happen this morning was sex with Ashton. Bugger, she should have put on a matching bra and knickers. With his eyes closed and eager fingers tugging at her bra strap, it didn't seem as if Ashton cared what she was wearing. At least she hadn't initiated it; he couldn't blame her this time for treating their relationship as just sex, and anyway, hadn't they properly split up?

Ashton pulled her top over her head and dropped her bra on the rug. If this was how they behaved when their relationship was over then they should have split up ages ago, Sienna thought, closing her eyes and kissing him. She was going to miss this. Miss him.

# *Pippa*

'What happens afterwards? I mean, would you want to have a second?' Sita asked as she and Pippa ate their sandwiches in the sunshine on the wall outside their office building.

'I'm only just twelve weeks pregnant. There's a long way to go yet and I can't even think that far ahead. But to be honest, at the moment having one healthy baby is more than I could have dreamt of – two would pretty much be a miracle. A friend of mine who's also gone through two lots of fertility treatment ended up having an early miscarriage just over a week ago. Anything can happen.'

'But it doesn't mean anything bad's going to happen to you. Are you excited about the scan tomorrow?'

'Excited and so nervous. I mean, I feel shaky just thinking about it so can you imagine the state I'll be in tomorrow?' Pippa took a bite of her falafel wrap and looked across the road to the Georgian houses opposite, imagining pushing her baby in a pram through Bath in a few months' time.

'It'll be absolutely fine,' Sita said. 'The wait for the twenty-week scan is worse because between twelve and twenty weeks all those early pregnancy symptoms fade away, yet it's too early to really feel the baby kick so you almost don't feel pregnant again, if that makes sense.'

'Totally,' Pippa said. 'All my early symptoms, like morning sickness and feeling wiped out, have already disappeared, so I get what you mean.'

'Make sure you enjoy the second trimester before you get too big and the tiredness kicks in again.'

'I will do, I promise.'

Pippa woke before her alarm went off and lay in bed thinking how the waiting was even more nerve-wracking than before the seven-week scan. Clive snored beside her, so she swung her legs out of bed, put on her slippers and padded downstairs to the kitchen to make a decaf coffee in an attempt to calm her nerves. It didn't work, and she had a lonely and nervous wait until Clive emerged an hour later.

Unlike the seven-week scan, the appointment was at the hospital in Bath rather than the fertility clinic in Bristol. Pippa and Clive didn't have to wait long before they were called through and she was asked to lie down, make herself comfortable and pull up her top to reveal her stomach.

The gel spread on her tummy was cold. The woman doing the ultrasound ran the scanner across her stomach; Pippa knew she was waiting to pick up the image of their baby before switching on the screen on the wall opposite to show them. Except, unlike the seven-week scan where they had been shown their little jellybean almost immediately, the technician was taking an age. Pippa studied her; she had been cheerful and welcoming, exactly the kind of person you'd want to be doing the scan, but her smile slowly faded.

When she paused, Pippa noticed her frown. Pippa gripped Clive's hand, but before she could say anything the technician turned towards them.

'I'm so very sorry to have to tell you this, but your baby doesn't have a heartbeat.' She turned the wall-mounted monitor on. It showed the most perfect image of a growing baby. No longer a jellybean, it had a large head and a body with arm and leg buds, but it was still and that wonderful flickering heartbeat they'd seen only five weeks before was no longer there.

'Please, no,' Pippa said, tears welling up.

'How can that be?' Clive put his other hand on top of Pippa's.

'I've had no bleeding, no pain…'

'Unfortunately this can happen when there's something wrong with the embryo so it stops growing. It's known as a missed miscarriage because it's exactly that – you have no indication of anything being wrong until we do a scan.'

Clive pulled Pippa close until her head rested against his chest and her tears made a damp patch on his T-shirt.

'What happens now?'

*     *     *

*20th July blog post:*

### Heartbroken

*I started this blog to detail my journey to become a mum, both the highs and the lows. This last week has been the lowest point and it's taken me a good few days to find the courage and will to write and form coherent words.*

*Seven days ago I was exactly twelve weeks pregnant and blissfully happy – naturally nervous about the dating scan I was to have the next day but life was as sweet as it could be. Twenty-four hours later I was heartbroken. I had suffered what is known as a missed miscarriage where our baby had died at around eleven weeks, but I'd had no clue as there was no bleeding, no pain, nothing. In hindsight I realise my symptoms had begun to tail off around that point – the nausea eased and the need to pee all the time had stopped too, but I'd put that down to the fact that I was getting towards the end of the first trimester. How wrong I was, and how heartbreaking to find out at a scan that should have been full of so much joy that our seemingly perfect little baby had no heartbeat, and hadn't for days and days. All that time I'd been living a lie.*

*And the pain didn't stop there. Then came the decision of how to remove the foetus from my body. It's a cold, hard world at times and the terminology doesn't help. To me, I'd had a baby growing inside; medically, it was a foetus and one that evidently hadn't been viable. I'd done nothing wrong and there was nothing I could have done to keep our baby alive and growing big and strong like it was meant to. It was nature's way of telling us that our baby, for reasons we will never know,*

114

wasn't healthy. To have so much hope – to feel pregnant and see our tiny baby with a heartbeat and then a few weeks later without one – seems cruel beyond words. At least the negative pregnancy test was a clean end to our first IVF cycle. What I'm going through now is messy in all senses of the word, emotionally and physically.

My husband told me last night to find the positive in all of this – that I can actually get pregnant. At the moment all I can focus on is the fact that I've lost our baby and all my hopes and dreams have been extinguished. The thought of going through another cycle fills me with absolute dread, but perhaps I've got to get past the horror of this week and the surgery to remove our baby before I can look to the future. I know I intended to post about everything on this blog, both the ups and downs, but some things are too personal and don't need to be shared. All I will say is this: I have the procedure in a couple of days' time. I hope then I can begin to heal both physically and mentally. I'm going to have counselling at the fertility clinic. I figure I need time to grieve, for the baby we hoped to have and for the tiny baby that I've lost. Then, when the time is right we'll decide what to do next, and hopefully I'll be able to share the next part of my journey with you.

With tears spilling down her cheeks, Pippa re-read her post before clicking 'publish'.

# Sienna

Was that a blue line? If it was, it was very faint. What the hell did that mean?

Sienna placed the pregnancy test on the shelf below the mirror and took a deep breath. Fuck this, she needed to know what she was dealing with. Leaving the test and its indecisiveness on the side, she went to her bedroom and squeezed into black skinny jeans, pulled on a white vest top with a short-sleeved black T-shirt on top and slipped on a pair of flip-flops. Grabbing her house keys from the sideboard in the hall, she slung her bag over her shoulder and headed out of the front door.

The pharmacy was within walking distance, so it would only be a few minutes before she knew the truth. She grabbed a box with two digital tests and queued up, wishing they had a self-service till.

'Perhaps congratulations are in order?' the girl behind the till said as Sienna placed the test on the counter.

Sienna looked her up and down and glared. She was barely out of her teens with big blue eyes and perfect skin.

'Really? You think that's appropriate to say to me? You have no idea about my situation or if I'd even be happy if it's positive.'

'I'm sorry, I just…'

'Assumed too much. Can I have a bag, please?'

Red faced and eyes watering, the girl handed Sienna a small plastic bag. Sienna snatched it from her and stuffed the pregnancy test inside. Screw her. Sienna didn't care if the girl was upset, because she wasn't as upset as Sienna was right now, with her stomach churning and negative thoughts spinning around her head. Oh God, was the churny feeling the beginning of morning sickness? With a curt 'thanks', Sienna rushed out of the door and stalked home.

Sienna paced up and down the bathroom, willing the test to be negative, but there was no denying it this time. She was 100% pregnant. How the fuck had that happened? Except she knew exactly how it had happened, and she hated herself for being so bloody stupid. Unprotected break up sex. She was pregnant.

Forget about Ashton, how the hell was she going to tell Pippa?

Sienna hadn't given Tulip any choice in the matter. Even though she wasn't working in London, a week after she'd done the pregnancy test, Sienna invited herself to stay. She needed someone to talk to; someone who wasn't Pippa or Ashton or her parents or sisters. Tulip was the safe option: a workaholic with no intention of having kids anytime soon or perhaps ever. She would understand what Sienna was going through and be able to offer sound advice, or at the very least a shoulder to cry on.

'Hey there, sexy lady,' Tulip said with a grin as she opened the door to her apartment. 'I don't see you for ages then you stay with me twice within a few months. You look like shit. Are you alright?'

Sienna nodded and dumped her overnight bag on the hall floor.

'Bit of travel sickness.' To hell with it, she thought. It was pointless beating about the bush. 'From the pregnancy.'

'From the what?' Tulip slammed the door.

'I'm pregnant.'

'You have got to be kidding me.'

'I wish I was.'

'Oh honey,' Tulip said, giving her a hug. 'Come on in. I'd offer you a glass of wine, but…'

'A cup of tea will do.'

'I have cake. Sticky toffee – makes anyone feel better.'

It was a warm evening, even for early August, and what Sienna really wanted was to be sitting in a leafy pub garden, sipping a glass of Pimm's with not a care in the world. She sighed, realising a cup of tea and cake would have to make do and that a lot of things in her life were going to change.

Tulip handed Sienna a mug of tea and sat down on the sofa next to her. 'Is it Ashton's?'

'Seriously? You have to ask that?'

'Um, yeah, the last thing you told me was that you two had split up.'

'We were on a break and there isn't anyone else.'

'So,' Tulip said, taking a bite of cake, 'the fact that you're knocked up means that you got back together again?'

'Not exactly.'

'But you had sex.'

'Oh yeah, we had sex despite my intention to try and prove to him that I wasn't only with him for his body. Obviously a few weeks abstaining made him horny. But we had actually properly split up before that, so this is a complete mess.'

'How pregnant are you?'

'Only about five or six weeks.'

'Do you know what you're going to do?'

'Nope. My main worry right this minute is how the hell I tell Pippa I'm pregnant? A baby is all she's wanted for so long.'

'She's your best friend; she'll understand and be happy for you.'

'But she might not be and I wouldn't blame her. It'll be a total shock, me telling her this – I've never wanted kids, you know that. I don't want a baby and she does. I'm pregnant and she's had a miscarriage. Life is so fucking unfair. I don't want to lose her as a friend and I know that could happen. She's not wanted to be around other friends of ours who've been pregnant. I've seen her looking at women with babies in cafes and I know all she's thinking is I want to be like them, and now that's me. I've got to tell her before I start showing. This is so messed up. Do you know what? I'd do anything – *anything* to swap places with her. She'll be such a great mum. I'm not ready; I don't think I'll ever be ready.'

'Sienna, honey, no one's ever ready to become a mum, even if they totally wanted the baby to begin with. It's a life changer.'

'Thanks for reminding me my life is over.'

'No, it's not; it's just going to be different.'

'A lot different.'

'Admittedly yes, but I know you – you always make the best of things.'

'I spend a huge chunk of the year away from home with work. I work twelve hour days – at least twelve hours. A film set is no place for a baby.'

'That's what nurseries are for, hun.'

Sienna tucked her legs beneath her on the sofa and sighed. 'Yeah, but to stick a really young baby in a nursery makes me question why anyone would want a baby to begin with.'

'That's the problem,' Tulip said, twisting her fingers through her blonde curls. 'You don't want a baby.'

'My mum's going to be overjoyed and kill me at the same time.'

'Can she not look after it?'

'Not for me to go back to work full-time she won't. I'm so screwed.'

'What about Ashton? Maybe he can be a stay at home daddy.'

Sienna shot Tulip a look and glanced down at her stomach.

'Oh. My. God,' Tulip said, sitting forwards and putting her plate down on the coffee table. 'You haven't told him, have you.'

Sienna shook her head. 'Before we split up, all he was

119

banging on about was us having a baby and becoming a family, as if that was going to fix all that's wrong with our relationship. In theory, he sounds like he'd be the perfect family man but he's as married to his job as I am to mine. As for having a baby, I know he'll be up for all the fun stuff, but he won't want to give up work, or his rugby, or Friday nights out with his mates. I'll be the one left to do all the shitty stuff. Seriously, I'm not cut out to change nappies or clean up sick.'

'Well, he'll have to step up, there are no two ways about it.'

'Except we're not even together any more.' Sienna took a bite of cake, felt nauseous and dropped it back on the plate. 'I'm supposed to be going to Wales next month for that movie we're doing together. I have work lined up all the way through to next year and I've just taken on the biggest, most exciting series to work on. A baby is going to fuck everything up.'

'Maybe you should have thought about that before getting knocked up.'

'No shit, you think I did this intentionally?' Sienna prodded her stomach. 'I feel like a careless teenager, except I'm in my mid-thirties.'

'There are always options. You could get rid of it.'

Sienna placed her hands on her thighs and sighed. 'I know, and I have seriously thought about it but I don't think I can. For whatever fucked up reason, I'm pregnant and I can't destroy that, however much it's not what I want in my life. Pippa has suffered a miscarriage and infertility – I simply can't abort a baby.'

'What about having the baby and giving it up for adoption?'

'I've always been someone who commits to something 100%. I've decided to go through with this pregnancy, and so that means bringing up this baby too, however difficult that will be. I don't think I could live with myself if I aborted it. How can I give something that's a part of me up? Yes, my life will never be the same again, and yes, I'll have to make some major changes, but maybe this was meant to be.'

# *Georgie*

Full of old filing cabinets, folders and broken chairs, the back office was hot and stuffy, but it had the big advantage of no one ever having any need to use it. Georgie had already thought of the excuse that she was looking for a bigger filing cabinet to go under her desk. As for what Felix was doing in there with his hand up her skirt, she just prayed that no one would discover them.

'I can't believe it's been five weeks since our weekend in Wales.' Georgie had missed his touch, the feel of his strong arms around her and the smell of his musky aftershave and peppermint breath. After two days and a night of sex, hot tub action and little else, Georgie hadn't heard from him for nearly a week, and he hadn't answered his work phone either. Her immediate thought was he'd simply used her for a weekend of sex and that was it – she'd never see him again. Then she'd had the horrifying thought that he'd been disappointed – in her, her personality, her body, the sex. When he had finally got in touch, he'd sounded awful: really down and emotional. He gave her some line about troubles at home, which panicked her into thinking his wife had found out about their affair.

'I've missed you,' Felix said, running his fingers along the inside of her thighs. 'The thought of you is the only thing that's kept me going over the past few weeks.' He kissed her lightly on her cheek and continued to kiss his way to her neck.

Georgie leant back against the wall and gave in to his kisses. 'Are you okay? I mean, are things better at home now?'

He muffled a yes into her neck, and after a while pulled

away and looked at her. 'Things are what they are. I can't change what's happened or make things better; I just have to deal with it. But seeing you today has made me feel properly happy again for the first time in a long time. Well, ever since we were at the cabin.'

'I have no idea what's going on with you at home or with your wife, and I don't want to know – unless of course you want to talk to me about it – but you've just made me so happy.' Georgie reached out and cupped his face in her hands. 'During our weekend it was pretty obvious I made you happy, but afterwards... I wasn't sure you wanted to repeat any of it.'

'Are you kidding me?' He kissed her lips. 'I'd have you right now if it wasn't too risky.' He pulled his hands out from beneath her skirt and smoothed it down. 'Seriously, we can't risk being caught.'

'I know.' She kissed him lightly on the lips and gestured towards the door. 'After you.'

He turned back to her. 'I'll be away for a few days next weekend, but after that I should be able to arrange another working weekend away, or a day at the very least. Any chance you can get some time to yourself?'

Georgie nodded. 'I hope so.' She reached forward and touched his arm. 'I'm going to be near Cardiff on Saturday with my sister. After we've finished, if there's time, we could maybe meet.'

Felix kissed her again. 'Text me what time and where and I'll see if I can get away.'

Friday arrived and Georgie said a silent goodbye when Felix left the office to go home to Cardiff. He gave her a brief smile and headed out of the door.

'He's always looking at you, you know,' Melinda said, peering around the side of her computer.

Georgie's heart slammed into her ribs. 'Don't be ridiculous.'

'It is understandable,' she continued. 'You are extremely

pretty.'

'Now you're being silly.'

'He probably wants a distraction.' Melinda leant further across her desk towards Georgie and whispered, 'Jeremy said Felix's wife had a miscarriage a few weeks ago. Poor guy.' She disappeared behind her computer before popping her head back round. 'Don't tell anyone, mind – it's not common knowledge.'

Georgie stared at her computer screen, the words she'd been writing a blur. Her heart thumped and her hands trembled. That was the problem he and his wife had been having after her weekend with him at the cabin? His wife had been pregnant? Tears welled in Georgie's eyes. Was that any worse than her having a two-year-old daughter, plus a husband wanting them to try for another one? No wonder Felix hadn't been willing to discuss what had been going on at home. If they'd been trying for a baby, why on earth had he started an affair? And why was he continuing to be interested in her? Maybe the baby hadn't been planned.

Unable to concentrate and with only twenty minutes left until home time, Georgie saved what she'd been working on and spent the remaining time mindlessly filing away and deleting emails. All she wanted to do was talk to Felix and she was very tempted to phone him but thought better of it – if he wanted to talk to her about it, he would.

All the way home on the bus, Georgie kept thinking how little she knew about Felix and how much he knew about her. She gave away too much of herself all the time. She'd always been like that, and both Pippa and their mum had warned her in the past that she was too open with people and she'd get hurt one day. After being on a high from seeing Felix, she crashed right back down faced with a weekend of family commitments stretching ahead. Tomorrow she'd promised to spend a few hours with Pippa and then they'd have a family day on Sunday. All she wanted was time by herself or a few hours out of her life, which seemed to be getting more complicated and confusing by the day.

Nathan was halfway through giving Daisy her dinner by the time Georgie walked in. She dumped her bag on the floor and kicked off her high heels. Then it was the usual madness of bath, story, milk and bed. It was gone eight by the time they sat down to a meal of pepperoni pizza, oven chips and salad. They ate in front of the TV with trays on their laps, watching the second season of *Game of Thrones*.

'This probably isn't the best choice of programme to be watching while eating,' Nathan said, taking a bite of pizza.

Georgie didn't really care about the blood and guts when there was Jon Snow and Jaime Lannister to focus on.

'Close your eyes when it gets gruesome.'

'But I don't want to miss anything.'

'Then don't complain.'

Nathan glanced at her. 'Are you okay? You seem snappy.'

Georgie sighed. 'I'm sorry, it's been a long week.' And my lover's wife has had a miscarriage…

She stabbed a chip with her fork and put it in her mouth despite not being hungry.

'I know the feeling.'

It took Georgie a moment to realise he was talking about work, she was so wrapped up in the private conversation in her head. Of course he knew that feeling; he seemed to live for work and it was always a long week for him. What had her life come to? At the grand old age of twenty-nine she was sitting having a TV dinner on a Friday night, resenting the fact that her husband was eating his pizza with his mouth open.

'Are you still meeting Pippa tomorrow?' Nathan asked.

Georgie nodded. 'If that's still okay with you?'

'Of course. Have you decided what you're doing yet?'

Georgie put her half eaten tray of food down on the coffee table and sank back into the sofa, clutching her glass of wine. 'Pippa wants to go for a walk so I suggested going to St Fagan's near Cardiff.'

'That's quite a way.'

'We used to go there a lot with Mum and Dad when we were younger. I thought somewhere familiar with good memories would cheer her up. I'll do whatever makes her happy at the moment.'

Nathan mopped the last bit of mayonnaise up with a chip and munched it then patted his lips clean with a napkin. 'Do you know what? We should have tried for a baby while we had the chance.'

It took a moment for Georgie to realise what he was referring to.

'You are kidding me?' She turned sharply, nearly spilling her wine. 'You mean while Pippa was pregnant and happy?'

'Well, she's going to be your excuse for not trying again.'

'Unbelievable.' Georgie put her wine glass on the table next to her tray with as much care as she could manage. 'My sister has recently lost her much longed for baby and you're turning that into the reason why I'm not wanting to try for a baby.' She stood up, suddenly needing to get as much physical distance between her and Nathan as she could. 'Yes, it would kill me to have to tell Pippa that I was pregnant after what she's been through, but the real reason why I don't want us to start trying for another baby is because I'm not ready. You don't seem to understand that I don't want to have another baby right now; maybe not at all. It's always been your dream to have a large family, never mine.'

She waited a second or two for a response, then stalked from the room, an image of Daenerys entering the House of the Undying imprinted on her mind.

# *Pippa*

Sunlight glinted off the lake at St Fagan's. It was a perfect August day with blue sky, high white clouds and a slight breeze. Pippa and Georgie had arrived separately and met at the ticket office before walking through the grounds, past the whitewashed cottages and historic buildings that looked exactly the same as the last time they'd visited more than fifteen years ago. Georgie looked good with her short blonde hair straightened, wearing jeans that flattered her curves, a colourful cami with a three-quarter-length-sleeved grey cardigan over the top and brand new pink trainers. This was as casual as she got; when she wasn't wearing work clothes she was usually in a skirt or a pair of fitted trousers. How different they were; it made sense they were only half-sisters. Pippa had always been envious of Georgie's proper blonde hair compared to her own dark blonde locks. Their taste in clothes was different too, with Pippa favouring comfort over fashion, and she'd always dressed older than her years. Now that she'd reached her mid-thirties, Pippa's wardrobe of White Stuff clothes suited her perfectly.

They'd been walking for twenty minutes, chatting aimlessly about the weather, how beautiful the gardens were and how their mum was, before Georgie stopped and turned to Pippa.

'How are you?' she asked. 'I mean really, how are you doing? Or not doing?'

Pippa took a deep breath of fresh air and soaked up the peaceful beauty of the place. 'I'm okay.'

'Really?'

'No, not really. I feel angry, like every day I feel angry and *so* sad. If I see a woman walking down the road with a pram, or even worse a baby bump, I have to walk in the other direction. It hurts too much.'

Georgie stepped off the path on to the grass and wandered down the slope.

'How about down here by the lake for our picnic?' She opened out the picnic blanket that had been attached to her rucksack before pulling out a bottle of rosé. 'I thought we could have a grown-up picnic.'

Pippa shrugged off her rucksack, sat down on the blanket and stared out across the lake towards the wall of trees on the other side.

'I don't know what to say to make you feel better.' Georgie sat on the blanket next to Pippa and pulled Tupperware out of her bag.

'That's the problem: there isn't anything anyone can say to make things better. Most things that people do say are so not helpful.'

'Like what?'

'Like "it'll happen" or "you can always try again" or "if it's meant to be".' Pippa took the lid off a box of snack eggs and took a bite of one. 'There's no guarantee that it will happen for us, none whatsoever, and I don't have other people's optimism…'

'Like Mum's?'

'Like Mum's or most of my friends'. It's only my friend Connie who's being helpfully realistic with me and that's because she's going through the same thing. And as for trying again, it's not as simple as trying next month. We have to fork out a few thousand pounds first and I have to go through weeks of sniffing, injections, blood tests and procedures with my hormones all over the place and no guarantee I'll get pregnant, let alone have a baby at the end of it.' Pippa leant back on her hands and gazed up at the sky peppered with wispy clouds. She closed her eyes for a moment and relished the warmth of the sun on her face and the stillness all around her.

'I can't even begin to imagine how difficult it's been for you,' Georgie said.

Pippa opened her eyes and looked at her sister. 'I know none of this has been easy for you. I'm sorry.'

'Pip, you really don't have to apologise.'

Pippa sat upright and crossed her legs. 'This is some picnic,' she said, taking a slice of feta and red pepper quiche and a handful of crisps and putting them on a paper plate.

'Well, I wanted to treat you.' Georgie dunked a carrot stick into the hummus and took a bite. 'And I do have sparkling elderflower if you prefer.' She waved the bottle of wine in front of Pippa. 'I wasn't sure if you were still cutting out alcohol.'

'I was, but what the hell – a glass or two isn't going to make any difference.'

Georgie poured them each a glass of wine and handed one to Pippa before knocking the rims together.

'It's good to spend time with you.' Pippa rested back on one hand and took a sip of her wine. Across the other side of the lake, grass sloped up towards neat hedges and a bank of bushes and plants before reaching a path and the whitewashed St Fagan's Castle.

'I'm sorry, you know, for not being there for you over the past couple of years. I'm trying to make an effort to be more involved in your life, like the way we used to be.'

'I know, thank you,' Pippa said. 'I also pushed you away when you first had Daisy. It was just unbearably hard seeing you pregnant and then with a newborn when our hopes of having a family were getting further and further away. I think if you'd already had Daisy before we started trying for a baby, I'd have been able to deal with it better – it was watching you experience everything I wanted that killed me so much.'

'And now? How do you feel about being around Daisy?'

'Oddly better in some ways. Maybe it's because she's older

and more fun and it was the baby stage that really got to me. Or maybe it's because I'm becoming resigned to the fact that we might never be parents and I don't want to miss out on being an auntie to her.'

'You can't think like that, Pip, it'll…' Georgie trailed off.

'You were going to say "it'll happen", weren't you?' Pippa smiled.

Georgie held her hands up. 'Guilty. I think it's human nature to be optimistic about these things.'

'If someone could tell me for certain that in two, three or even ten years' time we'd finally have our family, I think I'd be okay with everything. It's the uncertainty that's so difficult. It feels like I'm in constant limbo, putting our life on hold for something that may never happen.'

'You should be enjoying your childfree years,' Georgie said, biting into a slice of quiche and catching the crumbs in a napkin as they fell.

'I've had enough of childfree years. Life is revolving around fertility treatment, and even if we did want to do exciting stuff, we have no money.'

'We can always lend you some if…'

'No, thank you, really we're fine. We just don't have any spare cash to do fun things like holidays.'

Pippa appreciated the effort her sister was making; she understood the last few years hadn't been easy for Georgie either with a new baby and an older sister who was in no fit state emotionally to look after Daisy and help take the pressure off. She wished things had been different, that they'd both been pregnant at the same time and had children of a similar age. There was no point in daydreaming about what hadn't happened, though. The past was behind them. Somehow she had to make the best out of the hand she'd been dealt.

Feeling full and slightly tipsy, Pippa helped Georgie pack their picnic away before they wandered back through the grounds with the sun on their shoulders. They stopped to get bread and cakes from the bakery and said goodbye at the entrance to the car park.

'It was so lovely to spend time with you,' Pippa said, hugging Georgie. 'Send my love to Daisy and Nathan.'

'Of course,' Georgie replied. 'And you know where I am if you need to talk.'

'Thank you.'

Georgie put her arms around her sister and gave her a squeeze. 'Don't wait for me,' she said, pulling away and taking her mobile from her pocket. 'I've got to send a text before I leave.'

With a wave, Pippa walked back to her car, threw her rucksack down on the passenger seat and began to cry.

# *Connie*

'I've got to pop into work this afternoon… Connie? Did you hear me?'

Connie poked her head around the bedroom door to find Felix in the hallway, stuffing his mobile and wallet into the back pocket of his jeans.

'You've got to go now?' she asked. 'I thought we were going for a walk.'

'I'm really sorry, babe,' he said, kissing her on the top of her head. 'It's a bit of an emergency. I'll only be a couple of hours, though.'

Connie shrugged. 'Fine.'

'Ah babe, don't be like that.' He pulled her to him and gave her a hug. 'I was going to leave it as a surprise, but to make up for today we're going away next weekend.'

'We are? As in you're actually taking time off work?'

'I really am.'

'And you're able to take time off?'

He nodded. 'The advantage of being a boss.'

'The disadvantage of being a boss is that you never take time off.'

'Well, I thought you could do with getting away and I wanted to treat you. I've checked your diary and I know you don't have any meetings or fairs lined up, so I figured why not? It's on me. All you need to do is pack a few things and don't forget your passport.'

'I'm going to have to get a lot of work done by Friday.'

'You'll do it. The thought of a few days away will be

motivation enough.'

'You going to tell me where we're going?'

'Do you want to know?'

Connie nodded. 'How can I pack if I don't know where we're going?'

'Good point.' Felix glanced at his watch. 'Amsterdam.'

'Oh, you're a star.' She kissed him.

'Haven't seen that smile in a while.' Felix pulled her to him and kissed the top of her head again. 'Now, I really must go.'

It was quiet without Felix. It always was. At parties he was the person that people gravitated towards, and at home he always seemed to take over, either talking to someone on the phone, playing the music he liked or controlling the TV remote. When she was alone Connie enjoyed the stillness of their apartment with the TV and radio off – she could sit with a cup of tea and enjoy the view over the bay. Felix was always too busy; too preoccupied with work, his phone, his laptop – anything but her, really. So him taking her away was a surprise.

Her mobile rang and Pippa's smiling face appeared on the screen.

'Hi there.' Connie opened the sliding doors leading from the living area and stepped out on to the balcony.

'Hey, Connie, are you free to talk? I'm having a bit of a wobble today.'

'Of course. I'm home alone anyway as Felix has gone into work for a couple of hours, but he is taking me on holiday next weekend. He only told me about it before he left. He's hoping it'll cheer me up.'

'Where are you going?'

'Amsterdam. I've always wanted to go there.'

'Sounds nice. Hopefully it'll take your mind off everything.'

'Why don't you and Clive go away somewhere?'

'We can't afford it,' Pippa said. 'Well, that's not technically true – we could, it's just we're putting all our spare cash aside for another round of treatment.'

'You've decided to go for it again then?'

'I've not given up yet, and we've got those four embryos in the freezer so it's a no brainer really. Clive and I were talking about it last night – it's just deciding when to try again. I can't face the thought of it at the moment and I don't think I'd be able to handle another disappointment. Are you guys going to give it another go?'

'I don't know, we've not talked about it. We've not talked about anything much recently.'

'Well, a holiday will be the perfect opportunity.'

'I must be really miserable for him to be taking two days off work when he's so busy.'

'It's good. He's putting you first for once and he so needs to with what you've been through.'

'That's the thing, it feels like it's only me who's been through it.' Connie rested her elbows on the balcony wall and looked out over the bay at the calm water glinting in the late afternoon sunshine. 'I don't know – maybe he's just being a man and hiding his emotions, but he seemed almost relieved when I told him I'd lost the baby.'

'I'm sure he's just controlling his emotions. Clive's different, he wears his heart on his sleeve – always has done – and took my miscarriage almost as hard as I did. I think he really thought that this was it – we both did.' Pippa sighed. 'Everyone keeps telling me it'll happen and it's pissing me off. Fertility treatment feels like a lottery. There are so many things that can go wrong at so many different stages, not least of all after actually getting pregnant. I know people are only trying to be helpful and keep my spirits up, but it's an empty gesture as no one knows if it'll work out for us. Telling me it will because they have a good feeling isn't going to up our chances.'

'See,' Connie said, 'that's why I'm glad I haven't told anyone about trying for a baby or doing ICSI. What really gets to me is how people – friends, family and even people I don't actually know very well – ask me personal questions thinking it's absolutely okay to do so. Because of my age and because I'm married, people are always banging on about when Felix and I are going to have a baby, or even worse asking if I don't want to have children, or commenting that my biological clock is ticking. Don't I bloody know it? Anyway, enough about me. What happened to upset you?'

'Oh nothing, really,' Pippa said. 'I mean, it's silly because I actually had a lovely day. My sister took me out to St Fagan's – a place near you…'

'Yeah, I know it.'

'It's been a beautiful day and it was so good to be out in the fresh air, chilling by the lake, chatting to my sister. Except despite all that I ended up feeling really sad because the place reminded me of my childhood, and that got me thinking how amazing it would be to take my own children there, and then of course I started thinking about our baby and how pregnant I should be and whether I'd have had a proper bump by now.'

'Oh Pippa, I wish I was there to give you a hug. I know it won't make you feel any better but I understand how you feel. You're not alone.'

'I wish for your sake you didn't have to understand this feeling.'

Connie looked down at a couple walking hand in hand along the waterfront. 'Life can be truly awful at times, but I guess that will make us appreciate the good times when they eventually care to show up.'

The hotel room was one of two apartments on the top two floors of a family's beautiful home overlooking one of Amsterdam's famous canals.

'This must have cost a fortune,' Connie said once the landlady had left them alone. She wandered through the open-plan living and dining area with its cute kitchenette and into the separate bathroom that overlooked a small garden backing on to the gardens of the canal houses opposite.

'Pretty special, huh?' Felix said, kissing Connie on her forehead before taking her hand and leading her back out into the living area where a steep staircase led up to a snug bedroom on a mezzanine level. 'And you're worth it.'

It was pretty special and pretty unexpected too, although very welcome. Connie felt drained, emotionally and physically, and this was the first time in months that she'd actually felt excited about something. They had four days to themselves to relax and explore the city. She'd spent the week finishing commissions, packaging up rings and necklaces and posting them off before working into the evening to get on top of paperwork and emails and lining up further work for the next few months. Apart from the emotional side of things, she needed a break from her business, and her hands needed a rest from soldering and shaping silver into rings and bracelets.

'Where do you fancy going today?' Felix asked once they'd unpacked and freshened up after their early morning flight.

Felix loved busy beach holidays with temperatures of at least thirty-plus degrees, sunshine and plenty of water sports on offer – in truth, Connie's idea of hell, but she knew that city breaks, sightseeing and shopping wouldn't be his first choice either, so she was going to make the most of being able to decide what to do for once.

'Why don't we wander and see what we can find?' Connie pulled her jacket on and finished her look with a lightweight scarf. 'There's the Anne Frank Museum, the flower market – oh, and the Rembrandt Museum…'

They set off, hand in hand, and Connie could almost believe that they were on their honeymoon again without any cares in the world, the excitement of planning a family and buying a place together on their minds. Except seven years on from their honeymoon there was more uncertainty and disappointment in their life than excitement. She was determined, though, to enjoy this much needed break and relish the opportunity to spend time with her husband.

Not only that, Amsterdam was a place she'd wanted to

visit for ages and it didn't disappoint. The first couple of days were spent exploring the city, discovering hidden lanes, beautiful canals and bridges, eating *frites* in the street and soaking up the many museums across the city that even Felix seemed to be genuinely interested in. After dark they dined out before wandering through the gaudy yet fascinating red-light district. On the last evening they got a takeaway from a noodle bar, a couple of bottles of wine and ate in their apartment, then relaxed on the sofa by the large windows that overlooked the canal.

'Felix, thank you so much for this holiday,' Connie said, taking a sip of coffee. She'd drunk the wine and, with a head beginning to swim, she'd moved on to a latte with a double shot of espresso. 'I really needed this time away to do things that normal couples do – things that don't involve hospitals or needles or my hormones being shot to pieces.'

'Maybe we shouldn't try again.'

Felix's words hung heavily in the room. Voices drifted up from outside, the tinkle of a bicycle bell along with jazz music from across the canal.

Connie frowned and shook her head. 'What do you mean?'

'I mean, not doing another round of fertility treatment.'

'Where's this coming from?'

Felix moved his arm from the back of the sofa and picked up his coffee. 'Nowhere. I just want to make sure it is what you really want.'

'I want a baby and a family of our own more than anything.' Connie carefully placed her mug on the coffee table. 'But now I'm worried that it's not what you want.'

'I want a baby but I don't want to keep going through this hell with the treatment, the…' He waved his hands in the direction of Connie. 'You know.'

'The miscarriage.'

'Yes. I don't want you to go through anything like that again.'

'You do realise that fertility treatment is the only way for us to have a baby.'

'For *me* to have a baby,' he said quietly. 'As far as we know there's nothing wrong with you. It's me that's stopping you from having a family.'

Connie shifted along the sofa and took his hand. 'We're in this together. There is no me or you, it's us – it's *our* problem and we'll get there. You can't go blaming yourself, otherwise I'll have to take the blame for losing our baby. It sucks, a lot, but it is what it is and we have to deal with it in the best way we can, get through it together and in one piece.'

'You always have been stronger than me emotionally.'

'Don't be ridiculous. You're strong too, it's just you bottle things up.' She rubbed her thumb along the side of his hand. 'I'm glad you're talking to me about this. I want to try again. We did say we'd try three times if it got that far, and here we are looking at number three. But if you really don't want to I won't put us through it again.'

'Even if it means not having a baby?'

'Even if it means not having a baby of our own.'

'Then we'll try again, one more shot.'

# AUTUMN

## *Pippa*

Pippa took the photos from the seven-week scan and cut off the bottom picture. A tiny jellybean shaped embryo with a heartbeat. *With a heartbeat.* Their baby had been growing inside her for weeks. Her memory of seeing that tiny heartbeat flickering so fast on the screen was vivid; an image that would remain with her for the rest of her life. What had gone wrong? It hadn't been viable, the sonographer at their twelve-week scan had told them. Not viable – a horrible word and one she'd heard too many times before as none of the other embryos had been viable either – just this was the one that all their hopes and dreams had been pinned on. From a healthy growing embryo at seven weeks to a non-viable one by twelve weeks. Their baby, gone. And it was a baby, she didn't care what anyone said. Technically an embryo, but in her heart that had been her much longed for baby growing and so cruelly taken away. What was worse – a negative pregnancy test or a pregnancy that ended far too soon? Find the positives, Clive had told her – she could get pregnant, it was possible.

Pippa placed the remaining two scan photos back in the pregnancy diary she'd started to write and shut it away in her bedside table drawer. She then carefully slipped the scan photo into the pocket of her grey linen trousers and went downstairs. It was the 15th September and exactly two months since they'd had the twelve-week scan and found out that their baby had died. Even now nothing felt real, as if she was walking through a dream – nothing tangible, nothing she could make any sense of. No way of grieving. She'd cried, probably more in the last few weeks than she'd cried altogether in the past few years, and yet she couldn't get rid of the feelings of anger and sheer heartache. She needed somewhere and some way to grieve properly.

It was a perfectly clear and still day without the nip of autumn in the air yet. She opened the patio doors and let the fresh air flood into the kitchen. The house had been in a state of disrepair when they'd bought it – not the sleek period meets contemporary finish they now had with polished wooden floors, shiny white kitchen units and granite worktops. It had been the garden that had sold the place to her. Not the biggest in the world but a decent size for a city. Again, the garden was different to the overgrown version they'd first seen, but the apple tree at the end remained the same. Simply stunning in spring when it dripped white blossom on to the grass below, it was the focal point of the garden all year round, even in winter when frost often coated its bare branches.

Pippa stepped outside and lifted her face to the gentle warmth of autumn sunshine. She drew in a breath and wished she could stay in that moment forever, never having to face reality or deal with the emotions suffocating her.

The patio next to their house led to a lawn that gently sloped up to the apple tree. Pippa followed the path that snaked the length of the garden and picked up a trowel from the border on the way.

The soil beneath the apple tree was soft and damp. Pippa knelt on the grass and began digging a hole deep enough for cats not to disturb it. Once finished, she sat back on her feet and took the scan photo from her pocket. She held it in her hand and ran a finger across the picture before kissing the tiny embryo image. The what could have been – a boy or a girl? Would it have looked like her or Clive? Would it have been born on its due date, which she knew was the 25th January due to the accuracy of IVF? All futile questions.

With a shaky hand she placed the scan picture image side up in the hole and said goodbye. Her time to grieve; her place to grieve. She threw the first bit of soil over the image and let her tears drip down on top.

She'd bought a heather and before filling in the soil she planted it so it would continue to grow and thrive despite her baby not.

Pippa stood up and brushed off the soil that stained her trousers. The heather was dwarfed by the tree but its tiny pale pink flowers stood out against the soil and the deep green of the grass. It was her place; somewhere she could come to cry, to sit, to think, to hope, to wish; somewhere she could channel all the negative thoughts that were messing with her head. It was private, a place only she would know about, but that she could see from the kitchen or the moment she stepped outside into the garden. She wasn't even sure if she'd tell Clive about it. Was he hurting as much as she was? Maybe, in a different way, but he didn't have the longing for a baby like she did, and hadn't had the experience of their baby growing inside.

She wiped away fresh tears and took a deep breath. It was done; she'd said goodbye. She needed to let all her negative feelings be buried like the picture and try and look towards the future. Hard, she knew, and it would take time, lots of time, but that had to be the way forward. There had to be a better place than the hell she was living in right now.

# *Georgie*

'I'm going to be out two nights in three days,' Georgie said, slicking berry red lipstick on and following Melinda out of the ladies.

'Lucky you,' Melinda said, holding the office door open for her.

It was 5.15 on a Friday afternoon in mid-September, and the majority of the Goldman and Peabody staff were in the main part of the open-plan office where their boss, Henry Goldman, had gathered everyone. Georgie perched on a desk next to Melinda and peered between people. Felix was in a grey suit and pale pink shirt, standing next to Henry who was droning on about how good the working relationship was between Bristol and the Cardiff office. Felix had taken his tie off and unbuttoned the top two buttons of his shirt. Even from where she sat, Georgie could see the tanned hollow of his neck, which she'd kissed so many times before...

She shuffled on the desk, folded her arms across her chest and tried to concentrate on what her boss was saying.

'Although I'm sure we'll see him again,' Henry Goldman continued, 'I'm sorry to say that today is the last official day that Felix will be working with us in Bristol.' He turned to Felix. 'It's been a pleasure having you with us on and off over the past year, and in true Goldman and Peabody tradition we're sending you off with a bottle of champagne and no doubt a hangover in the morning.'

Everyone laughed and Henry shook Felix's hand.

'Speech!' someone shouted from the back of the office.

'Thanks, everyone,' Felix said, holding up the champagne bottle. 'I'll save this for a special occasion... who am I kidding? I'll have polished it off by nine this evening. Joking aside, I've had a blast working in Bristol and will really miss the place and the people. I hope that some of you guys get to come and work with me in Cardiff sometime. Now, let's make the most of finishing fifteen minutes early and head to the pub.'

Without a doubt, Georgie was going to miss Felix at the Bristol office. It made her day when she knew she was going to see him, even if she couldn't speak to him. And those few times they'd managed to have a fumble in the back office...

'Georgie, you coming?'

Georgie slid off the desk and hooked her arm in Melinda's outstretched one.

'It's a shame Jeremy doesn't get to work in Bristol.'

'I'd quite like to go and work in Cardiff, though,' Melinda said. They picked up their handbags from their desks as they went past and followed everyone out of the office door. Felix was up ahead talking to a junior account executive: a pretty twenty-something with short black hair and a killer figure. A tug of jealousy shot through Georgie, which was ridiculous considering she had no hold over him anyway.

'Georgie, are you actually listening?'

'Sorry, what was that?' She tore her eyes away from Felix and looked at her friend. Melinda glanced ahead of them and smiled.

'I said, Jeremy has asked me to move in with him.'

'What? Seriously? Oh my God, I'm so pleased for you.'

'I, of course, said yes, but now I really need a job in Cardiff.'

'You could commute.' Georgie let go of Melinda's arm as they reached the street.

'You have to be kidding. However much I love my job, a three hour commute each day would drive me insane.'

Melinda was excited about the impending next step in her

relationship and talked enough for both of them. All Georgie wanted to do was spend time with Felix, talk to him and snuggle up with him on one of the large leather sofas in front of the pub's fireplace like a normal couple would – like Melinda would have been able to do with Jeremy if he had been there – but even talking to Felix was difficult. They had no reason to talk to each other at work and so there didn't seem any opportunity to go over to him while out either. Not only that, their work colleagues constantly surrounded him – Georgie had discovered it wasn't just her who liked him. There was something about him that drew people to him – both men and women wanted to be his friend, and probably more.

Georgie was three cocktails down when Melinda took hold of her arm, manoeuvred her away from their colleagues to the patio doors that led to a terraced garden and leant towards her.

'What's going on with you and Felix?'

Georgie pulled away and frowned. 'What? There's nothing going on.'

'I wasn't born yesterday, Georgie. It's kinda obvious the way you two look at each other. I've seen the way his hand lingers when he brushes past you.'

'We get on well, that's all.'

'I don't doubt that – Jeremy says as much. Felix is always talking to him about you.' Melinda leant back and folded her arms. 'So, are you having an affair?'

Georgie glanced around, took Melinda's hand and led her outside, making sure no one from the office was out there.

'Georgie, seriously, you can talk to me in complete confidence.'

Georgie took a deep breath and fought back tears. 'I haven't been happy in my marriage for a while. I love Daisy but I don't think I was ready to have her and it's been a struggle. Felix... Felix turned up at the wrong time, or maybe it was the right time. I feel so alive when I'm with him.'

'That's because you're getting good sex. In fact, I bet it's great sex.'

'Melinda, it's not just about, you know, the sex,' Georgie said, feeling her cheeks burn.

'I'm teasing you. I'm sorry, I've drunk too much, ignore me.' Melinda squeezed Georgie's arm. 'I know how you're feeling. I was in a bad marriage too, although it was my ex who had the affair, but it was the catalyst for me to eventually get out.'

'The trouble is, I'm not in a *bad* marriage. I mean, Nathan treats me really well, I genuinely loved him…'

'Loved him, past tense. So that's it – you've fallen out of love with him?'

'I think so.' Georgie wiped away a tear streaking down her cheek. 'It's a total mess.'

Melinda wrapped her arms around Georgie. 'Do you love Felix?'

'I think so, yes, but it's crazy because I don't really know him. He's married, and the thing you told me about his wife having a miscarriage – I mean, why is Felix with me?' Georgie pulled away and looked at Melinda. 'Am I just a distraction? Does he actually have feelings for me?'

'Hun, you have to talk to him. Are you two hooking up tonight?'

'I hope so.'

'Then talk. Don't just do the dirty, otherwise you're going to end up more confused, resent your husband even more, and all for nothing.'

Georgie met Felix back at his hotel after they'd made their separate excuses and left within half an hour of each other. She had a knot in her stomach that Melinda in her drunkenness would spill the beans to Jeremy but by the sound of it he knew about her and Felix anyway. She had no choice but to put her trust in Melinda.

By the time Georgie joined Felix in his room he'd

changed out of his suit and into a white T-shirt and grey jogging bottoms. Even scruffy with a bottle of beer in one hand, he looked as good as she'd ever seen him.

'Hey,' he said, and gave her a long, lingering kiss. 'I've been dying to do that all day. How long have you got?'

'About an hour. I said I'd be home by midnight.'

He pulled her to him and slid his hands across her shoulders and down to the small of her back.

'We'd better waste no time then.' He kissed her again, more passionately this time, and she responded by sneaking her hands beneath his T-shirt and across his back. Her head swirled with too much wine and vodka, and when he undid the zip on her skirt she didn't resist.

'We need to talk…' she began to say.

He pushed her down on the bed and kissed the hollow of her neck right where she'd imagined kissing him earlier when they were in the office. Tugging down her skirt, he ran his hands up the inside of her thighs.

'Now is not the time for talking.'


For once there was no battle to get Daisy off to sleep, which, with her hangover from the night before, Georgie was thankful for.

'She's all yours,' Georgie said, handing the baby monitor to her mum and sitting down next to her on the sofa. 'I could do with putting my feet up and watching a film.'

'You'll enjoy it once you're out.'

It was her and Nathan's first night out together in almost a year, Georgie realised. In fact, since their last anniversary. They didn't spend any time with each other any more. The restaurant Nathan had booked was in the centre of Bristol and they drove past the hotel Felix had stayed in. Georgie flushed hot as her mind drifted to the night before. It was a long time ago that she'd felt that way about Nathan. Had she *ever* felt that way about him?

They had a table in the window overlooking the

Harbourside but Georgie wished they'd gone to the cinema instead. Her head throbbed and the last thing she felt like doing was making small talk with her husband.

'You were back late last night,' Nathan said, taking a sip of his wine and dabbing the sides of his mouth with his napkin.

She'd been waiting for this comment all day and took a deep breath. 'Melinda had some news she'd been dying to tell me all week, so she was gassing on and I got carried away, just didn't pay any attention to the time. I'm sorry.' She pushed a bit of bloody steak around her plate and wished she'd ordered something lighter, like the fish Nathan had.

'What was her news?'

'Huh?'

'Melinda's news?'

'Oh yes.' Georgie stabbed a chip with her fork. 'She's moving in with her boyfriend.'

'Have I met him?'

Georgie shook her head. 'No.'

Nathan cut a piece of salmon and popped it in his mouth. There was a sucking sound every time he chewed due to his mouth being slightly open. She tried to ignore it as best she could but after eight years of being with him it grated on her nerves. Close your fricking mouth, she wanted to scream.

'How's work?' she asked instead.

'Oh, you know, the same as usual.'

They got home before 11pm, and four hours of a meal and drinks had felt like eternity. When had it got so difficult to think of something to say to Nathan? Although she had to admit that a lot of her life was out of bounds to her husband, so what was left to talk about? Daisy and work.

Nathan poured them a glass of red and switched on the gas fire. She knew it was for effect as it was a balmy twenty-something degrees in their living room, so when Nathan slid across the sofa and tapped his glass against hers she knew where it was leading.

'Happy sixth wedding anniversary,' he said, kissing her lips.

He placed his wine glass on the coffee table and took hers out of her hand, kissed her neck and slid his hands beneath her top, just like Felix had done the night before. It took all her willpower not to pull away. She shuddered and wished it was Felix touching her instead.

# Connie

Connie's workbench overlooked the courtyard garden of the old warehouse that she rented studio space from. There may not have been a sea view or countryside stretching to the horizon, but the splattering of white and yellow flowers against the rust red bricks of the warehouse wall was better than nothing; better than working in the spare room of their apartment where Felix used to freak out about the mess she made soldering silver. Now their spare room was used as an office with a sofa bed for when friends stayed over.

Connie loved the peace and quiet of having her own small space to work in, and there were people to talk to in the communal kitchen along the corridor if she wished to. Other creative people. Her parents didn't understand why she didn't mind getting blisters on her fingers making jewellery and she knew they were disappointed in her choice of career, particularly with her older brother choosing a sensible and well paid career that they approved of. Even Felix didn't quite get her need to be creative, although he supported her choice.

September was a busy time of year with commissions lining up ready to be finished by Christmas. Keeping busy with work was at least taking her mind off not being pregnant. Amsterdam felt like an eternity ago, although it had only been five weeks. Since Felix's weekend of paying her attention and not working, he'd thrown himself into work and seemed busier than ever. Maybe it was a good thing as it made Connie feel less guilty about putting in so many hours at her workbench. At least their conversation in Amsterdam about trying fertility treatment again had allowed her to have hope and look forward to something, even with all the pain and emotion that went with it. They'd made a decision, and depending on dates they were planning on starting ICSI number three in November.

Her hands were sore and her neck ached from bending over the workbench and concentrating so hard all morning. Despite it being a Saturday, she'd decided to work as Felix had stayed over in Bristol the night before after working there all week and wouldn't be home until later in the afternoon. Although working in Bristol was temporary – or so he kept telling her – it had definitely brought an emotional as well as physical distance between them. He seemed preoccupied, but she guessed a new, high responsibility job would do that. That was where they were so different. Although she had deadlines, she worked for herself by herself and those deadlines were self-imposed.

Using tweezers, she picked up a delicate blue tourmaline and set it in the centre of the silver ring she was working on. It was an engagement ring commissioned by a young man planning on proposing to his girlfriend of three years when they went on holiday to Norway later in the year. There was so much promise and hope linked to the work she did. She held the ring up to the sunlight that streamed through the window. It was a wonderful thing to be able to bring so much joy to people.

The apartment was quiet when she got back. Felix had texted to say he was finishing some work and would be home by five. Connie had a shower, changed into her pyjamas, made herself a mug of hot chocolate and settled down on the sofa. The sunny day had turned overcast and all she wanted to do was curl up with a book or switch off completely and watch a mindless film. But her brain wouldn't switch off. She kept thinking about Felix's comment at dinner in Amsterdam about not trying for a baby again. Although he'd changed his mind after their conversation, it worried her. He never talked about his feelings so she had no idea how or if he was dealing with being infertile and the miscarriage. The trouble with telling none of her friends about going through fertility treatment was that she had no one to talk to. Pippa was dealing with too much heartache of her own for Connie to be offloading on her.

She flicked through Netflix trying to find a film she fancied watching. There was one person she'd always been able to talk to about anything, and she wasn't sure why she hadn't told her about the fertility treatment before now. She glanced at the clock and realised it was early evening in Tanzania so it'd be fine to call her aunt.

The line rang for ages, and then there was a pause and a woman's voice.

'Aunt Bella? It's Connie.'

There was a crackling noise, then what sounded like shuffling before her aunt's voice sounded loud and clear. 'Is that better?'

'Yes, perfect, I can hear you now.'

'It's good to hear your voice.'

'Yours too, I'm so sorry I've not spoken to you for ages.'

'Oh love, don't be silly. I know how life takes over, it does for me too.'

'Have you got time to talk?'

'Of course. I've just poured myself a rather large rum and Coke, have put my feet up and am sitting on the deck overlooking the ocean.'

'Way to go to make me jealous, Bella.'

Arabella Stone laughed. 'You need to get yourself out here for a couple of weeks, come join me on this deck.'

'I'd love to, it's just…'

'What? If it's money worries then I'll book your ticket, you know that. That husband of yours too if he wants to come, although I'd rather have you to myself.'

'It's not that. It's not even work that's the problem.'

'What is it, Connie?' The tone in her aunt's voice suddenly changed.

'We've been having fertility treatment on and off since the beginning of the year, that's why I can't come and visit. There are appointments, and the treatment itself doesn't really make me feel that great, plus I can't take malaria tablets. I don't want to risk flying…'

'Connie love, there's no need to explain, I understand. I'm just so sorry you've been having to go through all of this.'

'I had a miscarriage too.'

'Oh my… Connie, I don't know what to say. I'm so very sorry.'

Connie fiddled with the edge of the cushion on her lap. 'I should have told you ages ago, it's just I've not really wanted to discuss it. It's taken a while to come to terms with it.'

'How long ago did it happen?'

'In July. I haven't told anyone. Mum and Dad don't know and I don't want them to…'

'My lips are sealed, not that I ever talk to my brother anyway.'

'None of our friends know. The only person I've told is a woman I met online who's been having fertility treatment too, and she's really helped as she understands exactly what I'm going through. It's crazy how she's become such a close friend despite me only knowing her for a short time.'

'It's good that you've got someone to talk to. And you know I'm here for you, anytime you want to talk, even if it's the middle of the night. You know that, don't you?'

'I know, thank you.'

'You do sound sad,' Bella said. 'How many times have you tried?'

Connie took a deep breath. 'Twice so far. I'm sorry, I didn't mean to offload on you. It's just I'm home alone feeling sorry for myself and wanted to talk to someone I trust.'

'I'm glad you did. Where's Felix?'

'Working.'

'How's he been dealing with all of this?'

'Throwing himself into work. He doesn't really want to

talk about, you know, what's been happening. The fertility problem is his.'

'Uh-huh. You be careful about him bottling his emotions up, it's not healthy for anyone to do that. Watch he doesn't blame himself.'

'That's what I'm worried about too.' Connie took a sip of her hot chocolate and stared at the rain making patterns down the apartment windows. 'Anyway, how are you?'

'Oh, you know, living it up as per usual. Working hard, playing hard and enjoying the lifestyle and my beach bum existence.'

'Except you work ridiculously hard for a beach bum.'

'True, but there are worse jobs to have than owning a beach retreat on the Tanzanian coast.' Aunt Bella chuckled. 'I've hired a fabulous new manager who's living here permanently and so has taken a bulk of my work away from me.'

'Sounds good.'

'You should come over and visit... I know now's not the time, but when things in your life settle down I'd love to see you. I miss you.'

'I miss you too.'

Connie's dad was as different from his younger sister as any siblings could be. Connie had always got on better with her aunt than her own parents, and they made it clear that they thought Aunt Bella was a bad influence. But when had Connie ever listened to her parents? It was always Bella she went to with her problems. In her dad's eyes Bella was the reckless one of the family, going off to Africa backpacking when she was young, then winding up living and working in Tanzania, rarely returning home apart for an occasional family event such as Connie's wedding.

'Are you ready for bed already?' Felix asked when he walked through the door at just gone five with his travel bag slung over his shoulder and a bottle in his hand.

Connie shook her head. 'No, just wanted to get cosy. Did you have a good few days?' She glanced at him as he went over to the fridge, took out a bottle of beer and cracked it open on the side of the worktop. He looked good in jeans and a fitted dark blue T-shirt, his biceps bulging beneath the short sleeves, yet his forehead was etched with lines, and there were shadows beneath eyes devoid of even a hint of a smile.

'Are you tired?' She patted the sofa next to her and he came and sat down, immediately picking up the remote and flicking through the channels.

'It's been a long week,' he said, pausing on a replay of *The X Factor*. 'Oh God, this shite is on again.'

'And *Strictly*.'

He groaned. 'I made the mistake of going out yesterday evening for someone's leaving do.'

'Where'd you get the bottle from?'

Felix glanced to where he'd left his stuff by the door. 'Champagne for the work I've done on the latest project.'

'Nice,' Connie said, leaning over and kissing him. 'It's good to have you home.'

# *Sienna*

'It's seven o'clock in the fucking morning, I'm on location in a muddy field in the middle of Wales and I want to puke my guts up. Tulip, I can't tell you how glad I am that you're working on this film.'

'Well, you know me, always one to opt for the glamorous shoots.' Tulip winked at Sienna and squeezed her arm. 'Seriously though, how're you doing?'

Sienna pulled her coat round her and led Tulip away from the doorway of the production trailer.

'Sick – like I feel sick all the time but worse when I haven't eaten.'

'What are you now? Ten, eleven weeks?'

'Nearly twelve weeks. I have no idea how I'm going to carry on working feeling like this. It's like this freaking baby is slowly trying to kill me from the inside out.'

'They do say it gets better in the second trimester.'

'Yes, but then I've got the issue of showing.'

'You're going to get through this.' Tulip put her thumbs up to someone behind Sienna. 'I'm needed on set. If you're feeling down about things why don't you give Ashton a call and have a chat?'

Sienna sighed. 'It wouldn't be a quick conversation.'

'Oh my God! You've still not told him?'

'Tulip!' one of the runners shouted. 'You're needed asap.'

'Talk later,' Sienna said and headed in the opposite direction before Tulip had a chance to say anything else. She'd not told him because they still weren't together and hadn't actually talked to each other about anything, let alone having *that* conversation. She knew it was a conversation that she'd have to have soon – she couldn't avoid him forever, the same way she couldn't avoid Pippa. They spoke every week and texted each other almost every day, but this was something she needed to tell Pippa face to face. As for Ashton, she'd have to pluck up the courage to speak to him when she went home in two days.

Nausea crept up on her again, starting in her stomach and working its way up to her throat. Normally she lived on coffee when on location but the idea of decaf didn't cut it. She headed towards the food trailer, grabbed a digestive biscuit and started to nibble it, surprised that no one had guessed that she was pregnant. She knew all the signs were there: not drinking caffeine or alcohol; looking pale and like she was going to puke any second; avoiding eating seafood when they were out the other night. Being pregnant well and truly sucked.

'Justin,' she said, putting her hand on her assistant's shoulder and smiling at the pretty runner he was talking to, 'I'm going to scout the beach location now if you can hold the fort here.'

'Sure thing, Sienna.'

She'd already found the perfect location for the beach scenes but she needed to get away from set and find a bit of peace and quiet for an hour or two, plus another look at the beach wouldn't do any harm. The weather seemed to change at a moment's notice – raining one minute then brilliant sunshine the next – which was causing havoc with filming.

It was blustery on the Pembrokeshire coast with pale grey clouds shadowing the sun. Sienna was glad of her thick parka as she walked down the path on to pale yellow sand. Her boots left imprints as she paced across the beach until she was walking only a little way from the surf foaming on the darker, more compact sand at the water's edge. It really was the perfect setting for a medieval costume drama with the beach and sea stretching for as far as she could see, backed by a forest of trees. So early in the morning the beach was empty apart from the occasional person walking their dog. The further she walked, the fewer people she encountered until she felt well and truly alone. Alone in all senses of the word.

She'd always been popular and had a crowd of people around her. Her Facebook friends had reached four figures and her Twitter followers were in their tens of thousands. She shared her life on Instagram and jetted around the world working on movies and TV series her friends, who weren't in her line of work, would kill to be a part of. Apart from Pippa. Pippa had always been happy with who she was; had never craved fame or a more exciting life. As certain as she was that Pippa had never wanted to trade lives, Sienna hadn't either – until now. Now she envied Pippa's freedom of not being tied down by an unwanted pregnancy and she envied Pippa for having the ability to show so much love for something that didn't yet have a personality or a name; for something that wasn't even born yet.

She'd walked for a good twenty minutes before she sat down in the low dunes that sheltered the beach. There wasn't a person in sight; just the cloudy sky and waves tumbling on to the beach. She leant back and ran her hands through the soft sand, reaching cold damp grains the deeper she went. Fronds of long grasses sheltered her back and, despite the sun still being hidden, she felt comfortably warm after her hike along the beach. Life didn't stop for anyone; you simply had to get on with it and make the most of it. She still had time to get rid of the baby and then neither Ashton nor Pippa would ever have to know about it. The answer to her problem solved in one procedure. Tulip could be trusted to keep her mouth shut and she'd support Sienna whatever her decision.

That was it. Instead of going to see Ashton when she got back to Bath she'd make an appointment with a doctor and start the process to get this damn thing out of her. Life could then go back to normal. She wouldn't have to worry about having said yes to the biggest job of her life knowing that she'd be due to give birth just before she'd have to start. She'd never wanted a baby. Deep down, she knew having it would be wrong – she was too selfish, too busy, too unreliable, too focused on her career to be an okay mum, let alone a good one.

Sienna watched the surf break on the beach and felt a wave of nausea. This thing inside her wasn't going to let her forget that she was pregnant. She took a bar of chocolate out of her coat pocket and popped a chunk in her mouth. She did everything wrong – she drank too much alcohol and caffeine, ate crap when she was on location, had the occasional sneaky spliff and yet she was pregnant. Pippa had been teetotal for months, had never smoked even when she was a student, ate only organic produce and yet had lost a baby. Life was beyond messed up. What she'd do to trade places with Pippa.

The doctor's appointment was booked for 3.30pm the following day, and the only way she'd managed to get an appointment for then and not the following week was by crying and getting the receptionist worried about her mental health. Sienna was more concerned about her messed up hormones turning her into an emotional wreck about *everything*. She'd even thought about telling her mum that she was pregnant just so she could have someone to talk to, but realised that was a bad idea because her Italian mum would fly into a rage about her getting pregnant out of wedlock before berating her for waiting until she was thirty-five to get pregnant to begin with. And of course, once her mum knew, there was no way she could possibly go through with an abortion.

After going stir-crazy at home all day and not being able to eat any dinner because she didn't fancy anything, she made the really bad decision to walk over to Ashton's. She wasn't going to tell him; she simply wanted to see him to confirm to herself that she was making the right decision – that she was able to walk away from their relationship, the pregnancy, and move on with her life, single and uncommitted to anyone or anything.

There were many times she'd thought about moving to London – it would make her life easier being closer to where she was based work-wise a lot of the time, yet something always pulled her back home to Bath. She loved her house, the vibe of being in such an historic city – even if the tourists did drive her mad in summer – and the walk to Ashton's past grand Georgian houses and iconic sights summed it up perfectly. She felt relaxed and at home here. With her often nomadic existence through work, that was no mean feat.

Ashton buzzed the door open without an argument. She climbed the steps two at a time and realised that in a few months she'd be huffing and puffing upstairs with a huge bump... except she wasn't going to get that far.

'You're back in Bath, then,' Ashton called from the living room.

'Only for a couple of days.' Sienna closed the door behind her. The last time she'd been in his living room she'd ended up having sex with him. She froze in the doorway with the sudden realisation that they'd conceived this goddam baby that day back in July. She'd always been so careful but passion and a long relationship break had made her careless. Ashton too, but then he wanted a baby and marriage so why would he think about protection? It wasn't like she was some random one night stand.

'You okay, Sienna? You look pale.'

Sienna nodded. 'Yeah, sorry, just tired.'

'Why are you here?' Ashton turned the TV off and sat down right in the spot he'd been sitting when they'd kissed last time.

'I needed to see you.'

'Well, you've seen me and I'd really appreciate it if you'd stop messing with my head. The last time I saw you we ended up, you know...' He motioned to the sofa. 'And then, nothing. I've not heard a word from you in weeks. You ignored my calls and texts so I stopped trying in the end.'

Sienna bit her lip and looked around the room, clocking two beer glasses on the dining table along with two plates and two sets of cutlery. How stupid had she been? They'd broken up. Why wouldn't Ashton move on?

'I shouldn't have come. You've got company tonight.'

'What the hell's up with you, Sienna?'

'Seriously, Ashton, don't worry about it. I'll go. You enjoy tonight.'

'I will, thanks, but you don't have to leave.' He stood up, walked over to her, took her hand and gently pulled her back into the living room. 'Dan from work is coming round to chat about a business idea we've got. He's not going to be here until half eight, so stay and let's actually talk.'

Sienna reluctantly sank down on the sofa. So he hadn't moved on – she wasn't sure if that pleased her or made her feel more anxious. Why had she even come over? Her decision was made, the appointment with the doctor to discuss it booked, so why confuse things by seeing Ashton?

'I'm pregnant.'

# *Georgie*

It wasn't unusual for Georgie's period to be late, but it was unusual for her to feel dizzy when she woke in the morning. She lay quietly in bed and thought that maybe she was coming down with something. It was only 5.30am and the house was quiet apart from Nathan snoring beside her. She rarely woke up before the alarm or Daisy shouting for her, but something was bugging her. A niggling thought about what the other reason for the dizziness and late period could be but she dismissed it. She was just stressed about her marriage; her affair; where her life was heading. So much had changed for her in the last few months, it was bound to play on her mind.

She went through the day on autopilot, getting Daisy up and ready, grabbing a bite of breakfast while Nathan was in the shower, dropping Daisy off at nursery and heading to work. Although it had only been a couple of weeks, she missed seeing Felix working in Bristol. She'd always loved her job but it wasn't the same since he'd moved back to the Cardiff office.

After work she picked Daisy up from nursery and made a quick pasta dish for dinner, which Nathan managed to get home for. It was his turn to put Daisy to bed, so she sat down in the living room and turned on the TV. She'd been on the go all day long and had felt fine but now she was sitting quietly her head began to feel woozy again.

It was a weekday evening and there was nothing good on TV. She switched it off and reached for her Kindle. A bit of escapism was what she needed, but as she read her mind kept wandering to Felix, wondering what he did in the evening at home with his wife. Was he thinking about her? Wishing he was snuggled up on the sofa with her instead of the person he'd married?

'Nothing on?'

Nathan made her jump as he came into the room. She handed him the remote.

'Take a look.'

He turned the TV on and flicked through the channels. 'We could always go up to bed early,' he said.

Georgie pretended to keep reading but the words made no sense as she stared at the screen, wondering what on earth she was going to say.

'I need to put some washing on before bed and iron Daisy's clothes for tomorrow.'

'Surely that can all wait until the morning?' He shuffled closer and placed his hand on her thigh.

Georgie put her Kindle down and looked at him. There were more wrinkles around his eyes than she remembered and he definitely had more grey in his hair. She never really looked at him any longer, not properly.

'I'm kinda not in the mood,' she said, and lifted her Kindle back up and started reading again.

His hand left her thigh. 'So, we've got to the point in our marriage where we're just having anniversary sex then?'

Georgie placed her Kindle on her lap. 'Oh come on, that's not fair.'

'Really?'

'It's not exactly been an easy couple of years,' Georgie said, looking at Nathan. 'Having a baby and recovering from being pregnant and giving birth doesn't exactly make you feel like getting jiggy with it.'

Nathan dropped the remote on the sofa between them. 'Daisy is two years old now. How is that still an excuse?'

'It's not an excuse,' she said, a ball of anger rising from her stomach to her chest. 'It doesn't help that you're rarely home on time, and when you do get home you're always preoccupied with the flipping TV or preparing work for the next day.'

'So it's my fault now?'

'I don't think it's anyone's fault, it's just our life has changed dramatically in the past couple of years and it's not been easy.' Georgie leant back on the sofa, unsure whether the feeling in her chest was anger or nausea. 'You've been talking about having another baby and I don't feel like I'm coping with the child we have. If you remember, it was always you who wanted to start a family. I agreed to start trying in the end but I wasn't ready. These last two years have been the hardest of my life, so excuse me if I don't always feel like having sex. A bit of me time is preferable.'

'I didn't know you felt like that.'

'That's because we never talk. Our life is all about work and Daisy and getting through the day. I was so flipping young when we got married and started a family. You may have been ready but I wasn't. Hindsight is a wonderful thing.'

'What are you saying? That you wish we hadn't had Daisy?'

'No, of course not. I'm just saying that having a baby when I wasn't actually ready has been far from easy and I'm finding her being a toddler even harder. I miss my own space, my freedom, and if that makes me sound like a bad mother or wife then I'm sorry.'

An advert for Pampers came on and all Georgie could hear was giggling babies.

'Can't you switch the bloody TV off?' She stood up, stalked across the room to the kitchen and poured herself a glass of water from the fridge, took a sip, put the glass on the breakfast bar and turned back to Nathan with her hands on her hips. 'I'm sorry if I don't feel like having sex, I've just got too much stuff going on in my head at the moment.'

Nathan came over to her. 'It's good that you're telling me this, and I'm sorry if I've been pressurising you about having another baby.' He reached out and took hold of Georgie's hands. His hands were smooth, warm and comforting but there was no jolt like she got when Felix touched her. 'What can I do to help?' he asked, giving her hands a squeeze.

'I have no idea.' Georgie pulled her hands from his and left the room.

Again, Georgie woke early in the morning. It felt like Groundhog Day – 5.30am with Daisy still asleep, Nathan snoring beside her and that heady feeling making her nauseous. She'd gone to bed early and alone the night before after her unresolved conversation with Nathan.

She couldn't just lie awake thinking about things, so she carefully swung her legs out of bed and stood up, pausing to make sure Nathan was still asleep and to regain her balance. Tiptoeing out of their bedroom and across the landing to the bathroom, she locked the door behind her and opened the cupboard above the sink. It wasn't just dizziness she was experiencing but distinct nausea. She still had a pregnancy test left over from when she was pregnant with Daisy; with shaky hands she took it out of the cupboard and unwrapped it. Trying to calm her nerves and racing heart she stared at it, praying that all her instincts were wrong.

Waiting for the test result was the longest two minutes of her life. There was no denying it now – the result was clear with two defiant pink lines staring back at her. Pregnant. Her period missed by a few days. Georgie put the test back in the box and the box back in the cupboard so Nathan wouldn't notice that it had been used, put the toilet lid down and sat on it, leaning forwards with her elbows resting on her knees and her head in her hands. If her life had felt complicated and confusing before, it had just got a whole lot worse.

So much for anniversary sex – had that really got her knocked up? Her heart stilled for a split second and the nausea intensified as her thoughts took her to the night before her anniversary and the hotel room with Felix. They'd both been drunk, hasty, passionate, and she didn't remember him pausing to put a condom on. Tears ran down her cheeks and dripped on to the bathroom floor.

She had no idea whose baby she was pregnant with.

# *Sienna*

'I think we can safely say that your estimated due date will be the 3rd April. Congratulations,' the sonographer said, smiling at Sienna and then Ashton. 'You have one very healthy looking and active baby in there.'

They left the hospital in silence, Sienna clutching the scan pictures with her heart racing. Her palms were sweaty. Everything felt real, so horribly real.

'Are you okay?' Ashton asked, steering Sienna out of the path of people heading towards them. 'You look in shock.'

Sienna *was* in shock. She had been ever since she'd done the pregnancy test. Ashton had looked at her with disbelief when she'd told him she was pregnant five days earlier, then he simply wrapped his arms around her and hugged her until she hugged him back, allowing herself to let go of all the pent up emotion, fear, disbelief and regret she'd been holding on to for weeks. They weren't back together, far from that, but they were in it together, whatever that meant. Ashton would be a father to the baby and Sienna would be a mother; she made that decision the moment she'd picked up the phone the next morning and cancelled her doctor's appointment.

The walk from the hospital back to the centre of Bath took them through the Royal Victoria Park and past the Royal Crescent, and she felt calm enough to sit and talk by the time they reached her favourite coffee shop on George Street.

Cupping her hands around a large mug of latte, she looked at Ashton. 'I think this moment is one women are supposed to feel unbelievably jubilant and excited about, but I'm just scared.'

Ashton reached out and placed his warm hands over hers. 'I don't think every woman feels excited. I'm sure many are just as scared as you, even if it's a planned baby.'

'Even though this is something I never wanted, I went into that scan this morning hoping that everything was okay with it. I can't even begin to imagine how heartbreaking it must have been for Pippa to find out at her scan that her baby had died. I don't think I understood the enormity of having something actually growing inside you that has a heartbeat and that actually looks like a baby.' Sienna spread the scan photos out on the table. 'I mean, a weird alien-type baby, but that's definitely a baby. I don't actually know how Pippa is managing to function and keep going.'

'She's strong and she has a loving husband and good friends.'

'Except I don't think I've been a good enough friend to her, and now...'

'You can't change what's happened to you, or her; you have to make the best of what life's dealt you both. And you do realise that it may not be what you wanted but it is what I want.' He took his hands away from hers and sipped his coffee. 'Although I didn't bank on bringing a child into the world under these circumstances.'

Sienna took a gulp of her latte and wished it had more sugar in it and was caffeinated. Maybe even spiked with Baileys. She was in no mood to discuss what they were going to do about their non-existent relationship and she really hoped that Ashton didn't try and go there.

'I guess we tell our parents now,' he said.

Sienna breathed a sigh of relief and shook her head. 'Not now, not yet. I'm so not ready for that. I've still got to get my head around a lot of shit. The last thing I want is my fucking mother sticking her nose in or your mum questioning what's happening with us.'

'We have to tell them at some point.'

'I know and we will, just not yet. Anyway, the person I

need to tell before our parents is Pippa.'

'When are you seeing her?'

'We're supposed to be going out for Jen's hen do next week.'

'You can't tell her then.'

'I know that. I just need to choose the right moment – somewhere private where we can talk.'

'You'd better get a move on now you've reached twelve weeks.' Ashton shook his head. 'I'm sorry, I know how difficult it's going to be considering what Pippa went through at their scan. But the longer you leave it, the harder it will be.'

'Like you need to tell me that.'

There was no right moment. With a bright pink hen sash slung across her black cami and a dark grey short skirt on, Sienna met up with the bride-to-be Jen, Pippa and the rest of the hen party outside the Pump House in Bath. Sienna had wanted to wear her favourite black trousers but they were tight – like 'unable to do the zip up' tight. At least her skirt had more give in it, but it did panic her that people would be able to tell that she was pregnant. She'd stared at herself in the mirror for ages, trying to work out if she had the beginnings of a bump or not. She'd always been slim and kept fit with jogging and going to the gym, but her stomach was definitely rounder. Luckily the style of the skirt with the way it flared out took the attention away from her tummy.

Despite the garish sashes, the hen do started off in a classy wine bar on South Parade. Pippa gravitated towards Sienna and there was no way for Sienna to avoid her without it being really obvious and out of character. They'd been best friends since they were eleven, shared everything, told each other stuff they'd tell no one else, and now all Sienna wanted to do was to get as far away from Pippa as possible.

'What you having, Sienna?' Jen's maid of honour, Sadie, called across the table.

'Just a lemonade, thanks.'

Sadie pulled a face. 'What? That's not the Sienna I know.'

She had her line prepared. 'My stomach's still feeling tender after this bug I've had. Don't want to risk anything stronger – got to work over the weekend.'

Sadie raised her eyebrows. 'Should you even be out?'

Sienna laughed. 'I'm fine now. Vomiting and, you know, the other thing stopped well over forty-eight hours ago.' The lie slipped out so easily even Pippa didn't question it.

'Ah, you should have told me you were ill,' Pippa said. 'I'd have brought some soup over for you.'

Sienna squeezed her shoulder. 'I know you would have, hun, but I had the pleasure of my mother looking after me for two days. And anyway, I didn't want you to catch anything.'

Being out and not drinking was not enjoyable, Sienna decided. She didn't have to go out and get completely wasted the whole time but a cocktail or two would have been nice. And she still felt so tired. Weren't all the early and annoying pregnancy symptoms supposed to go once you reached the second trimester? At least she could put her yawning down to recovering from a stomach bug. Who would doubt her? After all, she was the last person anyone would expect to be pregnant.

Sadie came back from the bar and handed lemonades to Sienna and Pippa.

'You two go easy now,' she said and winked. 'Is there something you're not telling us, Pip?'

Sienna's heart jumped as she watched Pippa's face flush – what should she say to make Sadie go away? What could she say?

'No,' Pippa said with a hint of a wobble to her voice that Sienna was sure only she picked up on. 'I definitely have nothing to tell you. I'm just not drinking at the moment – a bit of a detox, that's all.'

As soon as Sadie turned away, Sienna touched Pippa's arm. 'Are you okay?'

'Not really, no. I don't get why people feel the need to ask such personal questions.'

'People don't think. I guess if they don't know anyone who has struggled to get pregnant it's not on their radar and they think it's a perfectly innocent question.'

'I guess it's like people always asking why you don't want to have kids. It's none of their damn business.'

It was Sienna's turn to blush. She sank back into the chesterfield sofa and willed the evening to be over and done with.

'So, what's happening with us?'

It was the question Sienna had been avoiding since she'd blurted out to Ashton just over two weeks ago that she was pregnant. She'd dreaded it because she really didn't have an answer.

'It's complicated. I mean, we're complicated.'

Ashton shook his head. 'Should I just go and forget about having a sensible conversation with you?'

'No.' They stood in Sienna's kitchen with the back door open and a cool autumn breeze filtering in from the garden. 'We've always been complicated. It's just we're now complicated with big life-changing decisions to make.'

'You know how I feel about things, about you,' Ashton said, leaning against the work surface and taking the coffee Sienna handed him. 'Move in with me. Or I can move in with you.'

Sienna fiddled with the edge of her top, self-consciously attempting to cover her stomach because of the way Ashton kept glancing at it. She was only thirteen fucking weeks pregnant – it was hardly like she was 'blooming' yet. This was everything he wanted and everything she didn't.

'We could sell our flats and buy a house together, whatever would make you happy.'

'Not being pregnant is what would make me happy.'

Ashton put his coffee down and pushed himself away from the worktop.

'Okay, I'm not doing this. You've always been one for

doing things on your own so you go figure how you're going to raise a kid and continue with the job and lifestyle you're so fucking accustomed to.' He took his jacket from the back of the kitchen chair and shrugged it on. 'It's fucking freezing in here.'

'I'm hot,' Sienna said, folding her arms across her chest. 'I keep getting hot flushes because of this damn alien thing growing inside me and messing up my hormones. Seriously, why anyone would willingly put themselves through this is beyond me.'

'Because, Sienna, the end result is a beautiful little family. Something I don't think you'll ever understand.' Ashton zipped up his jacket and stormed out of the kitchen.

Sienna sighed and rubbed her temples. 'Ashton, I'm sorry.' She followed after him and caught him by the front door. 'Do you really mean it that you'd move in here? Sell your flat?'

He leant his right hand on the door. 'If it means being with you, then yes, I'll do that.'

'I need more time. I've not got my head round having a baby. I've got to sort out my own feelings before I can think about us.' She gently laid her hand on Ashton's tense back. 'Is that okay?'

He turned to her. 'Take all the time you need but remember there is a deadline. It's October and the baby is due on the 3rd April. Don't leave it too long to make a decision.'

'I won't.' She grabbed Ashton's arm as he made to open the door again. 'What are we doing about Jen and Andrew's wedding? We were invited together, so are we going together or separately?'

'It's their big day,' Ashton said, 'so we go together. The last thing I want to do is muck things up for them.'

'And absolutely no mention of me being pregnant.'

Ashton turned back and folded his arms. 'You haven't told her yet, have you.'

'There's still time: there are four days until the wedding.

And anyway, after the hen do I'm not sure Pippa is even going to be at the wedding.'

'Well, won't that be lucky – Pippa not showing up.'

# *Pippa*

Pippa took a deep breath and stepped into the reception. She was only there because Jen was a close friend; for anyone else – apart from Sienna – she'd have gone straight home after the church service. Right now she'd do anything to be curled up at home on the sofa, in her pyjamas and munching on a big bar of chocolate, preferably with chunks of salted caramel in it. But she was at a wedding and not pregnant; in fact, as far from being pregnant as she could be with the miscarriage only three months ago and still so raw. The hen do had been hard, but she'd have felt too bad about missing the actual wedding to make an excuse.

Champagne bubbles sparkled in crystal glasses, vases of pale pink roses decorated the tables, and pink and silver 'Just Married' confetti was scattered over crisp white tablecloths. Everything was perfect – a young couple celebrating their love and about to embark on the rest of their lives together, right after two sun and sex filled weeks in the Caribbean. That had been Pippa and Clive only a few years ago. Pippa sighed and willed herself not to be so bitter. She remembered the feeling of disappointment when her period arrived after they'd got back from Thailand. They'd only just started trying for a baby. How many couples got pregnant the first time? Multiply that disappointment by God knows how many more months and years and it was no wonder she was a struggling hormonal mess.

With their arms linked and champagne clasped in their hands, the bride and groom toasted each other and then kissed. Cue applause. On autopilot, Pippa set down her glass of water and joined in.

A waitress came round with a bottle of white wine and Pippa automatically shook her head, but what for? She wasn't on treatment; she and Clive hadn't had sex since before the miscarriage, so there was no chance of her being pregnant – what the hell was she being good for? Even worse, what if the other guests at their table thought she *was* pregnant because she was abstaining, just like Sadie had thought last week at the hen do? A well-meaning but way too personal suggestion that she was pregnant would tip her over the edge.

'Actually, yes please,' Pippa said, catching the waitress's attention before she left their table.

Clive glanced at Pippa and then at her wine. Was that relief on his face? Concern? It wasn't like she was going to get drunk, even though that would probably help. She took a sip and swilled the dry and crisp wine around her mouth.

The food alone was worth making the effort to get dressed up and leave the house. Poached pears with Gorgonzola to start with, chicken wrapped in crispy pancetta served with broccoli, roasted carrots, a redcurrant jus and the creamiest mashed potatoes, rounded off with Eton Mess with autumn berries instead of summer strawberries. Making small talk with the other guests was the last thing Pippa wanted to do, particularly as the seating arrangements meant they were at tables with people they didn't know. Clive took the lead and talked enough for both of them, which Pippa was grateful for.

With Clive deep in conversation and the man to her left talking to his wife, Pippa took a sip of her wine and wondered how early into the evening they could leave without being rude. Sienna leant across from the table behind and squeezed her shoulder.

'How you doing, hun?'

Pippa shuffled round in her seat. 'Coping.'

'As weddings go it's a pretty lovely one. Not as good as yours and Clive's but then I did get to be bridesmaid at that one. Always wanted to be a bridesmaid, never a bride.'

'They have chosen a stunning place.'

'Must have cost a flipping fortune.'

'Well, Jen's parents aren't short of money.'

Sienna swirled her wine around in its glass. 'At least they've got taste.'

'You're back to drinking again tonight then?'

'Of course,' Sienna said, taking a sip of her wine. 'You know me. I just didn't feel too good at Jen's hen do.'

'When has that ever stopped you?'

Before Sienna could answer, the best man knocked a spoon against a glass and the chatter and laughter dissipated. Pippa turned towards the head table.

'Thank you all for joining us for Andrew and Jen's special day…'

The waiters and waitresses continued to walk between the tables topping up guests' drinks, and Pippa held her glass out.

'I've known Andy since he was a skinny kid, and if someone told me when we were eleven that he'd go on to marry someone as beautiful as Jen, I'd have laughed in their face – sorry, mate.'

The waiter moved on to the next table and offered the wine to Sienna who covered the top of her glass with her hand. Pippa turned her attention back to the best man and thought how awful it must be to wait all day to deliver one of the most important speeches of his life. He was doing a pretty good job, despite being red-faced and sounding like he'd had quite a lot to drink.

With the speeches done and the cake cut, more people arrived for the evening party. Pippa made her excuses to Clive and the rest of the guests at their table, picked up her wine and escaped outside on to the terrace that overlooked the mansion house's grounds. Surrounded by woods, grass sloped down to a lake that glinted in the moonlight. Pippa always felt calmer when she was outside; perhaps it was something to do with the fresh air blowing any negative thoughts away. Still clutching her glass of wine, she strolled down to the edge of the lake. Maybe she needed a job where she could work outdoors instead of being cooped up in a humid office all day. Although Clive mostly worked indoors managing various heritage sites in and around Bath, his was a far more interesting and valued job than her own, plus he got to travel. What she needed was a baby; maternity leave away from the job she hated; a little son or daughter she could play with in the park or take swimming.

Clive thought they should get a cat, something for her to mother and look after, but for her that wasn't the answer. A kitten couldn't replace or eradicate the longing she had for a baby, to be pregnant and experience the miracle of a life growing inside her. And it would be a miracle – their chances were so slim, everything had to be perfect for them to have any chance of conceiving, let alone carrying a baby to full term.

Pippa turned away from the lake and walked back up to the house. A few people had gathered by the patio doors, but a little further away on the edge of the terrace she spied Sienna with her head bowed and one hand clutched to her stomach.

'Hey, are you alright? What's up?' Pippa asked, running over.

Sienna's head shot up. 'Nothing,' she said. 'Fuck, you made me jump.'

'Sorry.' Pippa rested a hand on Sienna's shoulder. 'I know you, something's up. You're really tense.'

'Oh, you know how it is with work and stuff, this stress with Ashton,' Sienna said. 'I'm tired working on back to back films, that's all.'

'That's never bothered you in the past; you usually hate having too big a gap between films. Even getting you to go on holiday is a battle.'

'It's just burnout or this bug hanging about. I've probably drunk way too much today.' Sienna put her hands on her hips and gave Pippa a smile.

Pippa stepped back and glanced at Sienna's stomach, which was covered by her pashmina. 'I've been watching you,' Pippa said, frowning. 'You've had less than one glass of wine all day. It's not burnout, is it. You're not...' she motioned towards Sienna's stomach. '...are you?'

Sienna took a step forward. 'Pip, I didn't think you were going to be here. When I spoke to you earlier in the week you said you couldn't face it.'

'I changed my mind. After you, Jen is my closest friend. Despite everything, I really thought I should make the effort.'

Sienna visibly took a deep breath and reached for Pippa's hand. 'I wanted to come round and tell you in private, it's just I've been putting it off because I didn't know how to tell you.'

'That you're pregnant?' Pippa pushed Sienna's hand away and stumbled backwards as if someone had punched her hard in the stomach, really hard, knocking the breath out of her. Tears welled in her eyes and a burning heat rushed through her body to her face. Unable to say anything, she turned away sharply, dropping her glass with a crash on to the terrace paving slabs. Wine and glass splattered and scattered across the terrace, the shards glinting in the yellow light from the lanterns next to the lawn.

'Pippa.' Sienna's high-heeled boots crunched after her through the broken glass. 'Are you upset that I hadn't told you or that I'm pregnant?'

Pippa swung back to face Sienna. 'How many weeks are you?'

'Fourteen.'

'Oh my God.' Pippa buried her head in her hands then, ignoring the soreness of her throat from pent up tears, took a deep breath and looked straight at Sienna. 'I'm shocked because you of all people have never wanted children. I'm also upset that you're pregnant, and of course I'm fucking upset that you didn't have the decency or guts to tell me.'

'I didn't mean to keep this a secret – I didn't want to hurt you after what you've been through. It was so hard to know what was the best thing to do.'

'I'm sorry that losing my baby twelve weeks ago has made your life hard.'

'Pippa, I never intended…'

Sienna brushed her hand against Pippa's sleeve. Pippa shuddered and shoved her off.

'I can't do this now. We shouldn't do this now. It's Jen's day. Have the decency to tell her goodbye from me. Tell her I felt ill all of a sudden and I'll speak to her soon.'

Avoiding the glass on the terrace, Pippa walked back across the patio and through the open doors to find Clive.

'Pippa!' Sienna called after her.

Pippa kept walking as the tears she'd been fighting so hard to hold back finally escaped and rolled down her cheeks.

# *Sienna*

'I've fucked up big time.' Sienna pulled Ashton away from the bar where he was chatting to mutual friends of theirs and dragged him outside and on to the lawn, away from the noise, music and lights.

'What have you done now?' He sipped his beer and looked at Sienna with *that* look – the one that was so condescending and annoyed the hell out of her.

'You're too pissed to have a sensible conversation with.'

'It's a wedding, what do you expect?'

Sienna started to walk away, back towards the party. Ashton caught up with her and took hold of her arm.

'I'm sorry, I'm listening.' He placed his pint glass on the grass.

Sienna sighed. Ashton wasn't the right person to be talking to – the person she needed to confide in was the one person who'd just walked out, and the one person in the world she least wanted to hurt.

'Pippa found out,' Sienna said. Her words hung heavily in the chilly evening air.

'Oh. How did she know? Who told her?'

'No one. She just knew.'

'Where is she now?'

'She left.'

'Oh.'

'Is that all you can say?' Sienna wrapped her pashmina more tightly around her and folded her arms.

'No, I'm sorry, but I don't know what to suggest.'

'That's what I meant by I fucked up. I should have had

the guts to tell her as soon as I found out, like any decent best friend. It came across as me hiding a dirty big secret from her.'

'Maybe if you'd told me sooner about the baby then I'd have been able to suggest you tell Pippa sooner.'

'Oh, for fuck's sake, Ash, you really want to bring that up now and make me feel even worse than I already do?' Sienna struggled to hold back tears, panic bubbling up inside her. 'I realise I've messed up on so many levels: getting pregnant in the first place and tying myself to you when I don't want the whole marriage and kids thing. I'll be the first to admit I've screwed up big time.'

'Oh, that's perfect, Sienna.' He picked up his beer and took a large swig. 'Good to know you don't want either me or the baby growing inside you. You're thirty-five fucking years old, about time you grew up and thought about someone other than yourself.'

'The one time I could really do with you being on my side and here for me,' Sienna said, her voice rising with each word. 'You know what, us, this, whatever we're doing here…' she waggled a finger between Ashton and herself, '…isn't working and never is going to work. I'm not cut out to be part of a committed couple, never have been, never will, and that isn't going to change because I'm knocked up. You can kiss goodbye to *us*. Being a single mum will suit me just fine.'

She turned away and stalked back into the reception, fully aware of the outright stares she was getting. Pippa would have killed her for the scene she was making at their friend's wedding, but Pippa would have gone by now. In less than ten minutes she'd managed to make a fool of herself, lose a best friend, and split up with her boyfriend and father of her baby.

Despite the warmth and luxury of her hotel room, Sienna had never felt so miserable or alone. She and Ashton had booked separate rooms despite turning up to the wedding as a couple. Kicking off her shoes, she slumped down on the bed. She didn't want to read or watch TV and she couldn't sleep. All she really wanted to do was erase the thoughts tormenting her. She wanted life to go back to how it used to be: a non-complicated relationship with Ashton, a best friend she could talk to about anything and hadn't hurt so badly, and not being pregnant.

Lying down, she traced her fingers across her stomach – maybe there was a hint of a bump. Her stomach was definitely more rounded than usual. Most people thought of a baby growing inside them as the miracle of life; for Sienna, the thought of what was happening scared the shit out of her. Being pregnant and having a baby wasn't anything she'd ever wanted, and all the symptoms that went along with pregnancy, such as sickness, needing to pee all the time and lower back pain, weren't doing anything to help her come to terms with it.

She closed her eyes and snuggled back into the pile of soft pillows. It wasn't too late; she could still have an abortion. She shook the thought from her head – if she went through with that, Ashton would kill her and Pippa would hate her even more. Anyway, how could she? Despite freaking out at the twelve-week scan, she couldn't deny that there was a healthy embryo kicking and wriggling inside her with a very real heartbeat. However much she'd mucked up her own life, she couldn't destroy its life because hers hadn't panned out the way that she'd hoped.

There was no way she was going to sleep with so much crap swirling about her head. She opened her laptop to watch a film and realised she still had Pippa's blog open. Her heart felt as if it was going to explode out of her chest when she clocked the fact that a new post had been published only a few minutes earlier.

Not really wanting to, yet unable to stop herself, she clicked on the post.

*10th October blog post:*

### The Worst of Times

*This evening was one of the hardest since the miscarriage. Being happy for other people takes effort, and it wasn't even like it was someone announcing that they were expecting or an invite to a baby shower. It was simply the wedding of a really good friend, who also happens to be younger than me, not that that should make any difference. But at the moment it does, knowing time's not on my side and the older I get, the less chance there's going to be for things working out. Seeing my friend simply glow, knowing how much hope and expectation she has for the future and remembering what my hopes and dreams were on my own wedding day, crushed me.*

*Those dreams are in tatters. That hope and excitement I felt as we celebrated our union have been destroyed by disappointment, medical intervention and heartache. Overwhelming sadness is what I came away with tonight, despite it being a beautiful ceremony and day – in fact, probably because it was a beautiful day. I wouldn't wish what we've been through over the past few years on anyone, not even my worst enemy. No one who simply wants what comes easily to so many couples should have to battle so hard to have a family.*

*Then, to top it off, I discovered my best friend is pregnant. Fourteen weeks to be exact. Apparently, she'd been waiting for the right time to tell me. There's never a right time, but getting some balls to tell me before I guessed would have been preferable. If I hadn't lost my baby I'd have been thirteen weeks ahead of her, meaning she pretty much conceived around the time I found out my baby had died.*

*This should be a special time that we celebrate together.*

*I should be happy for her but I'm not convinced that she's even happy for herself.*

*She's never wanted children and has never been broody. Her career is everything to her. The worst part is she's been my rock throughout everything and now I can't even think about her without feeling uncontrollably resentful and jealous. My husband is convinced that it's all too raw tonight and I'll feel calmer about everything in the morning, but I'm not buying that. Friends since we were eleven, we've always been honest and told each other everything. One of the most important reasons for talking to me and she decides not to.*

*So, it seems my best friend, who has never wanted kids, has managed to get pregnant, while I, who have always wanted a family, remain childless with less and less hope. If someone was to ask me what's been the worst time of my life, then I'd say that right now my life is the worst it's ever been. Where to go from here? I should be feeling hopeful because in just over two weeks' time I'll be starting treatment again, this time FET (frozen egg transfer) instead of full IVF as we have four frozen embryos. It's ironic that I called this blog The Hopeful Years, because right now all hope has deserted me.*

Sienna slammed the laptop closed. What had she expected? For Pippa to smile sweetly, give her a hug and say 'Congratulations, it's absolutely fine that you've hidden your pregnancy from me and I'm totally cool with that despite having recently had a miscarriage following a second round of IVF'? She rolled on to her front and hugged a pillow, willing herself to go to sleep and escape her thoughts.

There was a knock at the door. Sienna buried her face further into the pillows, ignoring the second knock and the third and the fourth.

'Sienna, I know you're in there.'

There was a time not so long ago when Ashton wouldn't have needed to knock because they would have been sharing a room like a normal couple. 'Normal couple' no longer applied. Separate with separate rooms and separate lives, yet a shared baby growing inside her.

Bang, bang, bang.

All Sienna wanted to do was get shit-faced on all the drink from the mini bar. A few drinks wouldn't harm the baby, surely? Ashton was pissed – in more ways than one – and it wasn't fair that she wasn't.

'I have nothing to say to you,' Sienna shouted across the room.

'We need to talk.'

'There's nothing to talk about.'

'Yes, there is.'

'This isn't the right time.'

'There never is a good time with you.'

Sienna scrambled up to a sitting position and wiped tears and mascara on the back of her hand. 'It took you long enough to leave the party and get up here.'

'I'm not having this conversation in a hotel corridor.'

Sienna was tempted to lie back down, close her eyes and leave Ashton shut out both physically and mentally. She swung her legs off the bed and stalked to the door. 'What?'

'I'm worried about you.'

'There's nothing to worry about, I'm fine. I just need to be left alone.'

He stepped into the room and closed the door behind him. 'It's not fine. If I'm worrying about you then I'm worrying about the baby. Our baby.'

Sienna slumped back down on the bed. 'The baby's fine. Me getting upset isn't going to do it any harm.'

Ashton sat down in the chair by the window. 'One way or another you've got to come to terms with what's happening.'

The light from the lamp next to the chair cast a glow across Ashton's face, and Sienna thought how handsome he was with sun-kissed skin, the perfect amount of stubble, defined cheekbones and dark hair.

'I have come to terms with it,' she said, grazing her hand across her stomach. 'It doesn't mean I'm happy about it, but I got myself into this mess, so I'll deal with it. I *am* dealing with it.'

'Dealing with it doesn't sound like someone who has come to terms with having a baby and is happy about it.' Ashton leant forwards and his face was plunged into shadow. 'And it's our mess, not just yours.'

'No, Ashton, it's my mess. You wanted this…'

'Not like this, I didn't.'

'Maybe not, but you wanted a baby and I didn't. I should have been more careful or I should have broken up with you properly instead of having stupid break-up sex or whatever it was.'

'You're unbelievable,' Ashton said, standing up. 'No

wonder Pippa is pissed at you. You're pushing everyone away.' He walked to the door then stopped and turned back to her. 'You're dealing with it all wrong. Not telling me about the baby straight away and not telling Pippa at all was the worst thing you could have done. She'll hate you for it.'

'Like you hate me.'

He shook his head. 'I don't hate you, Sienna. The problem is, I love you.'

# Connie

Towards the end of October Connie finally phoned the fertility clinic and booked herself in for a third round of ICSI to start on the 9th November. With the date in her diary and medication ordered, she threw herself into her work with the aim of getting as much done as possible to enable her to ease up a bit when treatment started. She knew it was a good thing to have a distraction, but at the same time she remembered how tired and grumpy she got while on the meds, so she didn't want to stress herself out by having to work any more than she had to.

Three days into the treatment she met up with Pippa midway between Cardiff and Bath at The Harbourside, a cafe overlooking the waterfront in Bristol. It was a Wednesday morning and quiet so they had a choice of tables and opted for one on the raised part of the cafe, nice and private. Pippa was thinner than the first time they'd met – not that she'd been big before, but it looked like the last few months had taken their toll. Tiredness showed in dark circles below her eyes and there wasn't any real happiness when she smiled. She looked like Connie felt and considering what they'd both been through since the beginning of the year Connie wasn't surprised.

'Dare I ask how it's going?' she said as they sat down with two large mugs of latte.

Pippa took a sip of coffee and wiped away the foam from the corners of her mouth with a thumb. 'It's going okay. I'm about ten days into the sniffing but it feels different this time because I know we've already got the embryos to implant –

they just have to survive the thawing process.'

'So, you get rid of one stress only to have another worry. This whole fertility treatment shit is a bitch.'

Pippa knocked her mug of coffee against Connie's. 'I'll drink to that.'

'I'm on day one of sniffing and have got that "here we go again" kind of feeling.'

'You don't feel hopeful?'

Connie shook her head. 'I guess not. Or maybe it's because I'm scared of being disappointed again that I feel less excited.' She stirred her latte. 'Also, I get the feeling that Felix is only doing this for my sake and would stop fertility treatment if it was down to him.'

'Really? He's okay with not having kids?'

'Honestly, I really don't know what he is or isn't happy about. We talked through stuff when we went to Amsterdam, but since we've come back he's shut himself off again.' Connie drummed her fingers on the table. 'I know he doesn't like talking about his feelings but the way he's behaving...'

'Behaving in what way?'

'Oh, I don't know – a bit distant, preoccupied with work, just not his usual self. It makes me think he's struggling with the fact that he's infertile. I mean, I physically had the miscarriage, but it was his baby too and he's not really spoken about his feelings or, as far as I know, even cried about it.'

Pippa reached out and took Connie's hand in hers. 'I know it's a grieving process however early you end up losing a baby. Everyone's different, though, and deals with things in different ways. Maybe he finds it easier to work his emotions through by himself.'

'But that's the problem, he doesn't seem to be working through any emotions. It feels like I don't really know him any longer.' The place had a comforting buzzy atmosphere and a great location overlooking the water. Connie wondered if Felix had ever come here when he'd worked in Bristol. 'How's Clive dealing with things?'

'Oh, fine,' Pippa said. 'But then he's one for letting his emotions out and he talks to me. I've been the one struggling to cope.'

'Because of the missed miscarriage?'

'That and the fact that my best friend, who has never wanted children, is now pregnant – by accident, of course – and failed to tell me. When I found out, it was as emotional as it had been at the scan when I was told we'd lost the baby. I can't even begin to describe how hurt I felt.'

'Oh my God, that's tough.' It was Connie's turn to reach for Pippa's hand and give it a squeeze.

'I found out a month ago and I haven't even been able to speak to her, let alone see her. I can't bear the thought of her with a bump and experiencing her baby kick when that's all I've ever wanted. And I feel awful about it too because I know she's going to be struggling with it...'

'Being pregnant?'

Pippa nodded. 'Yeah. Her relationship is complicated and she's not the least bit maternal – her idea of a quiet night in is five bottles of wine and a sneaky spliff. It's so messed up – how unfair is it that she can get pregnant when she's desperate not to, while I can't even conceive naturally, and when I do via IVF it's taken away in the cruellest way?'

'Oh Pippa, I don't know what to say.' Connie handed her a tissue. 'In fact, there isn't anything to say. Life is heartbreakingly shitty at times.'

Pippa wiped away her tears, scrunched the tissue in her hand and gave Connie a weak smile.

'It's so good to have you to talk to. I feel like I've lost everything in the past few months.'

'Trust me, I've needed your friendship too.'

'Now we're getting soppy.' They both laughed. 'Do you know I'm writing a blog?'

Connie shook her head.

'I thought it'd be therapeutic to get my feelings out, so it was really for me to begin with, but people have started to read it and follow.'

'Cool. You should have told me about it before – I'll have to have a read now too.'

'After finding out my best friend was pregnant I wrote a really angry post, and then she tweeted this the next day.' Pippa turned her mobile round so Connie could read the tweet.

*My best friend @thehopefulyears blog – you should all read this and know what an utter idiot I am. Sometimes sorry just isn't enough.*

'Well, that's a sort of apology.'

'But this is the problem, she's hiding behind the safety of goddam Twitter instead of having the nerve to talk to me to my face. The even more annoying thing is the knock-on effect her tweet has had, with loads of people seeing it and then reading my blog. I don't know whether Sienna contacted anyone – she knows everyone, she's like a total networking guru – but a mummy blog wants me to write a post for them.'

'Pippa, that's amazing.'

'It is but now I feel like I owe her something when all I want to do is hate her and be angry at her. I loathe myself for feeling so jealous and resentful. I've never been like this in my life.'

'I think it's only natural with what we're going through. I feel exactly the same – ridiculously jealous of my brother and his wife and their two children. And none of my family, except my aunt, has any clue what I'm going through and I suspect even if they did they'd be far from helpful with comments or support.'

'Do you know what we need? Cake.' Pippa stood up and took her purse out of her bag. 'I'll get it. What do you fancy?'

'Anything chocolaty.'

Connie relaxed back into the armchair while Pippa went up to the bar to order. She didn't know what she'd have done without Pippa over the past year. In not telling any of her family or friends about her and Felix's struggle to conceive and then the fertility treatment, she'd completely underestimated her need to talk to someone other than Felix. Talking to her aunt had been a huge relief, but Bella was thousands of miles away and had never had children so didn't understand the raw emotions Connie was going through. Pippa – well, Pippa was a lifeline and someone who, without a doubt, understood the way she felt.

Pippa's phone alarm was beeping by the time she got back to the table with two chocolate brownies.

'Time to sniff,' she said, holding her nasal spray and waving it from side to side.

'We look like two druggies sitting up here inhaling God knows what.' Connie inhaled two squirts of spray and smiled as Pippa did the same with hers.

'Unfortunately it's second nature now,' Pippa said, tucking her spray back in her bag. 'I've done it so many times.'

'Well, here's to third time lucky for both of us.' Connie tapped her coffee mug against Pippa's.

'Wouldn't it be the most amazing thing,' Pippa said, stabbing a fork into her brownie, 'to be pregnant together and put the hell of this past year behind us.'

'When are you likely to find out if you are pregnant?'

'Should be towards the beginning of December.'

'I've worked out that if this treatment follows the same pattern as the last two I'll pretty much be finding out over Christmas,' Connie said.

'What a Christmas present that will be.'

'I'm a bit worried that doing this leading up to Christmas is even more pressure.'

'I don't think there is a good or a bad time. I guess I've made my peace with it and am thinking it will happen when it happens. Or not. We can't control it. That's the most frustrating thing.'

'I think I need to relax more and have your attitude.'

'Trust me, a month ago my attitude was the complete opposite.' Pippa took another forkful of brownie. 'Why don't you talk to Felix? It might make you relax if he opens up and you know he's okay.'

Connie gazed out of the window and watched an older man walking hand in hand with a younger woman. They stopped by the entrance to the cafe, and the woman reached up and kissed the man on the lips before walking away with a wave. The man watched her for a moment, then smiled and stepped into the cafe, joining a couple of men at a table by a window.

Connie turned back to Pippa. 'If I didn't know him better I'd think he was having an affair.'

# SECOND WINTER

## *Sienna*

'I know someone whose labour lasted three days,' Tulip said, tucking her legs beneath her on Sienna's sofa.

Sienna threw the remote at her. 'You're having a fucking laugh.'

Tulip snorted and shook her head. 'Afraid not. And she ended up having an emergency caesarean after going through all that.'

'I so don't need to hear your horror stories. Give me an epidural, I'm not going to suffer any longer than I have to. Seriously, the thought of what has to happen to get this out…' Sienna cupped her hands around her small bump, '… scares me stupid. I mean, how is it even possible?'

'Why not have a planned caesarean then?'

Sienna shuddered. 'And be sliced open while still awake?'

'They do numb you from the waist down, you know.'

'Urgh, to all of it. Whichever way this baby's going to come out scares me stupid, yet I can't do anything about it. It's going to come out one way or another.'

Tulip leant forwards and patted Sienna's knee. 'You'll be fine – you know that, don't you? You're one tough cookie and childbirth will be a piece of piss.'

'Ashton says I'll be able to do it without any pain relief. I told him it's easy for him to say when he has a dick instead of a vagina.'

'I'd have punched him.'

'I nearly did. I appreciate he was trying to be supportive when the lady at this birth preparation class was explaining all the pain relief options, but then she showed us a toy baby going through a pelvis. Head the size of a melon pushing through a hole the size of an apricot. Fuck me.'

'That's what got you into this mess to begin with.'

Sienna slapped Tulip's arm. 'You are so not helping.'

'How has it been, though, being pregnant?'

'Harder than I thought possible and more wonderful. The morning sickness that went on for weeks sucked big time, and so does the hip and lower back pain, and the tiredness – oh my God, the tiredness. It also doesn't help that I don't want to stay in bed in the morning because everything aches too bloody much.'

'It's your body training you for having a newborn.'

'Feeling the baby kick is the oddest sensation ever but also amazing. I mean, it's only been a week or two since I properly felt a kick but the first time I felt it I knew I'd made the right decision keeping it. I just wish I could share all these experiences with Pippa.'

'You can't talk to her about it at all?'

'Apart from the fact she's not talking to me, she's going through her third cycle of fertility treatment in less than a year and has had a miscarriage, so no, I can't share the ups and downs of my unwanted pregnancy with her. Life is so messed up at times – to give me a healthy pregnancy when a baby is the last thing I wanted, and then my best friend, who has always wanted a baby and will make a fabulous mum, goes through hell just to conceive. Then when she finally does, she ends up losing her pregnancy in the most awful way possible. Fucked up.'

'You do know you're going to make a fabulous mum too – unconventional, yes, but you're going to kick ass.'

'Have you been listening to a word I've said?'

'Of course. I'm sorry, I just don't want you to put yourself down. But yes, I totally agree life can suck, but it'd be boring if everything happened as we wished it to all the time.'

'Try telling that to Pippa.'

'You know I believe in fate,' Tulip said. 'You having a baby, even though it was the last thing you *thought* you wanted, was meant to be. As for Pippa, it'll be whatever is meant to be for her too – whether that's to have a baby only time will tell. And you do realise she is still your best friend. And from one friend to another, why don't you go over and talk to her? Apologise, grovel, make it right – do whatever you need to do to get your friendship back. It's too precious a thing to throw away because you feel bad that you're pregnant and she's not. Whether you realise it or not, you both need each other.'

'Hi Clive, is Pippa home?'

Light spilt from the open doorway into the darkness of early evening. Pippa's house was always homely. Even when they were students and Sienna visited her in Bournemouth, her room had always been clean, tidy, but most of all welcoming. Half of Sienna wanted to run away, while the other half wanted to be invited in to sink down on the sofa in front of the wood burner and make things right with her best friend.

'Hey, Sienna. Is Pippa expecting you?'

'No.'

Clive paused for a moment, then stood back and let Sienna past. 'Pip!' he called up the stairs. 'Sienna's here.' He led Sienna into the living room. 'Would you like a drink?'

'Just water, thanks.'

Sienna couldn't help but notice him glance at her stomach. Just over twenty-three weeks and there was no hiding that she was pregnant, with a small, neat bump forcing her into maternity clothes. Elasticated fucking waists – she hadn't worn clothes with elasticated waistbands since she was a kid. She unbuttoned her coat, placed it on her bag on the floor and sat down on the sofa.

True to form, the wood burner was glowing red and

Sienna began to warm up. Pippa usually got a tree and decorated for Christmas at the very start of December, but over a week in and Sienna realised that there were no decorations up apart from twinkling fairy lights draped around the large mirror above the fireplace.

'You have a nerve turning up.' Pippa appeared in the living room doorway, dressed in pyjama bottoms and an oversized jumper.

Sienna stood up and realised her mistake as soon as Pippa glanced at her bump.

'What are you now – twenty-two, twenty-three weeks pregnant?'

'Twenty-three.'

Clive stepped back into the room, squeezing past his wife to hand Sienna a glass of water. 'I'll leave you two to it,' he said, slipping back out and closing the door behind him.

Sienna took a deep breath and placed the glass of water on the coffee table. 'I'm sorry for just turning up but we need to talk.'

'No, we don't.' Pippa folded her arms.

This was her best friend who she'd shared everything with since they were eleven years old. Maybe their friendship had always worked because they weren't similar. And yet, their differences were now wrecking the very foundation of their friendship.

'I can't even begin to tell you how sorry I am for not telling you straight away about being pregnant. I was so confused about what I was going to do, and then by the time I'd decided to keep the baby it just got harder and harder to find the right time to talk to you. I know you won't believe me but I was trying to protect you. Excuses, I know, but it's the truth. I never intended to hurt you – that was the last thing I wanted.'

The words tumbled out. Pippa looked at her in stony silence and slumped down on the sofa. Sienna sat next to her, leaning forwards so her top hid her bump as much as possible.

'You were going to have an abortion?' Pippa asked.

'I thought about it.'

'What made you decide to keep it?'

'A few things. Not being able to lie to Ashton, the thought of what you were going through to try and have a baby, but most of all it was down to me taking responsibility. I didn't choose this, but I wasn't careful enough to prevent it and so I've got to deal with it.'

'Deal with it.' Pippa laughed. 'That's how you're thinking about that baby growing inside you?'

Sienna's cheeks flushed. 'Yes. Dealing with it because, unlike you, I'm not prepared for this. I would do anything to swap places with you. *Anything.* I know you'll be an amazing mum, but I'm a nutcase and I feel sorry for this baby having me as its mother.'

'You'll be a good mother.'

'Why? Why does everyone think that?'

'Because you care enough to keep a baby you never wanted. And you care enough to worry about what I think. You'll be mental but you'll be good.'

Sienna took a sip of water and tried to hold back tears. 'I don't want to lose you as a friend.'

'Then be honest and talk to me. You should have done that from the beginning, however hard it was.'

'I know, I'm sorry.' Sienna put the glass down. 'How are you? I mean, how's the treatment going? You haven't updated your blog for a while.'

'I wanted to see how things went this time before posting anything. But I'm actually pregnant,' Pippa said quietly.

'Oh my God, that's amazing.'

'I'll be five weeks tomorrow.'

'You don't sound happy.'

'You still don't get it, do you?' Pippa said. 'I've been here before, pregnant and happy and thinking about the future, only for it to all be taken away. It's too early to get excited. Do you know how many things could go wrong?'

Sienna nodded. 'I know, but there's every chance that they'll go right this time.'

'But I'm trying to protect myself in case they don't. I've got to get past the seven-week scan first, then the twelve-week and the twenty-week one before I can begin to relax. Even then there's no certainty.'

# *Connie*

'That is the most incredible news, Pippa!' It was the evening before the all-important egg collection operation and Connie was sitting on the sofa in her and Felix's apartment, removing the nail polish from her toenails while holding her mobile between her cheek and shoulder. 'Your little frozen eggs have done good. I can't believe two of them survived being thawed, let alone you getting pregnant.'

'It's taken a few days to sink in,' Pippa said. 'But it's weird – I don't have any symptoms. I don't feel nauseous like last time, which has got me worried.'

'Every pregnancy is different so don't dwell on that too much.'

'I know I shouldn't but it's hard. My best friend came over yesterday evening to apologise for how she let me find out about her being pregnant. It was so difficult seeing her with a gorgeous little bump.'

'That'll be you soon.'

Pippa sighed. 'Hopefully.'

'Are things okay again with your friend?'

'Sort of. I haven't fully forgiven her but I get why she didn't tell me. I know she's struggling with it all – being pregnant, the idea of becoming a mum, and having to deal with my emotional state on top of that hasn't been easy.'

'Well, hopefully you can both move forwards and support each other.'

'How are you feeling about tomorrow?'

'Quite positive. The scan showed I've got a good number of follicles so hopefully there'll be plenty of eggs. I guess we'll find out in the morning.'

'How's Felix?'

'He's alright. Gone to bed early with his laptop to do some work as he's taking the day off to look after me, plus he's missing his work's Christmas do tomorrow evening because I can't be home alone after the general anaesthetic. Think he's a bit pissed off about it.'

'Well, there's always next year, and anyway, this is way more important.'

'I know that.' Connie wiped the last bit of pink polish off and screwed the top back on the nail varnish remover.

'He's still not opened up to you?'

'No, but hey, we've got all day together tomorrow.'

Pippa laughed. 'That's the way, positive thinking!'

'Same goes for you: keep positive.' Connie pulled her socks back on and held her mobile properly to her ear. 'You do realise you could be pregnant with twins.'

Connie didn't mind going through the egg collection operation for the third time that year. Having a general anaesthetic was like having the deepest, most peaceful sleep – no dreams, no shuffling about, no being disturbed by anything or anyone. The only bad bit was feeling groggy when she finally came to. The clinic felt familiar and she knew the drill: getting changed into a hospital gown, waiting in one of the little cubicles for the nurse to do her checks, then the consultant doing the operation coming to talk to them.

There was one lady in before her, but soon enough she was saying goodbye to Felix and being led through to theatre. Holding her gown closed behind her, she went over to the open hatch where one of the embryologists was waiting to confirm her name and date of birth to match with Felix's sperm sample. This wasn't how most people conceived a baby; it wasn't quite so much fun with a general anaesthetic and a ruddy great long needle involved.

With her name and clinic ID confirmed, Connie was led to the operating table and asked to sit while the anaesthetist inserted a cannula into the back of her hand. She lay down, a mask was placed over her mouth and she was told to breathe in deeply and slowly and count down from ten. She didn't want to think about what they were going to be doing down in her nether regions, so being knocked out cold was a blissful release from the reality of it all.

Ten... Her future baby could be conceived today.

Nine... One of the eggs the consultant was about to collect could be the start of their baby.

Eight... One of Felix's sperm in the adjacent room could be the one chosen to be the all-important other half of that baby.

Seven... She would know her baby's journey from the very moment it went from being an egg and a sperm to an actual embryo.

Six...


Connie woke up back in recovery in one of the cubicles. Her mouth was dry and her head woozy as she slowly focused on the nurse's station in front of her. A stillness surrounded her as if all her senses hadn't quite returned. One of the nurses sat typing something on the computer. Vaguely she heard people talking, another couple perhaps, but she couldn't work out what they were saying.

Connie moved her head and groaned. Helen, one of the nurses she'd seen many times before, came over and raised the back of her bed so she was in a semi-sitting position.

'How are you feeling?' Helen asked, pouring her a plastic cupful of water.

'Okay, I think. Bit heady.'

'Do you fancy something to eat and drink?'

'Yes please.'

Helen patted her arm and left the cubicle, pulling the curtains closed. Connie lay back and shut her eyes, not wanting to think about anything, allowing sleep to take over for a moment.

Helen returned with a hot chocolate and a tray with a

sandwich, yogurt and banana on it.

'I've phoned your husband and he's on his way back. Oh, and they collected thirteen eggs,' she said with a smile.

'Thirteen!'

Helen chuckled. 'You've done good,' she said, walking away.

Thirteen eggs. Connie couldn't believe it. She knew the scans had been looking good with a reasonable number of follicles but thirteen was more than she could have dreamed of. They'd nearly doubled the amount from the second cycle. All they needed now was the small miracle of them all being suitable for ICSI and then to fertilise.

'I hear they collected loads of eggs,' Felix said. He kissed her on the cheek, then sat in the chair next to her bed.

Connie nodded. 'Way more than last time. Hope that's a good sign. I know it should be quality over quantity, but quantity does help. At least there're more to play about with now. You never know, we might make it to blastocyst stage this time.'

'You worry too much.'

'Can you blame me?'

Felix ran a hand through his thick black hair. 'No, I can't. It's a lot to deal with and you're being ridiculously strong.'

Connie watched him. Even though he was lounging back in the chair, his handsome features were pinched into a frown.

'What did you do while you waited?' she asked.

'Went to a cafe and did some work.' He coughed before mumbling, 'And had a full English breakfast.'

'You bastard.'

Felix smiled. 'Sorry. My stomach was rumbling, what could I do?'

'Share in my pain of not being able to eat or drink anything all morning. Remember your vows – "in sickness and in health".'

Felix leant forwards and pointed at the tray in front of

Connie. 'You've got some lunch now.'

'Mmmn, an appetising ham sandwich and a Müller Fruit Corner.'

'Have they said when you can go home?'

'Once I've managed to eat and drink something and go for a wee.' Connie shuffled into a more upright position. 'I'm so looking forward to getting into comfy clothes and vegging on our sofa.' She glanced at Felix. 'I'm sorry you're missing your Christmas do. I can always get my mother to come and stay until tomorrow. We can tell her it was an op for women's problems or something.'

'Don't be stupid, the Christmas party isn't important.' He took his mobile out of his pocket and checked it before looking up at Connie. 'You'd seriously want your mother to look after you?'

'I wouldn't want her to look after me, no. I was giving you the option, that's all.'

'I'll remind you of that offer when your anaesthetic has worn off, crazy lady.' He reached for her hand and held it in his.

Connie smiled and lay back on the pillow. 'It's incredible to think that our baby could be conceived in this building right this minute without us even having to touch each other.'

'Incredible and completely freaky. I'll be glad to get shot of all of this.' Felix motioned around the recovery bay.

'Well, let's hope it works out for us this time. We deserve a bit of good luck.'

# *Georgie*

'Are you looking forward to tonight?' Melinda slicked on lipstick in front of the office bathroom mirror.

Georgie stared at her reflection. It was a year ago that she'd met Felix at the last office Christmas party. She hadn't been looking for love or intended to have an affair, but there'd been something about him. They'd clicked, and a year on…

A year on and she was pregnant, although no one would be able to tell yet. She smoothed her sparkly top down over her stomach. When she'd told Nathan after the twelve-week scan about the pregnancy, he'd been delighted but confused as to why she'd only just told him.

'To get my head around it,' she'd said. In many ways that was the truth. Now at nearly fourteen weeks pregnant she was in two minds about telling Felix at the Christmas party about her pregnancy, but a text earlier that morning had left her disappointed when he'd said a 'family emergency' meant he wouldn't make it to Bristol. At least she didn't have to decide yet about telling him or not.

'Honestly, I could do without this tonight,' Georgie eventually replied as she took one final glance in the mirror and decided no amount of make-up or hairstyling would make her feel or look less frumpy.

'Felix not coming by any chance?'

'It's that obvious?' Georgie said, bashing through the door.

'You've been miserable all day.'

'I've got a lot on my mind, that's all.'

'Anything you want to talk about?'

Georgie took Melinda's arm and pulled her into one of the empty meeting rooms. 'You don't approve of my relationship with Felix, do you.'

Melinda folded her arms and took a long look at Georgie. 'I don't condone what you're doing. My marriage ended because my ex decided to have an affair, and trust me, it's no fun being on the cheated end.'

Georgie shuffled uncomfortably, wishing she'd worn lower heels and the heating wasn't turned up so high in the office.

'But,' Melinda continued, 'you and Felix are perfect for each other. I mean, I haven't met his wife so I don't know what she's like or what they're like together, but there's something about you two. You literally light up when you're with him. You do realise most people here know you're banging him?'

'Oh, God.' Georgie put her hands to her forehead and rubbed her temples.

'What I wish you'd both do – and this is coming from the point of view of someone who's been cheated on more than once – is come clean. Make a decision about your relationship with your husband and with Felix, and end one. You can't be so damn lucky to have your cake and eat it too.'

Melinda gave Georgie's shoulder a squeeze before leaving her alone in the room.

Georgie perched on the end of the conference table and rubbed her forehead harder, realising she was developing a headache. She knew Melinda was right and that she couldn't carry on this affair and pretence forever. Of course it was now complicated further with her not knowing whose baby she was carrying. What if she ended her relationship with the father? Her love life had turned into a nightmare. Would either of them stick around, let alone forgive her for not knowing which of them was the father? If she loved Felix and wanted to be with him, why was she still with her husband? And why did she have sex with Nathan on their anniversary? She hadn't wanted to. That was no way to bring a baby into the world.

She had an impossible decision to make, and no one, bar Melinda, to talk to.

Her heart wasn't focused on partying the night away. Without the addition of the Cardiff office it was a quieter affair than last year, and Georgie found herself longing to catch sight of Felix by the bar. She ordered a small glass of red wine as that was the only way she felt able to get through the evening, and she didn't want anyone questioning why she wasn't drinking. By the sound of it from Melinda, she and Felix were the subject of the office gossip anyway, and the last thing she wanted to do was fuel the flames.

'This is going to be my last Christmas in Bristol,' Melinda said, joining Georgie and Sue at a table by the window.

'Jeremy didn't fancy coming tonight then?' Sue asked.

Melinda shook her head. 'The Cardiff office's party is tomorrow so I think he figured two in one week was a bit much. I told him that's a sure sign of getting old.'

Georgie reached her glass across the table and tapped it against Melinda's. 'We're going to miss you, you know.'

'I know. I'm going to miss you too. Who am I going to gossip with at work when I move across the bridge?'

'Knowing you, you'll find someone.'

'Georgie, your phone's ringing,' Sue said, pointing to the mobile vibrating and flashing on the table next to her. 'Felix' the name on the screen said. Georgie snatched the mobile up, catching Melinda's eye as she did.

'I'll only be a minute.' Without waiting for an answer, she slipped away from the table and headed towards the door. 'Hello.'

'Hey, can you talk?'

'Yeah, of course.' She'd never been so pleased to hear his voice. 'Let me go somewhere quieter.' It wasn't exactly quieter on the waterfront with people clustered beneath outdoor heaters, so she walked a little further down until the bars were out of sight and she could look across the water to the M Shed. Without her coat and with only a thin cardigan on over her top, she shivered in the December air. What she would do to have him here right now, his strong arms wrapped tightly around her, his warm breath caressing her ear. 'Everything okay?'

'Yeah, sorry I'm not there tonight. My wife ended up having surgery today and she can't be home alone for twenty-four hours.'

'Oh, blimey. She's okay, is she?' Did Georgie really care? Or was she asking because that was the polite thing to do?

'Yeah, she's fine, thanks. In bed asleep now.'

There was a pause and Georgie shivered. She should have grabbed her coat before answering the phone. It wasn't even like she was drunk enough not to feel the cold – one glass of red didn't have much effect.

'Any chance you'll be able to get out the house and meet up this weekend?' Felix asked. 'It'll probably be the last opportunity before Christmas.'

Georgie felt a rush of warmth. 'I should be able to. I really want to see you.'

'Me too. I've already told Connie I'll be working in Bristol this weekend, so whenever you're free, even if it's only for an hour or two.'

So that was her name – Connie. He had to still care for her, didn't he? In her own way Georgie cared for Nathan, although she didn't actually love him any more.

'I'll sort something out,' she said before saying goodbye and heading back to the party, her colleagues and her nearly empty glass of wine.

# Connie

'Morning, is Felix there?' asked a man with a hint of a Welsh accent.

'No, sorry, he's working away this weekend. Have you tried his mobile?'

'I can't get hold of him on his personal or work mobile.'

'Can I take a message?' Connie grabbed a notepad and pen from the drawer of the console table in the hallway.

'You said he was away with work?'

'Uh-huh.' Connie took the pen lid off with her mouth and moved the phone into her right hand.

'This is Darren. I work with Felix and I'm calling the senior managers in for an emergency meeting this afternoon, so I don't quite understand what you mean by Felix being away with work. No one's away or having to work this weekend as far as I know.'

Connie dropped the pen back down on the table. 'He said something about doing work with the Bristol office.'

'He hasn't been working in Bristol for a couple of months now.'

'Oh.'

Silence, apart from the sound of Darren's breathing. He coughed. 'Um, well, sorry to have disturbed you. I'll keep trying his mobile.'

He hung up and Connie let the phone clatter to the floor. It all made sense now – the weekends 'working' away from home; trying so hard to please her, as if he was feeling guilty about something; the distance between them that hadn't been there before; that phone call from the woman before they'd gone to Amsterdam…

The phone call – had that been her? Was that who he was with this weekend?

Connie gripped the edge of the console table. Unless this Darren simply didn't realise that Felix was working this weekend. After all, Felix *had* been working in Bristol – that much was true. Maybe this weekend had been organised before he'd stopped going to the Bristol office…

With a tightness building in her chest, Connie replaced the phone in its holder, went back into the living area, sat up at the breakfast bar and pulled her laptop open. What was the name of the woman who'd phoned when they'd been in the restaurant celebrating Connie being pregnant? It had sounded like a boy's name… Charlie maybe? Definitely a name ending in ie. Susie? Julie? Georgie? Georgie, that was it.

Connie logged on to Facebook, clicked on Felix, found his friends and scrolled through the names.

Jeremy Boden

Darren James-Smith

Lucy Meckenborough

Charles Didier

Felix had a lot of friends – 452 in total, and Connie scrolled through a couple of hundred before getting bored and doubting herself over how silly this was. Anyway, if Felix really was having an affair, he wouldn't be so stupid as to be friends with the woman on Facebook, would he?

Mitesh Singh

Jonathan Bennett

Paula Yatton

Mike Clifton

Georgina Taylor

Connie paused and hovered over the photo of Georgina Taylor. She was pretty, like really pretty with short blonde hair, and Georgina could easily be shortened to Georgie. With her heart thumping, Connie clicked on her face and was taken to Georgina Taylor's profile page. She was even prettier close up, and young. Connie glanced at Georgina's date of birth and quickly worked out she was thirty years old – seven years younger than Connie and nearly ten years younger than Felix. She was from Bristol and was married too – no real surprise there. Connie clicked on 'About' and her fears were confirmed when she saw that Georgina worked at Goldman and Peabody, the same advertising agency Felix worked for.

She clicked back to Georgina's profile page and scrolled down. Her heart skipped a beat and tears welled up. Georgina Taylor had a daughter – there were photos of them cuddled up together on the sofa, reading a book, a few of them on the beach.

Connie slammed her laptop shut and took a deep breath. Her whole body felt tight and tingly. All she wanted to do was confront Felix. If he was really having an affair… how could he with what they'd been going through? She'd only had her third egg collection operation a couple of days ago; was he meeting up with this woman while their future baby was being conceived in a fertility clinic laboratory? But even if she knew where he was and how to find him, confronting him would be no good. She needed evidence; she needed to know he was actually having an affair before she said anything to him, otherwise, with his gift of the gab, he'd be able to talk his way out of it.

It was late on Sunday afternoon when Connie heard the key turn in the front door. She'd been tense for hours, reading the same page of a book for the last ten minutes, expecting him at any moment and trying to keep calm so she didn't fly into a rage and do something stupid like punch him.

'Hey, babe,' Felix said as he walked into the living room and slung his overnight bag on the floor.

Connie took a deep breath, turned to him and smiled. 'Hey there. Did you have a good weekend?'

'Yeah, got lots done, had some good client meetings.'

'Talking of meetings, Darren from work phoned trying to call you into one. He seemed confused that you were working away.' Connie looked back at her book and turned the page.

'Oh really? It's because it was organised through the Bristol office ages ago.'

'That's what I thought.'

Felix leant over the sofa and kissed Connie on the top of her head. It took all her willpower not to shudder.

'What are we having for dinner?' he asked.

'Takeaway. I can't be bothered to cook.'

'Sounds like a plan.' He sat down next to her and put his arm around her shoulders. 'I missed you.'

'Me too.' Connie gritted her teeth. Maybe he really was telling the truth… only one way to find out. 'I'm going to be away next Saturday for work as there's a Christmas market on in Cirencester. I hope you don't mind.'

'Of course not.' He smiled and kissed her again.


There was a Christmas market on in Cirencester the following Saturday. Early that morning, Connie made out she was going and packed up the jewellery, display boxes and flyers and put them in the boot of the hire car she'd parked in the underground car park. Before saying goodbye to Felix, she asked him what he was going to do.

'Ah, just chill at home,' was his reply.

She drove out of the car park and pulled into a space a little further up the road where she could still see the entrance. She usually wore her hair down so she tied it up and clipped back her fringe, then pulled a jumper over the top Felix had seen her in before she'd left their apartment and put on a pair of glasses. She'd put a lot of thought into today, leaving her car at the hire car place so he would be none the wiser if he ventured down to the car park.

She looked in the mirror – even she thought she looked different. On the seat next to her was a book, a blanket, a couple of bottles of water, a flask of coffee and loads of snacks. If she was wrong she was going to have a very long and cold day sitting outside their apartment building.

Feeling foolish, annoyed, upset and angry for being put in this position, she felt it was longer than twenty minutes until she spotted Felix's silver Audi pull out of their apartment building entrance. With her heart thudding and sudden sweaty palms, she released the handbrake and pulled out too, a car behind Felix. This was madness, she thought, and yet he'd already lied to her. Chilling out had very quickly turned into going out. Maybe he would head west towards the Carmarthenshire coast and go kitesurfing, but once they reached the M4 he headed east towards Bristol. Connie kept her distance but managed to follow and keep him in sight all the way to the M5 junction where he headed south. Maybe he wasn't going to Bristol after all; perhaps he'd decided to venture to one of the beaches in North Devon. But three junctions later, he turned on to the A369 and they were heading back towards Bristol.

Connie had never doubted Felix before. She'd put his being distant and not quite himself down to his reaction to fertility treatment and what they'd been through the past couple of years. It was enough to put a strain on anyone and she was aware that their relationship had been under pressure. Yet again she was in the middle of the dreaded two week wait and wasn't easy to live with at times, her hormones all over the place and the all-important pregnancy test due to be taken on Christmas Day. Christmas bloody Day. Could it get any more dramatic?

They were getting closer to Bristol when Felix, a couple of cars ahead, turned down a road on the left. Connie followed, driving past an entrance to Leigh Woods on the left and large, expensive-looking houses on the right. Felix indicated, pulled to the side of the road and stopped. Worried that pulling over as well would look too suspicious, Connie carried on, drove around the corner and parked. She turned the engine off and, apart from the steady and constant sigh of the wind through the trees, it was silent. It was only 11am on a Saturday morning in the middle of December and there was hardly anyone about. The road was tree-lined, quiet and exclusive. Only a man walking his dog and two cars passed by in the thirty minutes she sat there, getting colder and colder.

She was about to give up and drive off when a third car drove towards her, slower than the others. Something about the driver, who seemed to be looking for something or someone, made Connie pick up her book to obscure her face. Out of the corner of her eye she caught sight of a shock of blonde hair as the car went by. Despite the fact it was freezing, Connie opened her window. The car stopped around the corner and its engine was turned off. A car door slammed, silence, then another one opened and closed. An engine started up and within seconds Felix drove past with a pretty blonde, who looked just like Georgina Taylor in the Facebook photo, in his passenger seat.

Connie sat with her hands gripping the steering wheel, oblivious to the icy wind curling in through the open window and wrapping itself around her. There was no point in following them. Why would she want to see them check into a hotel somewhere or park up in an even more secluded spot for a quickie? There would have been no point in Felix lying to her if he had an innocent relationship with the woman. Her husband of eight years, who'd comforted her when she'd miscarried, taken her away for a romantic weekend a few months ago, agreed to try again for a baby, let her go through with having her eggs collected just a week and a half earlier before having a near perfect blastocyst transferred back five days later, was a lying, cheating bastard.

# *Pippa*

There was blood in the toilet. A lot of blood. Pippa sat back down, feeling weak and shaky. This couldn't be happening, not again. She'd had no warning; everything had been fine – no real symptoms to speak of but no pain either. Now she could feel a dull ache low down in her pelvis and there was too much blood for there to be any good news. She was six weeks and three days pregnant and her seven-week scan was in just a few days' time on the 23rd December.

'Clive!' Pippa managed to shout before tears choked her up.

He appeared in the bathroom doorway, a towel around his middle and his hair still wet from the shower. 'What's up?' He stepped into the bathroom. 'Oh my God, Pip, what's the matter?'

'Can you get my mobile?' Tears dripped on to her bare knees. 'I need to phone the clinic. I think I'm having a miscarriage.'

'Maybe you shouldn't have come to work today.' Sita had found her crying in the ladies and marched her straight to the small kitchen at the back of the office that people rarely used.

'I'd have felt worse being at home on my own.' Pippa wiped her eyes with the tissue Sita handed her. 'I'm sorry, I started thinking about things and it all got a little overwhelming.'

'You know for certain you've lost this one?' Sita put a steaming cup of tea in front of her and gently squeezed her arm.

'I haven't got a clue about anything any longer. It's like my body's toying with me – the first cycle was negative, the second I got pregnant only to have a missed miscarriage, and now with this third one I have hope, only for it to be taken away within a couple of weeks. It gets harder and harder to stay positive. I wish I could see into the future, know what the eventual outcome would be, know where we'll be in two years' time – if I knew we'd end up having a healthy baby then I'd happily wait; it wouldn't feel so much like putting our lives on hold. But the not knowing is pure torture.'

Pippa blew on her cup of decaf Earl Grey.

'Wouldn't we all love a crystal ball?' Sita said, taking a sip of her coffee.

'Time out of this emotional hell is what I want. It feels like there's something missing: a huge gaping hole in my life that can't be filled by anything else. The desire to have a baby is so strong, it's all I can think about.'

'It's taken over your life?'

'Totally. I don't know if I'll ever be happy again,' Pippa said.

'Of course you will.'

'How can you be so sure? This might never happen for us, and that's not me being negative. That's being realistic.'

'And if it doesn't, you'll find a way to move on and live your life and be happy again.'

Pippa bit down on her lip and struggled to hold back tears. 'I don't want to move on. Moving on means not having a baby, not having a family, and that's all I want. That's all I've ever wanted. I'm not like my best friend, totally focused on my career. I only have this job because I have to. I'd do anything to be a full-time mum and I don't care if that makes me sound old-fashioned.'

'Oh, Pippa,' Sita said, 'I'd do anything to make this happen for you. You deserve to be happy. I'm gutted you've had to go through all this. It's crap, truly crap what you've had to put up with.'

'I keep doubting everything, like the reason why it's not happening for us is because I wouldn't be a good mother.'

'You do realise you're talking total rubbish, right?' Sita tipped another packet of sugar into her mug of coffee. 'Life is just unfair at times. Really unfair.'

'It feels as if it's every woman's right to be able to have a baby if she chooses to. Otherwise why is this maternal instinct so strong if it's not what we're naturally meant to do? I envy women who don't want to have children and can be content with that decision. I sometimes wish my desire for a baby wasn't so strong. It'd make life much easier.'

'So you've cancelled the scan tomorrow?'

Pippa shook her head. 'They still want me to go. I've done a couple of pregnancy tests and they were both still positive.'

'But that's amazing.'

'But it might not be. They need to check if there's anything still there or if it's ectopic. I just have a really bad feeling about it all.'

Pippa shut the front door behind her, dumped her bag in the hallway and went into the kitchen. Tears were streaming down her face before she'd reached the end unit. She slumped on the floor, leant against the unit and looked out through the patio doors towards the garden. The apple tree was bare; pale grey branches against an even greyer sky. She could see the heather she'd planted in September, its fronds of green speckled with deep pink flowers giving a splash of colour to an otherwise dismal day. How could she mourn another baby, one that was only an idea, a hope for a brief few days; one that she never got to see a scan of or a flickering heartbeat?

She knew she was putting on a brave face, keeping it together as far as everyone else was concerned because it was awkward enough – what does anyone say to someone who has lost a baby before it's born, has a name or even a gender? All she'd really had was hope and the idea of what her future was meant to be. Without hope, what did she have left? She hadn't told many people about fertility treatment number three so now she felt she had to hide the sadness and bad news of failure number three and miscarriage number two. She didn't know what was worse. She didn't know how she was ever going to smile again or get past the desire to have a child of her own.

'There's still hope,' the clinic nurse had said over the phone, but hope had finally deserted her.

*'You could always adopt.'* When someone told her that she wanted to scream. Like it would solve everything, like it was the easiest thing in the world to do. It probably would be something she'd want to think about doing, but first she had to come to terms with not having a biological child; not being pregnant or giving birth; not knowing her child from the second they were born; maybe not even knowing her child until they were well into their toddler years.

How many times had she heard how lucky she was? She had a wonderful husband, a beautiful house, a good job... blah, blah, blah, blah. What did any of it actually mean without having a family to share the house with; to go to work for?

Pippa's bum had gone numb by the time she moved her aching limbs from the floor. It was dark too; she could see twinkling fairy lights in the windows of the house opposite. Pippa usually had the house decorated by now but three days before Christmas and their house was still bare. Celebrating Christmas simply wasn't on her agenda. Last year had been tough enough, another without a baby, yet at the same time she'd had hope and the focus of starting fertility treatment in the New Year, along with the belief that 'this time next year' she'd be looking after a newborn. Fast forward twelve months and that dream was in tatters. IVF and miscarriage had taken its toll.

*I have a wonderful husband, a beautiful home and a great job.*

Why would anyone think she was missing out on anything? How dare she want what came so easily to so many people? How dare she want something that was the most natural thing in the world, arguably what people were put on earth to do – procreate? How dare she mourn the loss of two babies? How dare she want to experience a baby growing inside her instead of opting to adopt a child abandoned or taken away from its natural parents? How dare she feel so miserable, so helpless, so angry when she was much better off than so many people? How dare she, how dare she, HOW DARE SHE?

Pippa picked up the glass vase filled with sorry looking roses from the kitchen work top and flung it across the room. It smashed against the wall, sending glass flying and leaving water and brown-tinged petals dribbling down the wall.

They were back in the waiting room, hands clasped tightly together, unable to talk. The last time they'd waited for the seven-week scan she'd been fearful but hopeful, sitting in the waiting room knowing she was pregnant. Now… now she was bleeding. She'd had no symptoms to make her think she was pregnant despite a third pregnancy test in the morning stating she still was. She dreaded being told it was her messed up hormones tricking her body into thinking she was pregnant.

'Pippa Green?' the same nurse who'd done the scan last time called out.

Pippa followed Clive and the nurse out of the waiting room and along the corridor into the now familiar room. They sat down and the nurse went through her list of questions.

'The bleeding could be down to a number of things,' she said, putting the lid back on her pen. 'As I'm sure my colleague said when she spoke to you on the phone, it could be one of the embryos coming away that's causing the bleeding, and the fact that you're still testing positive is a good thing.'

'Unless it's ectopic.'

'Of course, but let's not jump ahead of ourselves.'

'I've had no symptoms other than the bleeding – no nausea or sickness like last time.'

'That doesn't necessarily mean anything. Lots of women go through their whole pregnancy without experiencing any symptoms at all. I know it can be unnerving, but it's not always a bad sign.'

Clive took hold of Pippa's hand and gave it a reassuring squeeze.

'Right,' the nurse said, 'if you want to pop behind the curtain and remove the bottom half of your clothes and get comfortable, we'll take a look.'

Lying down, waiting for the nurse to tell them the news, good or bad, Pippa wished she was anywhere but there. Three years ago they'd been happy and carefree, not worrying about infertility and scans, miscarriages and their future. Life had been so much simpler when there was only the expectation of what the future would hold. Reality and uncertainty and disappointment had taken their toll.

Resting her head back on her hand, Pippa tried to relax. She needed to know one way or another – being in limbo was total hell. She wondered how Sienna had felt at her first scan – had she been hoping that the pregnancy test was wrong and there really was no baby? That she'd lost it? How did she feel when she actually got to see a real live baby on the screen? I should have been there for her, Pippa thought, because she was probably as scared as I am right now.

A tear trickled down her cheek and she wiped it away.

'There we go.' The nurse turned the screen round to face them. 'One embryo, in the right place, with a heartbeat. That's why you're still testing positive. You are still pregnant. It must have been the other embryo that implanted and then miscarried.'

'I'm still pregnant?' Clutching on to Clive, Pippa tried to focus on the screen. There it was, like last time: a single jellybean shape with a tiny pulsing heartbeat.

'I'm still pregnant!'

# *Georgie*

'Merry Christmas!' Six glasses clinked together across the table as everyone reached forwards. Georgie caught Pippa's eye as they said cheers and she smiled.

Nathan lifted his glass again and stood up. Georgie wanted her chair to swallow her; she wished she hadn't agreed to Nathan announcing their news over Christmas dinner in front of her parents, Pippa, Clive and Daisy.

'After Pippa and Clive's wonderful news on Wednesday, Georgie and I wanted to share our news with you, and that is we're also expecting a baby.'

There was momentary silence and Georgie bit her lip. She noticed Clive glance at Pippa and reach for her hand.

Her mum stood up. 'Another grandchild, how wonderful.'

'Amazing news,' Georgie's dad said, and then everyone was standing and hugging each other.

'Lots to celebrate this year,' Clive said, putting his arm around Pippa's shoulders.

'When are you due?' their mum asked.

'The 15th of June,' Georgie said, sidling over to her sister and giving her a hug.

'You're due in June?' Pippa asked, frowning. 'That's before me.'

Georgie nodded. 'Uh-huh, I'm fifteen weeks pregnant already.'

'Wow, you kept that quiet.'

'I didn't want to tell you while, you know…' Georgie wafted her hands in the direction of Pippa's stomach.

'I'm beginning to know that feeling all too well. Nobody having the balls to talk to me.'

'To be honest, I hadn't told anyone – not even Nathan until after the twelve-week scan.'

Pippa took a step back and frowned. 'Why?'

'Can I talk to you?'

'Of course.'

Georgie leant towards her sister and lowered her voice. 'I mean in absolute confidence.'

'You know you can.'

Georgie glanced around the room: their mum was already clearing the table, Daisy was in her highchair playing with a cracker, and Clive and her dad were still congratulating Nathan and nursing their drinks. She took Pippa's hand. 'Come with me.'

She led Pippa upstairs and into her and Nathan's bedroom at the front of the house. It was a large room and decorated to perfection in Georgie's style in pale pink and grey with a king-sized bed, soft carpet, dressing table filled with make-up and perfume, a wall of built-in wardrobes and a door leading to the en suite.

'What's up?' Pippa asked.

'I've got myself into a bit of a mess.' Georgie closed the door.

'I don't understand.'

'There aren't many people I can really talk to about this.'

'Should I be honoured or worried about what you're going to tell me?'

Georgie sat on the end of her bed and put her head in her hands. 'This isn't easy, you know.'

Pippa sighed and sat down next to her, placing her hand on Georgie's leg. 'I'm sorry. It's just…'

'I know, we've not properly talked for a very long time, and I'll be the first to admit that I've not exactly been there for you over the past couple of years with all the shit you've been through. You realise I am beyond happy that you're pregnant again?'

Pippa nodded and wiped a tear away. Georgie put her hand on top of Pippa's.

'We used to be good friends. We used to talk all the time, and now I really need some sisterly advice even if you don't approve of what I've done. In fact, I know you're not going to approve…'

'Georgie, for God's sake just tell me.'

Georgie let go of Pippa's hand, took a deep breath and turned to face her sister. 'I've been having… I'm having an affair.'

There was silence and Georgie could clearly hear laughter from downstairs mixed with a cry from Daisy. Pippa's face hadn't changed but Georgie could tell that she was working out what to say.

'Why?' Pippa eventually said, shaking her head.

'I don't expect you to understand; you're in a loving, stable relationship…'

'And you're not?'

Georgie rubbed her fingers across her forehead. 'No, not really.'

'You're married and have Daisy, and my God, you're pregnant again. How can you not be happy with such a beautiful family?'

'It's not as simple as that.'

'What is simpler than being loved and having a husband and children?'

'But I'm not in love with Nathan any more. I love Daisy to bits and wouldn't change her for the world, but I was too young when I had her. I should have had a career not a baby.'

'So this is about what you feel you're missing out on?' Pippa stood up and put her hands on her hips.

'Keep your voice down, Pip.'

Pippa shook her head. 'You're crazy, you know. Who is he?'

'Someone I met through work.'

'And is he married?'

Georgie clasped her hands in her lap. 'Yes.'

'Why are you telling me this if you knew I wouldn't approve? Surely you know what I'm going to say – finish it with this guy and work on your marriage, concentrate on Daisy and this new baby you're going to have… Oh.' Pippa went motionless before looking directly at Georgie's stomach. 'Whose baby is it?'

'That's what I really need some advice about. I don't know.'

Georgie could read her sister like a book – the slightest change in her frown made her face go from confusion to total disgust. Well, Georgie had never been an angel like her older sister was. She had always been the one to come home late, have boyfriends her parents far from approved of, and had even dabbled with drugs for a brief period. Even though it was Pippa who had been the one to go through the emotional turmoil of her parents divorcing when she was three, her mum getting remarried when she was four and then a new half-sister when she was five, she had somehow managed to avoid any real teenage rebellion and had always been very clear about what she wanted – a husband, babies and a lovely house to raise them in. Ironic then that it was Georgie who'd managed to get all of that while Pippa continued to chase her dream of having a family of her own.

'How do you expect me to help you with that?' Pippa said. 'How can anyone?'

Georgie stood up and threw her hands in the air. 'I don't know what to do.' Tears coursed down her face, streaking her flushed cheeks. 'Everything's such a mess. I should be happy – it's Christmas, we're home with all the family – but I feel so empty.'

'Welcome to my world. It's a horrible feeling, isn't it, when there's something you want so badly but you just can't have. And Christmas always amplifies things.' Pippa plucked a tissue from the box on the bedside table. 'You got yourself into this situation and only you can get yourself out of it. Or at least make a decision about what you actually want before you go and destroy other people's lives. You have no idea how much you have to lose.' She handed Georgie the tissue and left the room, closing the door firmly behind her.

Georgie shouldn't have told Nathan about the baby. She should have made an appointment at the doctor's. If this baby growing inside her wasn't a factor maybe she could have walked away from Nathan and her marriage, shared custody of Daisy. She could have been with Felix. That's why she hadn't told him about the baby when she'd hooked up with him the weekend before. He'd leave his wife for her, surely? The way he looked at her, touched her; the things he said.

Georgie leant on the dressing table and sobbed. Pippa was right – she had everything to lose.

# Connie

There were two red lines. Connie should have been happy, even overjoyed, but she wasn't. Staring at the pregnancy test wasn't going to change anything. She'd never felt as lonely as she did right then. It was Christmas morning, she and Felix were at her parents' house and she was the only one up, locked in the bathroom finding out what fate had dealt her. Even her brother, his wife and their two children were still asleep. She'd told Felix that their official test day was Boxing Day, and she had no intention of telling him or anyone else that she was pregnant for the second time that year.

Christmas with her parents was the last thing she wanted, apart from Christmas alone with Felix. The past week had gone by in a blur. After following Felix all the way to Bristol and witnessing his rendezvous with the blonde woman, she'd considered driving straight back to Cardiff to confront him when he got home, but she couldn't face it. Instead, she drove to Westonbirt Arboretum for a walk to clear her head, calm herself down and warm herself up with a hot chocolate before returning home, composed and with lies about her day at the Christmas market ready to flow as easily as they obviously did for Felix.

Connie stared at herself in the mirror. Pale face, mascara beneath her eyes and a sadness that wasn't going to be erased by enduring Christmas back at her childhood home. She wiped away her tears, wrapped the pregnancy test in a tissue and put it in her pyjama pocket to get rid of it later, somewhere no one would find it by accident. She had absolutely no one to talk to. It didn't feel right to phone Pippa on Christmas Day, and anyway she deserved a happy Christmas without Connie dragging her spirits down. There wasn't even the option of Skyping with Aunt Bella since her father's falling out with her years ago. Somehow Connie would fake that everything was okay between her and Felix so she could manage to stay in control of her emotions for the rest of the day. She knew Felix didn't want to be here any more than she did, but he had reasons for wishing to be elsewhere other than that he'd never got on with her parents.

She slipped back into her old room, which had been turned into a guest bedroom the minute she'd left home for university. The curtains were drawn and the room was pitch black, but Connie managed to creep across to where her bag was slung over the back of an armchair and tuck the pregnancy test safely inside. Felix was snoring gently but there was no way she wanted to get back in bed with him – the sound of his breathing alone was enough to make her want to hold a pillow over his mouth. She tugged a jumper on over her T-shirt and padded downstairs, crept into the large living room at the front of the house and turned the Christmas tree lights on.

The darkness erupted with hundreds of twinkling white lights and Connie slumped on the sofa, tucking her arms around her knees. She wondered what Georgina Taylor was doing right now. Was she up too, woken by an excited toddler dying to open presents from Father Christmas? Georgina fucking Taylor. Connie took a deep breath and ran her hands across her stomach. Her little blastocyst had hung on in there despite the odds; despite the stress. But did she really want to bring a baby into the world with a husband who was cheating on her?

Connie shook the thought from her head. She wouldn't confront Felix, do or say anything until they'd had the seven-week scan and at least knew what they were dealing with. The little life growing inside her was more important than anything in the world; more important than Felix's infidelity, his lies, and certainly more important than Felix himself. Keeping herself upbeat and healthy and as little an emotional mess as possible was going to be her goal over the next few weeks. Once she knew if she had a healthy pregnancy, then she'd think about confronting Felix.

Connie rubbed her temples and felt like screaming. Christmas bloody morning and she was pregnant and thinking about the woman her husband was screwing.

A door banged upstairs and there was a cry from Tobin. Footsteps sounded on the stairs. Connie's peace was about to be shattered. She untucked her feet, placed them on the floor and leant forwards. Her mum bustled into the room already perfectly made up and dressed in a tweed knee-length skirt and a cream blouse.

'What on earth are you doing sitting down here in the cold?' she said, going over to the grate and setting a lit match to the kindling.

'I couldn't sleep. I'm warm enough.' Connie watched the flames take hold, crinkling up and dissolving the newspaper curls with licks of flame.

Her mum stepped back, huffed and put her hands on her hips.

'I wonder if anyone will want a cooked breakfast.' She turned back to Connie. 'Glad to see your feet are off the sofa for once.' She turned on the lamp on the side table before bustling from the room.

'Happy Christmas to you too,' Connie said.


'I can't afford to take another day off work,' Felix said, taking a bite of his toast and fiddling with his tie. 'It's not like me being there is going to change the outcome.'

'I know you being there isn't going to change whether our baby has a heartbeat or not, but your support would be nice.' Connie threw her toast down on the plate. 'Do you realise how scared I am about this scan?'

Felix stood up and wrapped his arms around her. 'I'm

sorry, I know. You're scared, I'm stressed. I just can't face this today.'

He released her and sat back down on the stool at the breakfast bar.

'You can't face it because you're worried about what we're going to find out?'

He shrugged and bit into his toast.

'It's kind of natural to feel like that,' Connie said. 'It's a massive thing, to be finding out which direction the rest of our life is going to go in.'

Except Connie knew it wasn't as clear cut as that. She'd got through Christmas and told Felix the pregnancy news when they were back home and alone. For the last three weeks they'd been going through the motions of everyday life. There was a distance between them that she realised had been there a while, but was only now apparent to Connie since she had become aware of his affair. He'd been moody too and she could pinpoint that from the day of the egg collection operation – the day he'd missed his work Christmas party – and he'd only got worse since then. Work and the stresses of the fertility treatment he'd put it down to. But Connie knew better.

'Phone me as soon as you come out.' Felix left her with a hug and a kiss on the cheek, like it was a dentist appointment she was going to.

The drive to the clinic tied Connie's stomach in knots, and she felt a fool sitting in the waiting room on her own with no husband to hold hands with or give her shoulder an encouraging squeeze. Nausea crept up her throat. The nausea she'd been getting over the past couple of weeks had been a reassuring sign that her little embryo might be hanging on in there, but now she just felt sick, and she wasn't convinced it was pregnancy nausea. More likely sheer nerves.

Her phone pinged and Connie's heart skipped a beat, thinking it was a text from Felix.

*Pippa: Thinking of you this morning and sending you all the positive vibes I can. Hoping your little one has a good strong heartbeat. I have everything crossed for you. Xxxx*

Connie wiped away a tear. She had a better friend in Pippa than she did in her own husband. Did Felix not want to come to the scan because he was worried his true feelings might give him away – that he didn't actually want this baby with her? Did he think he wouldn't be able to fake joy? Maybe it would be easier if the nurse told her the baby wasn't viable. Her much longed for baby…

'Connie Vaughan,' a tall lady with short blonde hair and a welcoming smile said. 'If you'd like to come with me.'

Connie took a deep breath and stood up. Screw Felix. Deep down she wanted this baby more than anything.

# *Sienna*

'Mama, you know nothing about my relationship with Ashton.' Sienna stood in her kitchen, which had been taken over by her mother, Agnese. A bolognese had been simmering away for the best part of two hours.

'I know he's the father of your baby and you need to be with him and him to be a part of your and my grandchild's lives.' She lifted the lid off the frying pan and the smell of wine, oregano, tomatoes and meat escaped into the kitchen.

'I heard enough of your opinion over Christmas.'

'I'm your mother, of course I'll give you my opinion. And anyway, you were only with us for one day and didn't spend any time with Ashton at Christmas either.'

'He was with his family.'

'And you're telling me you weren't welcome?'

'Of course I was welcome but the last thing I wanted was to have his mother fawning over me and making unsubtle remarks about why we're not together. Our relationship has always been complicated and I'm not going to move in with him because we're having a baby. I tried it and I realised I like my own space.'

'You'll have no own space once you've had this baby. You'll be glad then of the extra help and who better than the baby's father?'

'I knew you were going to do this. Why d'you think I took so long to tell you I'm pregnant?'

Agnese huffed. 'Well, you're foolish not to want his help at least.' She opened the cupboard next to the cooker. 'Do you have tagliatelle?'

Sienna went to the cupboard next to the fridge, pulled out a packet of green and white tagliatelle and handed it to her mum.

'Living together will drive me mad. He's not going to be home with the baby; he'll be off out at work each day, so where's the advantage of me living with him?'

'Sienna, you're impossible.' Agnese wiped her hands on a towel. 'What about the evenings and weekends? Night feeds? Having some company, a shoulder to cry on, someone to hug when it all gets too much?'

'It's not like I'm not going to see him. He's going to be a part of our lives.'

'And is he happy with this arrangement?'

'We have no "arrangement"; we're still figuring all of this out.'

'My point exactly.' Agnese flicked the switch on the kettle. 'When was the last time you spoke to him?'

'Not that long ago. He came to the twenty-week scan and we did this stupid expecting couples yoga birthing type course. I'm trying to involve him but I need my space to figure out what I'm going to do once this baby is born before anything else.'

'You mean work.' Agnese folded her arms and shook her head.

'Of course work. I have a mortgage to pay, a career to somehow keep going.'

'You marry Ashton and you don't have to worry about all that.'

'Oh Mama, for f… I'm not marrying Ashton, and even if we were properly together, I wouldn't give up my career and everything I've worked hard for. I'm going to be a working mum. You may not like it but it's my choice, my decision, and that's what's going to happen.'

'You have no idea how hard it is raising a child.' Agnese poured boiling water into a large pan on the cooker.

'No, maybe not, but it's for me to find out and for me to

decide how I'm going to live my life. You really don't need to be telling me what to do.'

Ding dong. Ding dong.

'Saved by the doorbell,' Sienna said and left the kitchen. She'd waited until after the twenty-week scan to tell her parents that she was pregnant and right now she was wishing she'd waited until after the birth. Sienna had known her mother would have plenty to say. She'd invited herself to stay for the weekend to help out and spend some rare time with her daughter, but Sienna had always known it was about trying to fix her life for her. Her mother had never been happy with Sienna's desire to focus on her career instead of settling down and having a family, and couldn't seem to comprehend why she was still resisting all of that despite now being twenty-four weeks pregnant.

Sienna opened her front door and came face to face with Ashton.

'What are you doing here?' She clocked the bottle of wine and bunch of flowers. 'Oh. My mother, yes?'

'You didn't know I was coming?'

'Nope.' Sienna stood aside to let Ashton in. 'But I should have known and guessed by the amount of bolognese she's made.'

'It smells good.' He handed Sienna the flowers. 'Those are for you, the wine is for your mum.' He took off his coat and Sienna closed the front door on the icy January day.

'Right now I'd rather the wine was for me but I'd get another telling off from my mother, so best not. The flowers are beautiful, though, thank you.' Sienna led the way back through the living room and into the kitchen. 'Mama, look – what a surprise, Ashton's here.'

Agnese put down the wooden spoon she was holding, wiped her hands on her apron, took Ashton's head in her hands and kissed both cheeks. 'You need to talk some sense into my daughter.'

'I've been trying to for months,' Ashton said, placing the

wine on the wooden kitchen table.

'You really think it's a good idea to gang up on me?' Sienna put the flowers next to the wine.

'Ah, Sienna,' Agnese said, blowing on a spoonful of bolognese and tasting it. 'No one's ganging up, we're just concerned.'

'I can understand Ashton being concerned as he's the father of this baby, but Mama, it's actually none of your business and you're really not doing us any favours poking your nose in. You think playing happy families is going to help?'

'Sienna,' Ashton said, touching her arm, 'let's at least make the most of this. Maybe a mediator is exactly what we need.'

Sienna shrugged Ashton away. 'Then let's pay for a fucking counsellor rather than being emotionally blackmailed by my mother.' She paused at a vibrating sound. 'That's my phone,' she said, glancing at the number on the screen and scooping it up from the table. 'I've got to take this.'

She stalked from the room, anger coursing through her and her back aching from standing up for too long, went into her bedroom, closed the door and took a deep breath. 'Hello?'

'Hey, Sienna, it's Carly, one of the producers on *The Bloodstone Chronicles*. We met a few months back.'

'Hi there.'

'Is now a good time to talk?'

'It honestly couldn't be better.'

'Well, I'm very sorry to be the bearer of bad news, and there's no easy way of saying this so I'll come straight to the point. We've decided to go with a different location manager. We'd have loved to have you on board but considering the workload, time scales and the fact that you're due to give birth just two weeks before we'd need you to start work, it's really not feasible.'

Sienna sat down on the edge of her bed. 'Carly, trust me, I'd be able to make it work.'

'Sienna, I'm fully aware you're one of the best in the

business but there's simply too much riding on this to take that risk. We've already offered the job to Steve Pemberton, I'm sorry. Absolutely we'll keep you in mind for the future. We hope this show will run for years and I'm sure there'll be plenty of opportunities to work together, but right now is not the time. I wish you all the very best with the baby and I'll keep in touch.'

Sienna pressed end call and dropped the phone on the bed. It felt like a noose was tightening around her neck, squeezing the life out of her. With her mother and Ashton conspiring together in the kitchen, her career falling by the wayside and this baby taking over her body one uncomfortable day at a time, she felt suffocated. She took an overnight bag from the bottom of her wardrobe, stuffed it full of clothes and packed a wash bag. Screw Ashton and her mum; screw Carly and Steve bloody Pemberton (even though she knew and liked him); screw everyone and everything. Picking up her mobile, she slung the bag over her shoulder and crept from the room, grabbing her handbag from the hook in the hallway. She paused for a moment to check that she could still hear her mum and Ashton talking in the kitchen. Satisfied that they were, she opened the front door, quietly closed it behind her, got in her car and drove away.

# Pippa

*24th January blog post:*

### The Night Before the Dating Scan

*It's the night before my twelve-week scan and I feel sick to my stomach and not because I have morning sickness. In fact I've barely had any symptoms so far in this pregnancy. I think I'd feel so much better if I was throwing up constantly because then at least I would feel pregnant. But as my husband very rightly pointed out, I don't not feel pregnant either. At least being symptom free I've been spared the hell of last time, where at around ten weeks all my early pregnancy symptoms tailed off and that was because I'd lost the baby. I'm feeling as upbeat as I can. My good friend, who I met because of fertility treatment, had some fantastic news last week when she found out at her seven-week scan that her baby has a heartbeat. This is her third cycle too and she so deserves to be happy. The thought of us both having babies a few weeks apart is amazing. Yet, I've got to stop myself from rushing ahead when there are still so many hurdles to overcome before we're able to hold our babies in our arms.*

*Whatever the outcome tomorrow, I'll post about it. I've shared my journey so far and will continue to share it in the hope that I get a happy ever after. Wish me luck. Xx*

Pippa hit publish. It was 11pm and she wanted to think about nothing, sleep well and wake up calm and collected, ready to face their fate, but she had no idea how she was going to manage to sleep with her stomach churning and her head playing the different scenarios over and over again.

She did sleep but fitfully. Her blog post by the morning

had more than thirty comments on it wishing her luck. It had been shared on Facebook and Twitter numerous times. Maybe she'd been wrong in being so open – she couldn't imagine how hard it would be to write a post if they didn't get happy news. But she'd committed to it now, warts and all.

She and Clive went through the morning in a daze, showering, getting dressed, having breakfast. Pippa only managed a couple of mouthfuls of toast before having to rush to the toilet and be sick. The first time so far this pregnancy. That had to be down to nerves.

The waiting room in the maternity wing of the hospital was full of women with varying sized bumps. Pippa felt a fraud, not feeling pregnant, not looking pregnant, and worst of all doubting that she was still pregnant. She clutched Clive's hand and thought she was going to throw up again. Being here brought the memories of just a few months before flooding back, when anticipation and excitement had turned into absolute horror. Life wouldn't be so cruel as to put them through all that again, would it?

Walking into the same scan room felt like walking to the executioner's block. The man doing the scan knew their history and talked them through what they were going to do and be looking for before asking Pippa to lie down. Gel on her stomach. She closed her eyes. The sonographer eased the probe across her stomach. Clive clasped her hand. It felt like an eternity before the large screen up on the wall in front of them flickered to life.

'Everything's fine,' the sonographer said, pointing to the black and white image on the screen. 'There's your baby, perfect heartbeat and a little mover to boot.'

Pippa could barely make out the image of their baby through her tears.

'Look, Pip,' Clive said, his voice cracking. 'It looks like it's waving.'

Pippa wiped her eyes with the tissue the sonographer handed her and then watched transfixed as their tiny baby continued to wave its little arms and legs. The memory of that still image of a smaller, less formed baby last time was startlingly different compared to this. Her mum had told her that sometimes you had to go through the bad times to appreciate the good, and boy did she appreciate what she was seeing right now.

The sonographer handed her the scan printouts and she clutched them to her chest as they walked from the room. She couldn't help but think back to September when she'd buried the scan picture of their first baby beneath the apple tree. This time was different – this one was a fighter. This time she had real hope.

Pippa kissed Clive goodbye and he went back to work, while she headed home having taken the day off, pre-empting that she'd either be too upset or too overjoyed to concentrate and get any work done.

As she turned into their road, she could make out Ashton sitting on their front garden wall.

'Hey there,' she said as she reached him.

He stood up. 'Have you seen Sienna?'

'Not since before Christmas.'

'Your phone keeps going to answerphone so I thought she was with you and you were ignoring my calls.'

Pippa frowned. 'What are you talking about?' She took her mobile out of her bag and turned it on. 'I've had my phone switched off since yesterday. It was a pretty big day today and I didn't want to talk to anyone until I had some news one way or another.'

It was Ashton's turn to frown.

'We had the twelve-week scan this morning.'

'Oh right, of course, and it went well?'

'Perfectly. We have a perfect little baby.' Pippa took the house keys out of her bag. 'But yeah, Sienna's not here. What's up?'

'She walked out yesterday.'

Pippa slotted the key in the lock and turned back to Ashton. 'What do you mean, she walked out?'

'Her mum was staying and invited me over for a meal in an attempt to talk things through, and Sienna went and took a phone call and didn't come back. She'd packed some stuff and her car wasn't there and she's not answering her mobile.'

'Oh my God.' Pippa turned the key in the lock and pushed the door open. 'Come on in.' She ushered Ashton through to the living room and he sank down on the sofa. He looked like he hadn't slept all night and his usually tanned face was washed out. Pippa realised that it was around this time last year he'd gone to the Maldives with Sienna and had his proposal shot down. Twelve months later and he was still chasing the woman he loved, who was now carrying his baby – the one she didn't actually want. And Pippa thought her life had been messed up.

'Have you tried Sienna's friends?'

'The ones I know. Sienna knows everyone. She could be anywhere, with anyone, and no one's likely to tell me.'

'What can I do?'

'Try phoning her, please – she might answer to you.'

Once upon a time she might have answered, Pippa thought as she called Sienna's mobile and listened as it went straight to answerphone.

'Hey, Sienna, it's me. Everyone's worried about you and wants to make sure you're okay. Please give me a call when you get this message.'

'Thanks for doing that,' Ashton said. 'If it wasn't for her being pregnant I'd walk away. It's blatantly clear she doesn't want to be with me, and to be honest, although I'm stupidly in love with her still, I hate her for what she's doing. A family is what I've wanted with her ever since we met, and now that we are going to have a baby she's intent on doing it alone.'

Pippa perched on the sofa next to Ashton. 'I'm so sorry for what she's putting you through. If it's any consolation a few years ago she wouldn't have kept the baby and the fact that she has speaks volumes. It's probably all too much to commit to you at the same time as being pregnant. Wait until she has the baby.'

Ashton nodded. 'Do you know we're having a boy?'

'No. Oh my God, no, she never said.'

'We found out at the twenty-week scan but Sienna didn't want to tell anyone – she still refers to him as "it". I guess it's her way of dealing with things.'

'Or not dealing with them.'

'Tell me about it.'

They fell silent and Pippa played with her wedding ring. She'd always liked Ashton; of all Sienna's boyfriends he was the one Pippa had hoped she'd stay with. He looked defeated as he ran a hand through his hair and glanced again at his silent phone. There was nothing she could say or do to make him feel any better. She knew what it was like to want a family and go through the trauma of not believing it would ever happen – but to know the woman you loved was going to have your baby, it's just she didn't actually want to be with you any longer, must be pure torture.

'I'm really pleased for you, Pippa, about your baby,' Ashton said, standing up. 'You're going to be an amazing mum.'

'Sienna will be too, in her own way. Just give her a chance.'

Ashton grunted. 'We'll see.' He headed out of the living room and made for the front door. 'If you hear from her, please let me know.'

'Of course.' Pippa reached up and gave him a hug.

As soon as the door closed behind him, Pippa grabbed her mobile and rang Sienna. It went to answerphone again.

'Sienna, I love you. You're my best friend, always have been and always will be whatever happens between us. As your best friend I have to tell you, you're killing Ashton. Whatever you're struggling with because of this baby, Ashton is so ready to be a dad and loves you and your unborn baby unconditionally. You pushing him away isn't going to change that but he will resent you for it. He's beside himself with worry. I hope that you're okay. I know you, I've known you for twenty-four years but Ashton's only known you for four. I know you've always needed your own space, and I'm presuming that's what you've done – taken yourself off somewhere – but it'd be nice to know that you're fine.'

Pippa sat down on the sofa and realised she and Clive would need to get a fireguard for their fireplace, and that by the end of the year their tidy, grown-up living room would be littered with toys. She smiled and brushed her hand across her stomach, wondering if her little baby was wriggling around as much as earlier.

'We had our twelve-week scan this morning and I have one lively and healthy baby on board. We're going to be mums together, Sienna. You don't have to do this alone; I'll be with you every step of the way.'

# Sienna

Sienna had discovered the cottage while scouting for a location and building suitable to use for a few scenes in a British romance she'd worked on a couple of years back. It had been perfect: a yellow sandstone cottage in the Cotswolds with roses around the door and honeysuckle creeping past the windows. In the end she'd decided not to use it because of the difficulty in accessing it as she didn't want to pass that headache on to the cast and crew. But she knew it was a holiday cottage for rent, and on a cold and miserable grey day at the end of January she was relieved that it was free when she'd called ahead.

She saved Pippa's answerphone message and put her mobile on the coffee table in front of her. Despite the heat pumping out of the wood burner, she pulled the blanket tighter around herself. Pippa was right about everything. A weight lifted off her shoulders knowing that she still had her best friend on her side despite everything they'd been through. She'd been so wrapped up in her own problems over the past couple of days that she'd completely forgotten about Pippa's scan.

She wiped away her tears and resolved to be a better friend. A better daughter. A better whatever she was to Ashton. She had a lot of thinking to do and decisions to make.

She was about to get up when she felt a nudge beneath her ribs. The feeling made her hold her breath and move her hands to the top of her stomach. She still had nine weeks to go, yet already the movement was so strong. Any stronger and it would feel like the baby was going to burst out of her stomach like the scene from *Alien*. She shuddered, and then there was a nudge again just to the left of her hand. Was it a foot? A little fist? It had been a strange feeling to begin with and now she worried if she didn't feel movement for a couple of hours. She was comforted by the pummelling her insides were getting, although her bladder was suffering. She wanted to share this experience with Pippa and she so wanted Pippa to be able to experience her own baby somersaulting around inside.

Sienna nearly phoned Pippa back but paused before hitting call. She needed to figure some stuff out first. Throwing off the blanket and closing the air-hole on the wood burner to let it tick over, she went through to the country-style kitchen and pulled on her boots and put her thick winter coat on. It still did up over her bump as long as she left the last couple of buttons undone. She wrapped her scarf around her neck, put the house keys and her mobile in her pocket, pulled on her gloves and closed the back door behind her.

It was still and quiet with only the creek of the bare branches stirring in the breeze. Stepping out of her Victorian house in Bath, she would have been confronted by the noise of traffic, of people. There was always something going on or masses of tourists elbowing their way down Milsom Street. Sometimes she wanted it all to stop. That's why she loved her job. Even though lots of time was spent on set where there were always people and rarely any time to think, let alone time to herself, her job as location manager often took her off the beaten track on her own. She actively looked for jobs that would take her away from home for long stretches at a time and she never really questioned what it was she was escaping from.

She set off down the muddy track that led away from the cottage. The mud was ridged and frozen and leaves crunched and disintegrated beneath her boots as she walked. She took a deep breath of cold air and soaked up the smell of wood smoke. If it wasn't for the fact she loved socialising, meals out, after dinner drinks and having a coffee shop within walking distance, she'd give up the car fumes, noise and tourists, as well as the inspiring Bath architecture and history, for a peaceful country life.

At the bottom of the track, before she reached the lane that eventually led to civilisation, Sienna heaved herself and her bump over the stile and on to the path that meandered through the wood. It was warmer out of the wind, and although her cheeks burned with the cold, it felt good being flushed and free and alone.

Her baby was quiet now, she assumed rocked to sleep by the gentle sway as she walked along the frozen path. She paused when a pheasant shot out in front of her and rested her hands at the top of her bump. She wanted to feel the baby move; wanted to know that it... that *he* was okay in there. A tear rolled down her cheek and she leant back against the gnarled trunk of a tree, realisation dawning on her what a mess she was making of things. Despite not wanting a baby, she would now do anything to make sure he was fine. He... she was having a son. She and Ashton were having a son.

She wiped away her tears on her gloves and set off again through the wood, puffing as the path began to climb, curving its way between tree trunks until the trees thinned out to reveal a view that was worth the effort of walking while thirty-one weeks pregnant. The sun was high in the sky but watered down like it had been painted on with muted colours. A low lying mist collected in the dips of the hills and around the edges of the woods. The sloping hills, large stretches of open fields and clusters of wooded areas would make the perfect location for a battle scene.

She laughed. A beautiful and peaceful place like this and she was still thinking about work; still wanting to fill the place with actors and cameras, trailers and lighting. Maybe she should keep this place to herself.

\*    \*    \*

The wood burner was still glowing by the time Sienna had kicked off her boots in the kitchen, hung her coat and scarf on the hook on the back door and returned to the warmth of the living room. She flopped down on the sofa and rested her hands on her bump, waiting for her son to wake up, then reached for her phone and called Pippa.

'Sienna, I'm so glad you phoned back. Are you okay?'

A tear rolled down Sienna's cheek at the sound of her best friend's voice. 'I can't tell you how good it is to speak to you right now.'

'Same here. You've had everyone worried.'

'I know. I'm sorry, I just needed a bit of time.'

'I figured, and that's what I told Ashton, but he's kinda beside himself. What happened?'

'My mum and Ashton happened, but that wasn't what made me leave. I'm not even sure if I told you this, but last year I was in talks about the most amazing job as location manager on a new TV series that's set to rival *Game of Thrones*. That afternoon, when Ashton and my mum were there, I got dropped because they needed someone to start asap and not be giving birth anytime soon. I freaked out about how much my life is going to change and I needed some space. Plus, if either Ashton or my mum had said one more thing to me that afternoon, I'd have fucking killed them.'

'Oh Sienna, I'm so sorry about the job. In a weird way I understand what you're going through, only the other way round – losing out on what I wanted most in life…'

'A baby,' Sienna said, rubbing her bump.

'A baby,' Pippa said quietly. 'You'll get your career back on track. It might take a bit of time but the wait will be worth it in the end. And trust me, I should know. Right now I'm holding the scan picture of our little baby – everything's fine this time.'

Sienna laughed. 'Oh Pip, I wish I wasn't on the end of the phone right now. I am beyond happy for you. I should have asked you a long time ago about this, because as far as I'm concerned you're family, and apart from Ashton you're the only person I want to be with me when I give birth. Will you be there when the time comes?'

There was an intake of breath and Sienna knew that Pippa was crying.

'Yes, absolutely, I'll be with you at your baby's birth. It's the sweetest thing you could have asked and done for me. I know my reaction to your pregnancy must have been as upsetting for you as it was for me, but deep down all I really wanted was to be involved – however much it may have hurt me. But I got good news today.'

'You so did, and I'm so happy that we're going to be going through this together.'

'What about Ashton? He asked me to let him know if I spoke to you.'

'Tell Ashton I'm fine – that we're fine.'

'Why don't you tell him yourself?' Pippa asked.

'I will do, I just want to tell him in person and not over the phone. I'm going to stay here for a couple more days – this place is like therapy, but cheaper. I need this time by myself. I don't expect Ashton to understand but I hope he can respect my decision.'

'What are you going to tell him when you do see him?'

'That's what I still need to figure out.'

Three days later Sienna stood outside Ashton's and rang the buzzer to his flat. Now they were about to become parents she really needed the keys back to his place. He buzzed her in and she took the stairs slowly, feeling like she needed a lie down by the time she reached his flat on the second floor. Ashton stood with the door held open and for the first time Sienna got the sense of coming home. It was ridiculous how emotional she'd felt over the past few days – pregnancy hormones were a bitch.

Before he could say anything, she started speaking. 'Ashton, this is how it's going to be, and I don't want you or my mother or anyone else trying to change my mind or interfere with how I want to live my life.'

'I feel like I need to sit down for this.' Ashton walked into the living room, sat down on the sofa and waited. Sienna took a deep breath and followed him but remained standing.

'First of all, I love you. It may not seem like it at times, but I always have loved you and always will, and I've never felt this way about anyone before.'

Ashton ran his hands along his jean-clad thighs and Sienna could see him visibly trying to control his emotions. She put her hand on her bump.

'I want you to be a real father to our baby and a part of his life so we'll live together, but for the time being we're going to keep your place and mine and live at both. The baby's going to be sleeping in a Moses basket in our room for the first few months so we don't need to worry about his own room or whose place to live at or about buying a house together just yet. Trust me, pushing this baby out is going to be enough for me to deal with without house hunting too.'

Ashton began to stand up. 'Sienna, this is just per…'

'Wait.' Sienna held up her hand. 'Before you go all gushy and totally girlie on me, there's more.' He sat back down. 'I want to work. I need to work, and I don't want to have to restrict myself to working on projects close to home. I don't mean I'm going to go out of my way to work on a film abroad, and if something exciting and interesting comes up that's going to be filmed at, say, The Bottle Yard Studios in Bristol, I'll jump at it, but I'm not going to let having a baby stop me from doing the job I love. I can make it work. I'll take him with me, work around him, pay for childcare whenever I need to – whatever it takes. But I want your blessing because you're his dad at the end of the day.'

Ashton leant back and folded his arms. 'We're going to have one well-travelled son by the sounds of it.'

'You're with me on this?'

Ashton stood up and wrapped his arms around Sienna. 'If

it means being with you and raising our son together, then yes,
I'm with you 100%. Somehow, we'll make this work.'

# *Connie*

It was a day that would remain imprinted on Connie's mind forever. The 2nd February and she was nine weeks and four days pregnant. *Was* pregnant. She knew the moment she started bleeding that it was all over. She'd woken up with a pain, said goodbye to Felix, taken a paracetamol and thought nothing more of it until she'd gone to the loo with terrible cramps. Only one embryo had been put back at the blastocyst stage, unlike Pippa who'd had two transferred back, so she knew there was very little hope of remaining pregnant.

The more she bled, the more anger surged through her until she was unable to focus on work or do anything apart from get more and more angry and wait until Felix walked through the front door. She was in the bathroom at the time and heard the door slam closed, the thump of his bag landing on the floor, the Nespresso machine pouring a coffee and then music from the living room. She finished doing the third pregnancy test of the day and there was no doubting the results this time. She chucked the stick in the bin, washed her hands, glanced at her pale make-up free face and walked into the living room.

'Hey,' Felix said without looking up from the sofa where he was leaning over his laptop.

'Who is Georgina Taylor?' She watched him carefully. He didn't look up and remained calm, barely giving anything away save a slight tightening of his jaw – just enough for Connie to notice.

Still focusing on his laptop, he said, 'Who?'

'Georgina Taylor.'

'Never heard of her.' He picked up his coffee and took a sip.

'That's funny because she works at your Bristol office.'

'A lot of people work there.'

'You'd probably remember her – short blonde hair, very pretty. Maybe goes by the name of Georgie.'

That got his attention. He closed his laptop. 'What about her?'

'You should have been more careful than using working in Bristol as an excuse on the weekends when your boss phoned before Christmas, calling you into the office for the meeting.'

'Oh that, yeah, that was all a big misunderstanding. My boss didn't realise I was still doing some work in Bristol.'

'Oh, is that so?'

'Uh-huh. All my work's now back in Cardiff.'

'Good to know.' Connie paced across their living space, painful cramps worsening with each step, stood in front of the window and looked out at the night sky and the twinkling lights across the bay. She'd always loved this view, but now it felt tainted, dirty – a view she'd shared with the man she loved, the man she'd wanted a baby with, and the man who was now lying through his teeth about a woman he was screwing. 'So, if you're no longer working in Bristol, what took you there the weekend before Christmas?'

She turned to face him.

'The weekend before Christmas?' She saw the frown, then the realisation cross his face. He stood up.

'The weekend I went to the craft fair in Cirencester.'

'Oh, that weekend. I was here.'

'No you weren't.' Arms folded and fists clenched, Connie walked back towards him. 'What is she to you?'

Felix held his hands up. 'Connie, I have no idea what you're talking about.'

'I didn't go to Cirencester. I followed you when you left here and drove all the way to Bristol and picked up Georgina

Taylor. Let me remind you – blonde woman, very pretty, young, married, got a fucking kid.'

'Hey, calm down, I can explain.'

'Don't you dare tell me to calm down. And I don't want you to explain, I want you to tell me the fucking truth.'

Felix shook his head and stepped towards her. Every muscle in her body clenched and she stepped back, not wanting him anywhere near her.

'I do know who she is. I did work with her and we had a fling, but that's all it is – all it was. I just think with everything that's been going on…'

'You complete bastard,' Connie screamed, letting months and months of pent up anger, frustration and hurt come flooding out. 'Why would you do it? I know what we're going through is shit – no, more than shit, it's been the worst couple of years of our lives. I thought we were going to get through it together, but your idea of getting through it is to shag someone else.'

'I didn't plan it, Connie,' Felix said.

'Oh, well that makes me feel so much better. You total bastard.'

'You've not exactly been the easiest person to talk to…'

'Oh. My. God. I can't believe you've just said that. You've obviously not noticed that I've been sniffing and injecting a cocktail of drugs on and off for the past year. I'm hormonal, what do you expect? My body's been tricked into thinking one minute that it's menopausal, the next bursting with eggs, then actually being pregnant, and then…' Connie took a deep breath, '…and then losing our baby, not just once but twice. You're an absolute wanker. Of course having fertility treatment was never going to be easy and we've had an even shitter time of it than I thought possible.'

Connie looked around their apartment and realised everything they'd built together was based on a lie. They'd simply been playing house and pretending that having a family would complete them – the wood burner for cosy family nights cuddling up on the sofa; the multiple picture frames on the wall all ready for gorgeous photos of their newborn; the soft low-pile rug for tiny feet to toddle across. It meant nothing now.

'What do you mean, losing our baby twice?'

'I'm having another miscarriage,' Connie said, her voice cracking and fresh tears spilling.

'Oh Connie, I'm so…'

'Don't you dare say you're sorry. Why would you let me carry on having treatment? If you didn't want to be with me, why did you think it was a good idea to carry on trying for a baby?'

'It's not that I don't want to be with you.'

He stepped towards her again and Connie took another step back.

'Do you love her?' she asked.

'Connie, you're upset. We don't need to talk about this.'

'Of course we need to fucking talk about it!'

Felix sat down on the sofa and patted the seat next to him. Connie stood her ground and thought about how much she'd like to punch him right now. Break his nose and make him bleed. Suffer just a fraction of the hurt she was feeling.

'I do work with her,' he said after a pause. 'Not in the same office, she works at the Bristol office, but we met at a work get together.'

'How long ago?'

'Just over a year ago but nothing happened straight away.'

'Well that's fine then.' Connie flexed her fingers and cracked her knuckles, conscious that Felix hated her doing that – enough to have an affair? 'When did "something happen"?'

She watched Felix shuffle and wipe beads of sweat from his forehead. 'I really don't think we should be talking about this in the state you're in. Shouldn't we be going to hospital?'

'*We* don't need to be doing anything. All I want you to do is answer my fucking question. How long have you been having an affair with her?'

'Six months.'

Connie worked the dates out in her head, rewinding six months to July last year. Her blood ran cold. 'You're kidding me. That weekend you said you were going away with work? The one when I miscarried? You utter bastard.'

'Connie, I didn't know that was going to happen.'

'I was pregnant! I'd just had weeks of treatment, an operation, the stress of that two week wait and then I was pregnant. *I was pregnant*. You dealt with all that by starting an affair?'

Connie put her head in her hands and sobbed. Suddenly Felix had his hands on her shoulders, trying to pull her into a hug. She pushed him away with all the strength she had.

'Get out! Get the fuck out of here!'

Connie dragged the razor across her wrist and watched as blood oozed and pooled bright red against her skin. It didn't hurt as much as she expected or wanted it to. She leant back against the kitchen cupboard door and let the blood drip, drip, drip on to the tiled floor, crimson against pale grey. The cut wasn't deep and she wasn't going to die from it or even pass out, but the packet of paracetamol next to her might do the trick. She hadn't made her mind up about that yet; she just wanted the emotional trauma to be erased by physical pain.

The brief sense of relief gave way to numbness. She hit her head backwards against the wooden door, sending a thudding pain across her skull. Collapsing forwards with her head in her hands and blood smearing her cheek, she sobbed and reached for the paracetamol.

# *Georgie*

Even if it was a bad idea, Georgie had made up her mind. She couldn't continue to live a lie; she didn't want to pretend any longer that she actually loved her husband. He'd been increasingly working late so they rarely saw each other in the evenings – which suited Georgie just fine – and then on the weekends, in between entertaining Daisy and taking it in turns to do their own thing, they were effectively already leading separate lives. Maybe Nathan was having an affair too. As she'd discovered, work was the perfect cover up.

Georgie re-read the text message from Felix for at least the twentieth time. She hadn't seen him since the 19th December, and after not hearing from him for most of January she got a text out of the blue towards the beginning of February.

*Felix: I need to see you. I need to know how you feel about us. When can we meet?*

With Daisy staying overnight at Georgie's parents and Nathan working late yet again, that evening would have been the perfect opportunity to see him, but she didn't just want to say to Felix how she felt – she wanted to prove it to him. It was Nathan's turn to take Daisy out on the weekend so she'd texted Felix back and arranged to meet at their usual place on Saturday morning. She just had to get through this evening and then her life could really begin again.

The road by Leigh Woods was as quiet as usual with only a couple of cars parked in front of the large houses screened by trees. Felix was already there, parked on an empty stretch of road. Georgie's heart thudded as she pulled up behind him. The things she'd thought about doing to him on the back seat of that car. The things they had done in hotel rooms and at that cabin in Wales. The memory made her flush and her heart pound faster.

She stepped out of her car and slammed the door shut. Her breath frosted in the icy air and she shivered as she walked the short distance to his car. Her coat covered her bump and she hoped Felix would forgive her for not telling him about it sooner. The time before last that she'd seen him they'd conceived this baby. She opened his car door and slipped inside, grateful that he'd kept the engine running and the heater on, leant towards him and kissed his stubbly cheek. He turned, cupped her face in his hands and kissed her lips.

'It's so good to see you,' he said.

Georgie had been waiting for this moment for weeks. Without a doubt she knew she'd made the right decision. She pulled away from him, took his hands and smiled. 'I ended it last night with my husband. I told him everything.'

'My relationship with my wife is pretty much over too. She found out about us.'

'I can't tell you how I've been longing for this moment,' Georgie said, running her thumbs along the sides of his hands. 'And there's something I've been wanting to tell you in person for quite a while now… I'm pregnant.' She let go of his hands and unbuttoned her coat to reveal her rounded stomach. 'Twenty-one weeks, in fact. I wanted to tell you the last time I saw you, but…'

'It's not my baby,' Felix said, turning away from her, gripping the steering wheel and resting his forehead on his clenched hands.

Georgie frowned and covered her bump again with her coat. 'How can you be so sure?'

'Because I'm infertile.' He lifted his head up from where he leant on the steering wheel and looked out of the window.

Georgie shook her head. 'But your wife had a

miscarriage… I'm sorry, I know I shouldn't know, but Melinda told me.'

'We were having fertility treatment – that's how she got pregnant. Naturally, there's no chance.'

Despite the heat in the car, a coldness spread over Georgie with the realisation that she really was carrying Nathan's baby. How naïve she was to think that because the night she and Felix had spent together was so passionate that was when the baby had been conceived. Instead, it had been conceived out of a sense of duty on her wedding anniversary to the man she'd fallen out of love with.

'Felix, it's you I want to be with. I did the right thing – I'm not in love with my husband any more but I am with you, so I ended it with him.' A tightness crept across her chest.

'Neither of us have done the right thing, Georgie.' Felix held his hands against the vent pumping out hot air. 'The right thing would have been not to have had an affair to begin with and lie to our partners for months. You're pregnant with your husband's baby.'

'But you love me?'

Felix stroked the stubble on his chin. 'I do. I did. I really don't know any more.'

'You mean you did before I told you I was pregnant.' Georgie bit her lip and looked out of the passenger window. Bare branches were being whipped by the wind and high above them the sky was grey, a reflection of her mood. It may have been honest telling Nathan about her affair but it could also have been the worst decision of her life. The future she imagined with Felix was disappearing as quickly as their relationship had begun.

Felix turned to her. 'My wife's in hospital after trying to kill herself. She found out about us before Christmas but didn't say or do anything until last weekend when she confronted me. She was upset – I mean, like out of her mind upset because she was pregnant again and having a miscarriage.'

'Hold on – you were still trying to have a baby all the time we were having an affair?'

'That's the bit that caught your attention? Not the bit about my wife attempting to commit suicide?'

'Actually, I'm trying to understand what we've been doing this whole time. Why would you want to be with me when you were trying to start a family with your wife?'

'The same goes for you, Georgie.'

'I don't love my husband any more and things hadn't been right between us for a while.'

'And yet you're pregnant with his baby, unless there's someone else other than me.'

'No, of course there isn't. I'm still married, we still share a bed, it doesn't mean there's actually any passion left. This baby was a complete accident.'

'So you were screwing both of us.'

Georgie's nostrils flared. 'Really, you're going to get all saintly on me? You can't talk – you screwed your wife over in a far worse way than I did with my husband. At least I had the guts to be honest with him in the end. You've been leading your wife on for months, and why go to all the trouble and expense and trauma of fertility treatment if you didn't want to be with her? Oh.' Georgie stopped and rested her head back on the car seat. 'I'm so stupid. I was just a distraction, wasn't I, from all the crap going on in your life. You still love her, don't you?'

'I think I'll always love her,' he said slowly. 'I've never been able to talk about the way I feel, and I know I've dealt with my infertility in the worst possible way. I guess I wanted to feel like a man again.'

Georgie laughed, a hollow sound, bereft of emotion. 'And so I was someone you could use to make you feel better about yourself. Surely a one night stand would have done the trick? Why the hell lead me on and say the things you've said to me over the past year?'

'Because I care about you and you made me feel so good.'

'But if everything had worked out with your wife and her pregnancy, you'd have ended it with me.'

'I have no idea what I intended to do. Life just kept on getting so fucking confusing.'

'And if I wasn't pregnant?'

Felix really looked at her then with his deep blue eyes, making Georgie want to both kiss him and punch him.

'If you weren't pregnant then maybe we'd have had a chance.'

# *Pippa*

Pippa didn't know how she was going to walk into the hospital ward Connie was on knowing that she was nearly fourteen weeks pregnant, while Connie had lost her second baby and her husband in the space of a few months. She paused, her hand hovering, ready to push the door open. What would she want if she was in Connie's position? It was what she'd wanted all the time she'd been trying desperately for a baby – to be included, talked to; for people to be honest with her. She ignored the knot of tension in her stomach, pushed open the door and strode straight over to Connie's bed.

In the short time she'd known her, Pippa had envied Connie's looks: her glossy dark hair, flawless complexion, the beautiful jewellery made by Connie herself, and a quirky bohemian dress sense that Pippa wished she could get away with. She hardly recognised the pale make-up free woman in a hospital gown with bandages on her wrists.

'Hey there,' Pippa said quietly, before leaning over and kissing Connie on the cheek. She pulled the chair next to the bed closer and sat down.

'Thanks for coming,' Connie said, her voice cracking.

'You don't need to thank me, it's what friends do.' Pippa poured a glass of water and handed it to her. 'I've got to ask – and you don't have to answer – why did you do it?'

'Because I was in so much pain emotionally I wanted to erase it all with physical pain.'

Pippa folded her hands in her lap, half covering the tiniest hint of a bump beneath her blue and cream dress. Her nails were neatly filed and painted pale pink, her dark blonde hair shiny and carefully brushed and she finally felt at peace with herself, while Connie looked lost – out of control of her emotions and her life.

'I don't expect you to understand why I did what I did,' Connie said after a while.

'But I think I do,' Pippa said. 'I mean, with what you've been through over the past year or so I can imagine how you got to this point. And then finding out about the affair… there's only so much a person can take.'

Connie nodded and wiped away the tears that had begun to inch down her face.

'What I mean, though,' Pippa continued, 'is that I sort of understand why you did it. I never hurt myself but I thought about it after the miscarriage. At a particularly low point I remember scratching my nails really hard across my wrist just to feel something… I don't know, hurt that was physical rather than all in my mind. It seems easier in some ways to fix physical pain, doesn't it?'

Connie nodded and took a deep breath. 'It's the not knowing when this feeling of complete hopelessness and loss will end, or if it ever will. And then on top of that there's Felix's betrayal. I wanted a baby more than anything but in a twisted way I'm glad I'm no longer having a baby with him.'

Pippa's hand automatically covered her stomach.

'You don't have to hide your bump from me.' Connie reached her hand out and placed it on Pippa's. 'I'm happy for you, I really am, I'm just devastated for me. The wounds on my wrists will heal, but what I'm going through won't, at least not until I either hold my baby in my arms or come to terms with being childless and on my own.'

Pippa took hold of Connie's hand and they both remained silent for a while.

'After the second failed IVF and the miscarriage,' Pippa said, 'I remember feeling completely lost, like there was no hope – ironic really, given my forum name. I wrote about it on my blog and it's been a really cathartic process, but I realised I was grieving.' She paused, not sure how to continue or if anything she said would actually help Connie.

'Go on,' Connie said.

'A friend – although that's a loose term – didn't understand how I could be grieving when I'd only been six weeks pregnant, but to me it wasn't just the loss of a tiny foetus, it was the loss of our baby. In a matter of minutes our whole future changed from becoming a family to being a childless couple again. It may sound corny but to grieve properly I buried the picture from our seven-week scan. I buried it in our garden beneath our apple tree. I was on my own; Clive didn't know and I don't think he would have understood, but it helped me to move on as there's somewhere I can go and sit and cry or simply think about things when it all gets too much. I know I'm saying this from a position of being pregnant, but it truly helped when I had no hope left.'

# Connie

Apple blossom. Connie suddenly remembered the apple tree at the arboretum and the promise she'd made to herself the year before to keep loving life whatever was thrown at her. At the time she hadn't added an affair and marriage breakdown into the mix along with two miscarriages and the ever-fading hope of having a family, but here she was with a whole heap of awful things having happened to her. It may not feel possible at the moment but she would get through it – she had to get through it. She had no choice, because what was the alternative? Giving up? Giving in to those all-encompassing thoughts? Trying to take her own life again? That wasn't an option.

It couldn't be an option.

'There are good things in my life,' Connie said slowly.

Pippa still had hold of her hand and gave it a squeeze. 'Of course there are.'

'Do you know what I need? Closure. At least some kind of closure. I'm done with Felix, which means I'm done with fertility treatment, but I need to confront the woman he was having an affair with. I need to find her and see her and speak to her and know what it was about her that attracted Felix. I need to know what he is to her.' Looking up at Pippa from her hospital bed, Connie asked, 'Will you come with me?'

'When you're fit and strong again and discharged from hospital, then yes, I'll come with you. But be warned, I'm liable to give her a piece of my mind too.'

# SECOND SPRING

## *Georgie*

It had been exactly four weeks since she'd last seen or heard from Felix and it hurt. There was no denying that she longed for him but did that really mean she loved him? Her present situation would make anyone long for what they'd lost, even if the person they'd lost had been the cause of her life falling apart. Actually that was a lie – she was the cause of her life falling apart, just as Pippa had warned at Christmas.

The house was empty. Daisy was at Georgie's mum's and Nathan was... she had no idea where. He'd moved out despite the fact that she'd offered to be the one to leave. She was unsure if he was at a hotel or staying with a friend. Either way it didn't matter; he'd not even given her the chance to explain herself. When she'd got home after telling Felix she was pregnant, Nathan had already packed a few things and had made it quite clear that he'd be having Daisy two evenings a week and every other weekend. Georgie hadn't argued.

The baby had started to kick properly only a few days after she last saw Felix. Around seventeen weeks she'd recognised the fluttering feeling that she'd had with Daisy and had done her best to ignore it, but there'd been no mistaking the sensation once she'd reached twenty-two weeks. There was no ignoring the fact she was well and truly pregnant and her life was utterly fucked up.

Georgie sat on one of the stools at the breakfast bar and shivered. The heating was on a timer and only came on for a couple of hours in the morning and the evening. Georgie had no idea how to alter it and didn't have the energy or inclination to try.

A key turned in the front door and she shuddered, whether from the cold or nerves she wasn't sure.

'It's flipping freezing in here,' Nathan said, walking into the room.

'Thank you for coming,' Georgie said.

'I've not come for your sake.'

'I know.'

His manner was as icy as the house, which she knew she deserved. She drank him in: the familiar way he was dressed in a jumper and smart trousers even though it was the weekend; the flecks of grey in his brown hair and the creases of stress etched across his forehead. There was no pang of regret or longing for him; no rush of love; no feeling whatsoever.

He folded his arms and remained standing in the doorway. 'Let's get this over with. What do you want?'

'It is your baby.'

He snorted. 'You had sex with another man and you expect me to believe that?'

'He can't have children.'

'Go to hell, Georgie, I don't want to hear another word of bullshit coming out of your mouth.'

'I'm willing to try, Nathan. I'm willing to do whatever it takes to give us another go and be a family.'

'You don't know the meaning of the word.' He couldn't even look her in the eye, let alone down to her bump, prominent beneath a tight grey maternity top. 'I'm filing for a divorce and I want full custody of Daisy.'

Georgie slid off the stool. 'You can't do that.'

'I can and I will. I thought you'd be glad to be shot of your daughter so you have time to concentrate on your precious career.'

'I love Daisy. Whatever you may think of me, I've never not wanted her in my life.'

'Well, you'll just have more time to concentrate on your bastard baby.'

His words smacked her in the centre of her chest. She'd never seen her calm, benign husband look or sound so angry. He turned to go and Georgie decided she'd use the only leverage she had left. She placed her hands protectively over her bump.

'If you go ahead and do that then you'll never see this baby and never be a part of its life. Obviously if you're 100% sure that it's not yours then it won't matter.'

Georgie saw him falter, his forehead creasing a little more as he glanced at her bump for the briefest of moments. Then he turned and walked out.

'Hello?' Georgie called as she closed her parents' front door behind her.

'In the living room!' her mum shouted back.

Georgie dropped her bag on the hallway floor, shrugged off her coat, hung it on the hook next to the front door, rubbed the small of her back and walked into the front room to be faced with her mum, dad and Pippa.

'What is this? Some sort of inquisition?' Georgie folded her arms and shuddered when she realised the top of her bump brushed her elbow.

'Sit down and let's talk,' her mum said, patting the empty space on the sofa next to her.

Georgie surveyed the room – her mum all dewy-eyed with concern; Pippa stony-faced, her hand resting lightly on her small, neat bump; and her dad with his head down, not meeting her eyes, looking like he wanted to be anywhere but here.

'I'm fine,' she said, and made for the door.

Her mum stood up. 'You're not fine. You're twenty-six weeks pregnant and are losing weight – that's not good.'

'Twenty-five. I'm twenty-five weeks pregnant.'

'Either way, you need to talk to us. We want to help you.'

'I don't need any help.'

Her mum stepped towards her. 'Daisy may not be three yet but she says enough for me to get a decent idea of what's going on.'

Georgie felt a rush of heat in her chest. 'Well, you know what? It's no one's business but mine what's going on in my life.'

'You're my daughter, Georgie, of course it's my business. I look after your daughter three evenings a week before you get back from work and I'm concerned about my unborn grandchild, so yes, I'm making it my business whether you like it or not.'

'Bridget, go easy on her,' Georgie's dad mumbled from where he sat in his armchair by the window.

'You need to talk to someone, Georgie,' Pippa said, getting up from the sofa and standing next to their mum.

'Yeah, cos you were so bloody helpful the last time I talked to you.'

Their mum swung around to face Pippa. 'You know what's going on?'

'I only know what Georgie told me at Christmas – I really don't know what's going on now.'

Bridget turned back to Georgie. 'I know Nathan's moved out – Daisy's said as much, saying how she doesn't like her room because it's painted blue. She told me yesterday that Mummy and Daddy are never together, and when I asked her what she meant and when was the last time they were together, she couldn't even remember. And yet you've been carrying on like nothing has happened, telling me that Nathan's working late whenever I ask where he is.'

Pippa looked at Georgie. 'So you told him.'

'Told him what?' Bridget asked.

'About the affair,' Pippa said.

Bridget turned back to Georgie. 'He's been having an affair? Oh love, I'm so sorry.'

Georgie glared at Pippa. 'No, Mum, I was the one having

an affair.' She wanted to burst out laughing at the silence that descended over the room. Her mum, who was rarely lost for words stared at her open mouthed, and her dad simply got up and walked out.

Bridget turned to Pippa. 'You knew about this and didn't tell us?'

'Hey, don't have a go at me, it wasn't my place to tell.' Pippa pointed at Georgie. 'She confided in me and asked me not to tell anyone, so I didn't. I told her what I thought and how reckless she was being – what more was I supposed to do?'

'Get her to see sense!'

'You know how pig-headed Georgie is. When has anyone been able to make her change her mind when she doesn't want to?'

Georgie stepped between Pippa and her mum and clicked her fingers at them. 'I am here, you know.'

Her mum took a deep breath and reached for Georgie's hand. 'You go to Nathan and grovel. Do whatever it takes to make it up to him.'

'Mum, it's over. He wants nothing to do with me.'

'But you're having a baby. How on earth are you going to cope on your own with a newborn?' Her mum squeezed her hand tighter until Georgie flinched. 'Oh my God. The baby.'

'The baby is Nathan's,' Georgie said. 'Not that he believes me.'

'How can you be sure it's his?' her mum asked.

'I just know.'

'Is it over?' Pippa asked. 'The affair?'

The burning sensation lodged in Georgie's chest worked its way into her throat and she couldn't hold back tears any longer. 'I think so.'

'Oh Georgie,' her mum said, pulling her into a hug.

'But you don't want it to be,' Pippa said, and sat back down.

# *Pippa*

The confrontation with Georgie played on Pippa's mind all the way back to Bath. However much she didn't agree with what Georgie had done, she was still her sister, pregnant and vulnerable with her whole life turned upside down. At least Georgie had done the right thing in the end telling Nathan the truth, even if it had all ended in tears. As for the affair, Pippa guessed that's what she got for playing around with a married man.

'Well, that was fun,' Pippa said when she got back home. The rugby was on and Clive paused the TV when Pippa flopped down on the sofa next to him.

'A bit of a family drama?'

'Something like that. The short version is Nathan's moved out because Georgie told him about the affair she's been having since last summer and both her marriage and the affair seem to be over. She's on her own and pregnant.'

'Shit.' Clive shook his head. 'She's always been a bit... what's the word?'

'Stupid?'

'Wilful.'

'I call what she's done stupid.'

'Her and Nathan never did seem compatible.'

'Then she shouldn't have married him,' Pippa said. 'She had a choice, it's not like anyone forced her into it or anything.'

'True. But I guess people change.'

'Enough to warrant having an affair?'

'Well, no. Is there ever a good reason for that?'

'The funny thing is I'm going with Connie tomorrow to confront the woman her husband's been having an affair with. How ironic is that?'

'How is she?' Clive asked.

'Georgie or Connie?'

'Connie.'

'She's okay, considering.'

'They discharged her from hospital?'

Pippa nodded. 'The other week, and I had to persuade her to wait a bit before going charging over to have a face-off with this woman. An overdose, slashed wrists and a miscarriage are not things you recover from quickly.'

'I take it her husband isn't still at home with her.'

Pippa shook her head. 'She presumes he's moved in with the woman he was having the affair with.'

'Are you going to be okay going with her after what happened today?'

'Of course. It's Connie I'm worried about. I think I need to be there to make sure she doesn't do anything stupid.'

Pippa picked Connie up from Bristol Parkway train station after she finished work. It was obvious from the moment Connie got in the car how much the past few months had taken their toll on her. Pippa leant across to hug her and felt her shoulder blades through her coat. Her face was pale and dark shadows circled her eyes; she looked as vulnerable as she had done in hospital.

'Are you sure you're feeling up to this?' Pippa asked, pulling out of Parkway. Connie directed her right at the mini roundabout and straight over the next two.

'As ready as I'll ever be. It's long overdue. I think the only way for me to move on is to meet the woman who took my husband from me. I need to understand what it was that made him unfaithful in the first place. Go right here.'

Pippa indicated and turned, finding herself on a familiar road she'd driven along many times before to her sister's.

'What do you know about her?'

'Quite a bit. It's incredible what you can find out from Facebook.'

'Like what?'

'Like where she lives, for starters. She uses an app to show her jogging route, starting and ending at her house. I worked out the house number from a photo. I know she worked with Felix at Goldman and Peabody, and I know her name is Georgina Taylor and she's married and has a kid…'

Pippa was just about to say, 'How weird is that? She has the same name as my sister', when her heart felt as though it had dropped into her stomach. A shudder wriggled down her spine as all the pieces slotted into place. How could it possibly be? Of all the people Georgie could have had an affair with… Connie's husband? But if they worked together it wasn't that odd that she'd met him. The strange bit was that infertility had thrown Pippa and Connie together via an online forum.

The drive to Georgie's house was automatic and Pippa had to make herself wait for Connie to give her directions before turning. She should tell her, she knew she should tell her, but how could she? There was no way Pippa could knock Connie's confidence in confronting the woman when she'd built herself up to face her, not after what she'd been through in the last few weeks.

Any shred of doubt that it was simply a huge coincidence and it wasn't really Georgie who'd been having an affair with Felix disappeared as soon as they turned into her sister's cul-de-sac. Pippa pulled over a little way down from number twelve.

'Maybe you should go on your own and I'll wait for you in the car.'

Connie turned to her with tears welling in her eyes. 'Pippa, I can't do this on my own. Please, I need you with me. Please.'

Without thinking about the consequences, Pippa released her seatbelt, stepped out of the car and waited for Connie to join her on the pavement.

'Come on then,' she said, hooking her arm in Connie's.

They walked up to the front door and, almost without hesitation, Connie rang the doorbell. Pippa tried to shrink backwards, wishing she was anywhere but here. She hoped to God Daisy wasn't home, or her mum hadn't popped round. It was taking a long time for Georgie to answer the door. Pippa got a rush of hope that she wasn't in but that quickly turned to her heart pulsating and sweaty hands as the door swung open and Georgie appeared wearing leggings and a long T-shirt. With minimal make-up on and her short hair swept up into a messy ponytail, she looked every inch a tired mummy-to-be.

Georgie looked at Connie first with no recognition crossing her face, and then her gaze fell on her sister.

'Pippa?' Georgie said. 'I wasn't expecting to see you.'

Connie glanced from Georgie to Pippa and frowned. 'You know her?'

Pippa turned to Connie and took hold of both her hands. 'I'm so sorry, I didn't know how to tell you in the car. I literally only realised when you said her name a few minutes ago.'

'What are you talking about? How do you know her?' Connie's voice began to rise as she took a step back, the calmness she had been exuding rapidly leaving her.

'She's my sister... my half-sister,' Pippa said as calmly as she could.

'Excuse me.' Georgie stepped out from the shadow of her porch. 'Can you please tell me what's going on?'

Pippa swung back to Georgie, anger swelling inside her. 'This is Connie...'

Before she could say anything else, Connie pushed past her, her attention firmly on Georgie's bump now obvious in the porch light.

'My God, you're pregnant,' she said and spat in Georgie's face.

'What the hell?' Georgie staggered back, wiping the spit off her face with the back of her hand. 'How dare you...'

'I'm Felix's wife and I'm just beginning to understand how well suited you both are – screwing around with other people's lives. You know what? You're welcome to him. I take it he'll be back from work later?'

Georgie turned on Pippa. 'You know her?'

'Let's do this inside,' Pippa said firmly.

Georgie stabbed a finger in Connie's direction. 'She's not coming in this house.'

'Yes, she is.' Pippa took Connie's hand and marched her through the doorway so Georgie had no choice but to step back and let them in. The door slammed shut behind them.

# Connie

With Pippa still gripping her hand, Connie could feel herself shaking, whether from anger, adrenalin or both she wasn't sure. Georgie had her back to the front door, a hand held protectively over her bump, and all Connie wanted to do was tear into her and hurt her physically as much as she'd been hurt emotionally.

Perhaps Pippa sensed how out of control Connie felt because once she released Connie's hand, she stepped between them, turning to Georgie. 'I had no idea it was Connie's husband you were having an affair with but you know full well what I thought about it.'

'Yeah, that I'm some kind of slut and bitch, no doubt.' Georgie took her hand from her bump and stepped forward. 'You do realise it's not just my fault the affair happened?' She turned to Connie. 'What about Felix? He's as much to blame as I am.'

'Of course he is,' Connie said, trying to contain her emotions and get the words out without bursting into tears. 'And I'm done with him. We've split up and he's all yours. I just wanted to know what made him stray to begin with. Why I wasn't enough.'

'You've left him?' It was the first time there was no anger in Georgie's voice, just a quiet disbelief.

'He's not living with you, is he?' Connie said.

Georgie shook her head.

Without meaning to, Connie chuckled. 'He wasn't up for being with a lover who was pregnant with her husband's child, was he? Not after he lost his own baby his actual wife was carrying.'

'You bitch!' Georgie launched towards Connie but Pippa was quick and grabbed hold of her.

'Georgie, for God's sake, calm down. Connie is certainly not the one who's the bitch.'

Georgie struggled away from Pippa. 'Oh, I see you're siding with her then.' She folded her arms across her chest.

'If you want to put it like that, as if we're kids in a playground, then yes. Connie's my friend and I'm going to do everything I can to support her through this.'

'I'm your sister.'

'True, but you have no idea what Connie's been through and the pain your actions have caused her. And the problems in your life, I'm sorry, are nothing compared to hers. Your affair, your marriage breakdown and your pregnancy are all your doing, no one else's. Connie is the victim here.'

'What, just like you've always been the victim?'

'What are you talking about?'

'You know exactly what I'm talking about – being the poor big sister with divorced parents and always milking that whenever you wanted to get extra attention from Mum, then playing the infertility card for years, making us feel bad that we were happy to be parents and Mum and Dad to be grandparents.'

Connie stepped forward. 'You don't get to talk to Pippa like that. She may be your sister but she's my friend and you have absolutely no understanding what it's like to long for a baby and watch everyone around you get pregnant, grow beautiful bumps and give birth, while all the time your own dream of having a family slips away. What she's been through over the past couple of years is beyond comprehension.' Her voice finally cracked and the tears she'd been holding back trickled down her cheeks. Pippa wrapped her arms around her and Connie sobbed into her shoulder, feeling the hint of Pippa's bump pressing against her own stomach.

'I'm so sorry, Connie,' Pippa said. 'I wanted more than

anything for us to be pregnant together.'

Connie pulled away and brushed her tears from the shoulder of Pippa's coat. She smiled. 'You have nothing to apologise for. You absolutely deserve to be happy. And pregnant.'

Pippa turned to Georgie. 'You have no idea how lucky you are.'

'No, Pippa, I'm not lucky. I've made bad choices to end up in an unhappy marriage and to have an affair with a man who obviously doesn't care about me.'

'You don't get it, do you?' Connie said, shaking her head. 'Pippa's not talking about your stupid marriage or your fucking affair with my husband, she's talking about that beautiful little girl you've got and that miracle of a baby growing in your belly. That's what makes you lucky. Family is everything.'

'I love Daisy, I do, but I wasn't ready to have her, and this', Georgie pointed to her bump, 'this baby is all kinds of wrong – conceived during an affair by a man I no longer want to be with. You're absolutely right, the baby is my husband's, although I was convinced it was Felix's – he put me straight about that, the fact that he couldn't be the father. So yes, I have actually told him, and it seems clear from the fact he's no longer living with you but hasn't been in touch with me that whatever it was we had is over. So go ahead and gloat. Lap it up, why don't you?'

Georgie shoved past Pippa and Connie before slamming the living room door closed behind her.

Connie and Pippa remained in the dusky hallway and looked at each other. Connie wanted to laugh but there was nothing funny about the situation. So many lives had been ruined because of Felix and Georgina bloody Taylor.

'How is it possible that I now feel bad?' she said, playing with the thick silver bangles that covered the scars on her wrists.

'Because she has a way of manipulating the situation so

everyone feels sorry for her.' Pippa put her hands on her hips and leant back against the hall wall. 'She's always done it, playing Mum against my stepfather and vice versa. I was the one who went through the hell of my parents divorcing, but with the way she behaved as a child and a teenager anyone who didn't know us would have thought it was her who'd had a traumatic childhood.' Pippa pushed away from the wall and made for the living room door. 'Before we leave I need to make sure she's okay, for her baby's sake...' She took the car keys from her pocket. 'You don't have to be here.'

'No, it's fine,' Connie said, pushing open the door and walking into an open-plan kitchen and living area. A bold-print flowered wallpaper decorated one of the walls, the sofa and armchairs looked like expensive ones from Habitat and there was an unlit gas fire in the blocked-up white painted fireplace. The place was modern, spotless, not to her taste and completely soulless; if there had been any sign of a toddler living there it had been cleared and stored away. It was a house for grown-ups, not a family, and without wanting to, Connie got a stab of sympathy for Georgie leading a life she didn't want.

Georgie leant on the edge of the sink looking out of the window to the garden, which Connie imagined to be as organised and well maintained as the inside of the house. Pippa made to go towards her but Connie grabbed her hand and shook her head.

'I'll go.' Taking a deep breath, Connie walked over and stood behind Georgie. 'I'm not gloating,' she said. 'I don't know what I expected to find or get from coming here today – whether it was some kind of understanding or peace. Am I glad that Felix is no longer with you? I guess so, yes, but that doesn't change anything. I'm not taking him back; I'm done with him. He had an affair with you while I was having the worst year of my life. To be honest I think you're well shot of him and should be glad that you're having another baby with your husband.'

Georgie's shoulders shook with sobs and when she turned around tears streaked her face. She really was pretty, Connie realised, with lightly tanned skin, large pale blue almost grey eyes and silky blonde hair. Even with the oversized T-shirt and baby bump, Connie could plainly see what had attracted Felix. The other thing was that Georgie was nothing like her – the complete opposite, in fact. Maybe he really had been trying to forget about everything going on in his life.

'My husband has left me and wants custody of our daughter, so no, I'm not glad that I'm having another baby with him because I'm having this baby on my own.' Georgie waved her left hand in the air and tugged at the rings on her wedding finger. 'I can't get these fucking things off because my fingers are so swollen from being bloody pregnant. If you've said your piece, then I'd appreciate it if you'd leave.'

Pippa stepped into the kitchen. 'Georgie, you need to ca…'

'You too.'

'Georgie, you need someone to talk to…'

Georgie swung towards Pippa. 'Well, it's not going to be you, seeing you're best bloody friends with the wife of my ex-lover.'

Connie took hold of Pippa's arm. 'Come on, we should go.'

Outside, the air was as chilly as Connie felt. She didn't feel better for confronting Georgie; she didn't really feel anything, just a mixture of confusing emotions. Pippa unlocked her car and they clambered in and sat in silence for a moment before Pippa started the engine.

'I'm sorry I dragged you into this,' Connie said, blowing on her hands to warm them up. It was early March but it felt like it was still the middle of winter instead of the beginning of spring.

'Don't be,' Pippa said, turning on her headlights, pulling away from Georgie's house and doing a three-point turn. 'You weren't to know she was my sister. The whole situation is beyond ridiculous but it's of her own making. I'm just so sorry her actions impacted your life in the way they did.'

'I hope this doesn't affect your relationship.'

'Our relationship is complicated; this is just another layer to add to that.' They pulled out of the cul-de-sac and headed away from suburbia. 'Maybe it's the wake-up call she needs.'

# *Sienna*

'Should it feel like this?'

'You're asking the wrong person,' Amy said, rubbing Sienna's back. 'But if it hurts like hell, then yes, I'm guessing that's what it should feel like.'

Sienna groaned. 'I started getting contractions a couple of hours ago and they're already six minutes apart. How the hell is that possible? I didn't think it would happen so quickly.'

'He's eager to meet you, that's all.'

Sienna picked up her mobile, glanced at the screen and threw it back on the sofa. 'Of all the times to have his mobile switched off.'

'I'm sure he'll phone back soon. Maybe he's somewhere with no reception.'

'I told him it wasn't a good idea to go to this meeting today.'

'He's only in Reading, it won't take long for him to get back.' Amy handed Sienna a glass of water. 'Drink.'

'I think I need something stronger than that.'

'I really don't think alcohol is a good idea right now…'

Sienna looked up from where she was perched on the edge of the sofa, leaning forwards so the strain was off her back.

'Seriously, you thought?' She shook her head. 'There's Lucozade in the fridge and call Pippa for me, could you?'

Amy disappeared into the kitchen and Sienna took a deep breath as pain contracted across her lower back and stomach. How the hell she was going to get through this she had no idea. It was a drizzly, cold afternoon on the last day of March and she wanted to go to sleep and wake up to find that not only had the pain stopped but the pregnancy had been a dream. She'd go out tonight and meet friends and then tomorrow get her next job lined up, preferably somewhere hot and sunny to escape the gloomy British weather.

'Lucozade,' Amy said, handing her the bottle and bringing her crashing back to reality. 'And Pippa will be over as soon as she finishes work.'

'Have you got your hospital bag packed?' Pippa asked as she removed her coat and gave Sienna a hug. Sienna was pretty sure Pippa, ever the organised one, already had her bag packed with over four more months to go.

Sienna nodded. 'Ashton made me pack it last week.'

'Have your waters broken?'

'No. Just proper contractions. I wasn't expecting the pain to be so bad and so regular this quickly.'

Pippa grinned. 'I'm so excited for you.'

'At least one of us is.'

'I can't believe you're going to be a mum before me.'

'Trust me, you're not the only one who's in denial about that.'

Pippa reached into her bag and pulled out a TENS machine.

'I thought you might want to use this, help manage the pain.' She untangled the cables. 'Lean forward a bit more.' Pippa rolled up Sienna's top and stuck the pads of the TENS machine on her lower back, then turned it on.

'Really, this is going to help?' Sienna frowned and fiddled with the button until it pulsed more strongly. 'I guess it might be a distraction if nothing else.'

'It's all about managing the pain and breathing through the contractions.'

'You and your pregnancy yoga shit. Oh, oh, oh, fuck, it hurts.' Sienna gripped Pippa's hand as another contraction washed across her.

'Breathe in through your nose and slowly out through your mouth. That's it – in through your nose, out through your mouth. Better?'

'Like I'm being tickled with a feather,' Sienna said and laughed. 'Oh God, it hurts.'

'Stop being a smart arse, then.'

Sienna continued to breathe in and out until the pain of the contraction dissipated and she could breathe easily again. She stood up and shook her arms and legs and rolled her hips in a circular motion to loosen her aching joints.

'I hope this isn't going to freak you out, you know, watching me give birth.'

'Well,' Pippa said, 'just don't do anything like start screaming or pushing before we get to the hospital and I'll be fine. Talking of which, have you phoned the delivery suite?'

'Uh-huh. They wanted me to stay home, told me to relax as much as possible, move about, watch a film, have a bath. Have a fucking bath like this is some kind of spa retreat.'

'It'll help with the pain,' Pippa said.

'This baby not being in here any longer will help with the pain.'

'You good?' Amy said, hovering in the doorway of the living room. Pippa nodded and Sienna shot her a look that she hoped conveyed 'of course I'm not fucking good, I'm about to push a baby the size of a watermelon out'. 'I'll be upstairs if you need me.'

'You know, you can do this,' Pippa said once Amy had gone. 'This is what our bodies are made for.'

Sienna humphed. 'I'd feel better if Ashton was here. He got me into this mess, the least he can do is make it back in time for the birth of his baby.'

'I'll call his mobile again.'

Sienna grabbed Pippa's arm before she left the room. 'This is really happening, isn't it?'

'It really is and you're going to be fine.'

\*     \*     \*

Sweat dribbled down the side of her face and her fringe stuck to her forehead. She hadn't had a shower in forty-eight hours and being submerged in the birthing pool didn't count. As it turned out Ashton had plenty of time to get back from Reading, and Sienna was still at home with Pippa when he did arrive.

The water in the birthing pool was warm and Sienna relished the weightlessness and the way it eased the pressure on her back and bump as she bobbed gently up and down – until the next contraction when it felt as if a red hot poker was splitting her in two. She writhed in pain, sending water lapping at the sides. Gas and air were her saviours, along with the steady presence of Pippa and Ashton repeating over and over for her to breathe through the pain. She almost told them where to go, then remembered in a few months' time Pippa would be in the same position.

Night and day had merged into one long period of being awake and in agony. All she wanted was to sleep, but there was no respite from the waves of pain that kept on coming, getting closer and closer until they were almost unbearable. Almost. Somehow she managed to push on through, overcoming the worsening pain of each contraction, telling herself she wasn't going to be beaten by a baby trying to get out of her body. *There was an actual baby trying to get out of her body.* Shit, shit, shit, shit, shit…

'No, no, no! I. Can't. Do. This.' She gripped the sides of the birthing pool as another contraction ripped through her. She bit down on the mouthpiece of the gas and air to stop herself from screaming, but her whole body shook with a pain like she'd never felt before.

'Breathe in slowly and deeply,' a calm voice said. She wasn't sure, and didn't care, if it was Pippa's or Ashton's.

'Focus on holding your baby in your arms,' the midwife said, but that was what scared Sienna the most. At least being pregnant she could be in denial about the inevitable. Now there was no choice but to face the reality of a screaming red-faced poo-emitting baby that she had no clue how to deal with.

'I think I need to push.'

'Then push. Let your body guide you,' the midwife said, rubbing Sienna's back as she rolled over until she could rest her arms and head on the side of the pool and her knees on the seat below the water. 'On the next contraction, push, but push from your bottom like you're having a poo.'

There was no resisting. Her body took over like it knew exactly what to do, just as Pippa had told her hours before. She kept her eyes closed and allowed Ashton's, Pippa's and the midwife's words of encouragement to wash over her. Each contraction brought her closer to the pain being over, so she balled her hands into fists, focused on breathing in the gas and air and pushed and pushed and pushed and pushed.

Jacob Fasano-Blake was born at 16.34 on the 1st April, around thirty hours after Sienna had gone into labour. Sienna thought it was nothing short of ironic that her son was born on April Fool's Day.

Was it a rush of love she felt when her son was placed in her arms for the first time? She wasn't sure but she knew she felt something. Still in the birthing pool and feeling exhausted, relieved, elated and confused all at once, she looked down at her tiny baby with his red screwed-up face and shock of dark hair and then up at Ashton, who had tears pouring down his face and a smile that screamed 'I love you', whether to her, their son, or both of them she didn't know and she didn't care. This was what she'd been trying to avoid all her grown-up life. After a few accidents and morning after pills in her late teens and twenties, she had managed to get knocked up in her mid-thirties, just when she felt she was at the pinnacle of her career.

Her eyes blurred with tears as she tried to focus on her son, take in his features and work out who he resembled. She reached for Ashton with her free hand and pulled him to her until his arms encircled her and the baby. She looked over at Pippa, standing by the side of the birthing pool, one hand resting on her bump, the other wiping away her tears with a tissue.

Sienna smiled and mouthed, 'Thank you'.

After an overnight stay in hospital they were home the next morning and dealing with nappy changes, breastfeeding and getting used to their lives revolving around a little person. Home for the time being was Sienna's flat, with Jacob's Moses basket next to the bed and Ashton a permanent fixture.

'I'm so proud of you,' Ashton said, handing Sienna a glass of orange juice. He kissed the top of Jacob's head and then Sienna's before sitting down in the chair opposite and grinning.

Sienna adjusted her position on the sofa, cradling Jacob's head while he continued feeding. She rested her gaze on Ashton. 'Don't you go all soppy on me.'

'I'm not,' he replied. 'I just want you to know you're doing an amazing job.'

'And you're surprised, right?'

'Well yes, actually.'

Sienna laughed and Jacob stopped feeding momentarily and gurgled. Ashton's reaction didn't surprise her; in fact, in the last forty-eight hours she'd more than surprised herself, managing to give birth with little more than gas and air and taking to breastfeeding with relative ease, despite having been adamant that she was going to bottle feed. Had she lucked out so far with an easy baby and a great midwife team who supported her through that first night and those tricky feeds? Only time would tell, but for the moment at least – until lack of sleep took over – she felt better than she'd dreamed possible.

'I'm going to phone my parents and sort out when they're going to visit.' Ashton stood up. 'Do you need anything else?'

Sienna checked off everything she had next to her – her mobile, a drink, a plate of biscuits, a spare muslin and her laptop.

'We're good, thanks.' With one hand she positioned her laptop on her knees behind where Jacob lay, opened it up and clicked on Pippa's blog.

*2nd April blog post:*

## *A New Life*

*My best friend gave birth to her son yesterday afternoon and I was honoured to be a part of the most amazing experience, witnessing a new life enter the world. The midwife said it was a textbook birth and she managed to push a 7lb 12oz baby into the world on just gas and air and a hell of a lot of willpower. In the birthing pool in a room lit by fairy lights with just the midwife, the baby's daddy and myself, I can honestly say it was a serene and moving experience, the serenity only broken by my best friend dropping the F-bomb just as little Jacob came shooting into the world.*

*With my due date of the 10th of August approaching I'll be more than happy if I can have a birth experience like my friend's. Her life has changed and I can't wait for mine to as well. The love and bond I saw between her and her son was the most beautiful thing and I can honestly say that's what I've been waiting for all my life. Welcome to the world, Jacob. Xx*

# Connie

Connie had imagined that they'd sell their apartment one day, but that daydream had been because they'd run out of space after having a baby or two, not because they'd split up and both needed the equity to move on and find somewhere new. The apartment she'd once loved now made her feel sad every time she stepped through the door. It reminded her of what she'd lost, and despite the happy times they'd once had, it was now tainted with unbearable sadness.

Felix had moved out as soon as he realised Connie had no intention of trying to rebuild their relationship. Connie had decided she couldn't be there when the estate agent showed the first lot of potential buyers around, so she'd gone to her studio to do some work. In fact, she'd thrown herself back into work, catching up on commissions she'd let slide while she'd been undergoing fertility treatment and then in hospital following her suicide attempt. She had no such distractions any longer – rebuilding her business and making some money were her main priorities; having something tangible to focus on was the only thing keeping her going.

She stayed away until she was confident the estate agent would have left then rode up in the lift that had always given her the first sense of being home but now left her feeling lonelier than she'd ever been.

The lift pinged open and Connie stepped into the hallway that led to the apartment. A woman with silver hair, bundled up in a coat, scarf and gloves – despite it being nearly the end of April – leant against the wall next to the apartment front door with a small suitcase beside her. For a moment Connie thought it must be someone from the estate agency until she got closer and recognised the woman's high cheekbones, tanned skin and familiar profile.

'Aunt Bella?'

Her aunt turned towards her and grinned.

'What on earth are you doing here?' Connie asked, quickening her pace.

'If I'd told you I was coming you'd have stopped me, so here I am.' Bella pulled Connie close and wrapped her arms around her, squeezing her tight. For only the third time since the second miscarriage and confronting Felix then Georgie, Connie let go in front of someone and sobbed.

'I thought you'd vowed never to come back to the UK,' she said into her aunt's shoulder.

'Sometimes there are things more important than sticking to a silly vow, and family is one of them.' Bella released her niece from her hold and wiped away Connie's tears with her thumbs. 'Now, let's get inside and stop making a scene.'

Connie smiled, a rush of love for her aunt's down to earth banter flooding through her. She unlocked her front door and let Bella inside. Suddenly the empty apartment felt filled with warmth and no longer the lonely place it had been since Felix had moved out.

'You're selling it then?' Bella asked, taking off her scarf and gloves.

Connie nodded. 'I don't want to be here any longer. It's not home. It's never going to feel like home ever again. I need a new start.'

'Good. A new start sounds like a very positive step.' Bella shivered. 'I remember now one of the reasons I never wanted to come back to this godforsaken country – British weather.'

Connie laughed. 'I'll turn the heating up.'

'Twenty-eight degrees it was when I flew out of Dar es Salaam.'

'And it's not even particularly cold today, or raining.'

Bella humphed. 'I'm sure that will change.'

Connie turned up the radiators in the living room and set about making hot chocolate. Bella sat down on the sofa and looked around.

'I like what you've done with the place – it's definitely got your style and taste about it and not as manly as I thought it would be.'

'Felix…' Even his name was hard to say out loud. 'Felix didn't really mind what I did with it as long as he got his wide screen TV and coffee maker.'

'That figures.'

Connie brought two mugs of hot chocolate over to the living area and placed them on mats on the coffee table.

'You never did like Felix, did you?' She tried to contain her emotions but she could sense the wobble in her voice.

'It's not that I didn't like him, it's just he reminded me too much of my ex-husband. There's a reason why he's an ex and Felix just happens to be a lot like him – certain personality traits, plus he's good looking and knows it. In my mind that spells trouble. Unfortunately, my instincts were right.'

Connie sat down next to Bella and cupped her mug of hot chocolate in her hands. 'Mum and Dad were never particularly keen on him either.'

'Yes, but my brother's reasons were different to mine. He was never keen because he wanted you to marry someone with a good standing in society – a doctor or a lawyer, not a cocky Welsh lad working in advertising.'

'Tell it how it is then, Bella.'

'I'm sorry. It's just this is what I dreaded, seeing you get hurt. Felix's job never bothered me; it's the fact he reminded me of Geoff that did. I hoped I'd be proved wrong.'

'You know, he wasn't that clever about hiding it. He had an affair with a woman he worked with and then used weekends working away as an excuse to go hook up with her. It's almost like he wanted me to find out.'

'What I don't understand,' Bella said, taking a sip of her

drink and smacking her lips together, 'and tell me to sod off it it's none of my business, is why he allowed you to go through all the trauma of fertility treatment if he was having an affair.'

'Of course I don't mind you asking, and it's something I've thought about a lot. The only thing I can put it down to is him wanting to keep his options open.'

'Having the best of both worlds, more like.'

'I met her, you know, the other woman, a few weeks ago. She happened to be my good friend's sister, which was the weirdest and most upsetting coincidence for both of us.'

'I hope you gave her a piece of your mind.'

'I did, but I wouldn't say it made me feel any better. I left her house realising her and Felix's actions have left behind two broken families, mine and hers, and my friend Pippa now has a strained relationship with her sister because she's friends with me. Felix isn't even with this woman, and I don't know if that's because she's pregnant with her husband's baby or if he never intended to be with her anyway. Not that I care. All I know is he's not in my life any more.'

'Sounds like she got herself into quite a mess,' Bella said, holding Connie's hands in her lap. 'But you know what? You'll get through this. You will do, I promise.'

'I know I will, it's just all so raw at the moment. I'm thirty-seven and less than a year ago I thought I'd have a family with Felix by now and be blissfully happy. Like we used to be.'

'Sometimes you don't really know the people you're closest to – they can surprise you in all sorts of ways. Unfortunately with Felix it wasn't in a good way.'

'I'm glad I'm not pregnant with the wrong man's baby but my heart still aches for a child.'

Bella squeezed Connie's hands and took a deep breath as if she was holding back tears. 'I know, sweetheart. I can imagine the pain of carrying a child and then losing it.' Bella took a deep breath before pulling Connie close. When she pulled away, she was smiling. 'Come back with me,' she said. 'Spend some time with me and get over all of this. You know there's no better tonic than being thousands of miles away in Tanzania.'

# *Georgie*

Georgie's due date of the 15th June was just under three weeks away and despite not wanting to deal with the reality of a newborn, she was longing not to be pregnant any longer. She became more and more uncomfortable, swollen and tired as the days passed by. Her mum checked in with her every day, either phoning or popping over to make her some food for dinner or simply to fuss about. Since Nathan had found a more permanent place to live, and once it got within a month of her due date, Georgie relented and temporarily let Daisy stay with him four days a week instead of just three.

By the evening, and despite her mum begging her to come and stay with them, Georgie was on her own with little more to do than be annoyed by Braxton Hicks or fall asleep in front of the TV. She had plenty of friends but either they had kids of their own and were mostly home in the evening or they wanted to go out. At gone thirty-seven weeks pregnant that was the last thing Georgie wanted to do. She missed Melinda, her one reliable friend who wasn't tied down by children but was old enough to prefer a quiet night in with chocolate and a DVD. Since Melinda had moved to Cardiff and left Goldman and Peabody, their relationship had turned into one on Facebook rather than real life.

Her mobile rang and Melinda's smiling image flashed up on the screen. Georgie thought about ignoring it, then moaned and dragged herself upright from where she'd slumped over a birthing ball.

'Hi,' she said, rubbing her bump as another Braxton Hick tightened across her belly.

'Hey, how are you, chick?'

'Oh, you know, fed up and wanting this goddam baby out.'

'How're you holding up with all the other stuff?'

Georgie realised this was the reason why she had faltered in answering the call, questions like that. Having to talk about the catastrophe that was her life put it firmly back to the forefront of her mind when all she wanted was to forget about the crap going on.

'My life is still a car crash, if that's what you're asking.' She shifted positions but couldn't get comfortable and figured a little foot was tucked beneath her rib. 'Nathan won't talk to me about anything other than Daisy. Daisy's been with him for the past four days and doesn't seem to miss me, and I'm due to give birth to another baby who I'm going to have to bring up as a single mum.'

'What about Felix?'

'What about him?'

'What's happening with him?'

'Surely you can get all the gossip from Jeremy.'

'Felix hasn't spoken to him for a while.'

Georgie snorted. 'Well, at least I'm not the only one he's not talking to. I've not heard from him in months, which speaks volumes considering I found out from Pippa the other day that his wife's filed for divorce.'

'Pippa's talking to you again?'

'Not exactly. I kinda begged her to let me know what was going on.'

'Maybe he needs time,' Melinda said. 'To come to terms with everything – you, the baby, his divorce…'

'Melinda, you know as well as I do that he wanted escapism and sex, not a divorce and a lover pregnant with her husband's baby. I'm hardly an enticing prospect at the moment.'

With the TV on mute, the house was deathly quiet once she'd said goodbye to Melinda. How ironic was it that when she had been with Nathan and Daisy she often longed to be on her own and treasured the rare moments she got to herself? Now she was alone, she loathed it. Not that she wanted to be with Nathan...

Her mind wandered back to the weekend the summer before that she'd spent alone with Felix in the cabin in Wales. For a couple of days everything had been perfect and so simple – nothing more complicated than her and Felix, their bodies and love. There had been love, she was certain of that.

A pain ripped through her lower stomach and back, shocking her from her thoughts. She gasped at the realisation that what she felt was no longer a Braxton Hick but the real thing. How had it started so quickly and early? Her heart thudded in her chest. It was really happening, the moment she'd been dreading. She'd been in labour with Daisy for over forty-eight hours and the pain she'd just felt was equal to forty hours in.

She stood up and paced up and down, remembering from last time that keeping moving had helped, but soon enough the pain forced her back down on all fours. She waited until the wave of pain eased then with shaky hands phoned her parents. No answer. Unable to focus on the screen, she waited until the next contraction finished and tried her mum's mobile. Still no answer. She phoned the delivery suite and the midwife told her to come in. Despite the coolness of the room, sweat trickled down her face and her heart raced. She opened up the contacts on her mobile and rang Pippa. She knew it would go to answerphone even before it did.

'Pippa, I wouldn't do this unless I had no other option but I can't get hold of Mum and Daa...' Her voice broke off as another contraction gripped her, taking her breath away and forcing her forwards, clinging on to the side of the sofa. She breathed hard, trying to work her way through the pain, cursing Pippa the whole time for ignoring her call – and she knew she was being ignored – and her parents for not being there when she needed them most. Why the hell hadn't they answered? Where the hell could they be?

Finally, she was able to speak again. 'Can you come. Take me to hospital. Please? If I don't hear from you soon, I'll call. A. Taxi.'

She put her mobile down and realised her face was wet with tears. Her mum was supposed to be her birthing partner but her sister used to be the one person who was always there for her. How had life ended up like this?

Another wave of pain took hold, making her gasp with shock at its intensity. She hadn't timed the space between contractions but she knew there'd barely been any time at all. Gripping a cushion, she screamed as the pain stepped up a notch. Wetness trickled down her legs as her waters broke. Her breath was short and sharp, and there was a heaviness so low down in her pelvis that she could barely calm the fear coursing through her body with the realisation that even if Pippa listened to her message, she'd get to her too late.

With an effort, Georgie picked her mobile back up and dialled 999.

'By all accounts you made quite a mess of your living room carpet.'

Georgie's eyes flickered open to see her sister smiling down at her. Pippa swept a stray lock of hair from out of Georgie's eyes and tucked it behind her ear.

'I did get your message,' Pippa continued, 'and I'm so sorry I didn't answer straight away. If I'd known it was all going to happen so fast...'

Georgie shuffled to a sitting position and glanced across the room to where her mum cradled her new granddaughter in her arms. 'It wouldn't have changed anything. You wouldn't have got there in time and she'd still have been born on the living room floor.'

'At least you had the sense to call the paramedics.'

'I didn't think a taxi was appropriate in the end.' Georgie managed a weak smile. 'How long have I been asleep for?'

'Only an hour.' Pippa looked over her shoulder. 'She's beautiful, you know. She's the spitting image of Daisy.'

Georgie gritted her teeth and nodded. That was the problem – no paternity test was needed. The baby had fair hair rather than a hint of Felix's dark locks, and as Daisy looked way more like Nathan than she did Georgie, there was no denying who the father was. A tiny part of Georgie had clung on to the hope that the baby would turn out to be Felix's rather than Nathan's. One look when the drama of her unplanned home birth was over and she was safely on her way to hospital with her newborn daughter in her arms and Georgie knew. She knew, and didn't have a clue how she was expected to love her.

# SECOND SUMMER

## *Pippa*

*29th August blog post:*

### Olivia

*However much you plan these things, in the end, when it comes to giving birth, the birth plan goes out the window. I wanted as natural a birth as possible, in the midwife-led unit with music playing and to have the baby in the birthing pool. In reality I was twelve days overdue, was induced, had a back to back baby, an epidural and ended up with a forceps delivery. Not the birth experience I was hoping for, but despite all of that, the outcome was a healthy baby – our much longed for daughter, Olivia Hazel Green.*

*I've never known a feeling like it, the rush of emotions – relief, love, sheer joy when our daughter was placed on my chest just seconds after taking her first breath. The room, the midwives, the doctors, everything seemed to peel away, leaving just me, Clive and our daughter. Our daughter. I'm not sure I'm ever going to get used to that idea. All I know is it was something that during our darkest times I never believed would become a reality. But there we go, sometimes miracles do happen.*

Pippa pressed save, closed her laptop and gazed into the Moses basket where her seven-day-old daughter was sleeping. Finally sleeping. Somehow, Sienna had made motherhood look easy in those first few weeks. Through exhaustion and tears, she and Clive had survived the first week with a baby who didn't sleep for more than ninety minutes at a time, who struggled to latch on when breastfeeding, who wasn't putting on weight and who they had to top up with bottles of both breast milk and formula. All Pippa had done since giving birth was feed, pump and feed again. But despite all of that, she relished every moment and spent every waking second studying her daughter, cradling her in her arms and kissing her perfectly smooth plump cheeks.

Pippa sat in the shade of the apple tree with Olivia lying next to her. She looked so peaceful and Pippa finally relaxed back into the wicker chair and closed her eyes for a moment. It was a perfect summer day in late August and she wanted to bottle this feeling of bliss after months and years of struggling through infertility and loss.

'Clive let me in.'

Pippa opened her eyes to see Sienna in a white vest top, yellow summer skirt and flip-flops, long tanned legs striding towards her with Jacob clamped to her hip and a changing bag slung over her shoulder.

'I brought ice cream,' she said, pulling two Magnums from the top of her bag and placing Jacob down on the picnic blanket at Pippa's feet with the bag behind him, propping him up. 'They might be a bit melted by now so eat it quick before that gorgeous little girl of yours wakes up.' Sienna kissed Pippa on the cheek and sat down in the wicker chair next to her. 'You were made for this, you know. You look amazing.'

'Even with bags under my eyes and greasy hair?'

'Seriously, for barely having slept all week, you look incredible. You do realise while she's sleeping you should be asleep too?'

'Your company will be a break enough.' Pippa unwrapped her Magnum, took a bite and felt cold ice cream run down her chin. She grabbed a baby wipe and cleaned her face.

'I use those damn things for everything,' Sienna said, handing Jacob a set of plastic toy keys. He shook them violently before letting out a gurgly laugh.

Clive poked his head around the kitchen door. 'Do you

want a drink?'

'A jug of Pimm's would be great, thanks,' Sienna said with a laugh. 'Whatever you've got that's cold, please.' She turned back to Pippa. 'You've got him well trained.'

'He's making a massive chilli so we can put some in the freezer. This is the first day since Olivia was born that we've felt able to do something other than change nappies, put washing on, feed her…'

'Domestic bliss.'

'And for you too.' Pippa leant down and kissed Jacob on the top of his head. He reached his hands up and grabbed her hair. 'He's so gorgeous.'

Sienna smiled. 'He looks just like Ashton.'

'Oh, I don't know, he's got your eyes and your lovely dark hair.'

'He's desperate to move,' Sienna said as Jacob toppled over on to his side. She picked him up and put him on her lap with her arms hugging his middle. Pippa could hardly believe that this was the Sienna she knew – the die-hard 'I'm never going to have kids' best friend who was the image of a yummy mummy right now. 'Then there's going to be trouble trying to contain him.'

Clive emerged into the sunshine with a tray of drinks and placed the jug and two glasses on the table between Pippa and Sienna.

'Not quite Pimm's, but a jug of lemonade instead,' he said.

'Ooh, posh cloudy stuff too.' Sienna smiled and poured. Olivia let out a wail from her Moses basket.

'Right on cue,' Pippa said.

'I'll take her.' Clive leant in and picked her up. Her little toes poked out from her bodysuit and she looked tiny snuggled against his chest.

'She probably needs feeding,' Pippa said, getting up to take her from him.

'I'll try her with the bottle of expressed milk in the fridge; you sit down and relax for a bit.'

'Do as you're told, Pip,' Sienna said with a wink. 'He'll be back out in a minute when he realises it's boob she wants.'

Without arguing, Pippa kissed Olivia's little foot, reached for her lemonade and sat back down.

'I have a bit of news,' Sienna said with a grin. 'You know the job on this new series *The Bloodstone Chronicles* that I lost out on because I was pregnant?'

Pippa nodded, and once Clive and Olivia had disappeared inside she focused her attention fully on Sienna.

'Well, everything's been delayed, and now the location manager they hired to replace me can't continue working on it because it clashes with him working on the next Bond movie. So they came to me.'

'But I don't understand. How are you going to do it with Jacob?'

'He's coming with me.' She bounced Jacob up and down on her lap. 'It's not a problem when filming's in the UK and when I go to Croatia he'll come too.'

'But what about Ashton? Surely he's not going to agree to this?'

'That's the best bit – he's coming too.'

'Seriously?'

'He's already handed his notice in. He's been working on his own project with a friend for the last few months and he's going to give that a go as he can work from anywhere and look after Jacob as much as he can.'

'That's amazing.'

'I think I should marry him really…'

Pippa laughed. 'I never thought I'd see the day when you were married with kids.'

'I am joking about the marriage thing – having a baby is a way big enough commitment for me.'

'Never say never.'

Sienna grunted and put Jacob back down on the blanket with a soft book to play with.

'You're a natural at it,' Pippa said.

'I do feel like I've lucked out with a very easy going baby,' Sienna replied. 'And Ashton has been incredible.'

'So you're seriously doing this? Taking on this job even if it means being on location and away from home for months at a time?'

'Yep, I'm doing it. Jacob's going to be one well-travelled little boy.'

Pippa took a sip of her lemonade. She always missed Sienna when she was working away but she was going to miss her even more now they both had babies.

'Oh, by the way, my friend Connie's popping over in a bit to say goodbye. It was the only time she could make as she's off to Tanzania in the morning.'

'Is she the one who lost her baby when your effing sister was shagging her husband?'

'That's Connie.'

'I should go then, really,' Sienna said, motioning towards Jacob.

'No don't. The last thing she needs is people avoiding her because they have a baby – I want her to feel involved. I know seeing me with Olivia and you with Jacob will be upsetting, but trust me as someone who knows, it'll be far more upsetting for her if she's simply not included.'

Connie arrived looking better than she had done in months. She wore a long white skirt with a jewelled low-slung belt about her waist and a peppermint green short-sleeved top. Her silver jewellery jangled on her wrists as she walked towards them and it was a proper smile she gave Pippa as she reached down to hug her and stroke Olivia's cheek while she was feeding.

'I'm so happy for you,' Connie said, giving Pippa another hug.

'This is my best friend, Sienna.'

'Hey there,' Sienna said, standing up and giving Connie a hug. 'I've heard lots about you.'

'I've heard lots about you too.'

'I bet you have and probably not all good.' Sienna reached down and plucked Jacob from the picnic blanket. 'This monkey is Jacob.'

'How old?'

'Nearly five months. Do you want a cuddle with him?'

'Oh, I, um…'

'Don't worry, he only bites occasionally,' Sienna said and laughed. She put Jacob into Connie's arms and he rested his head against her.

'He's too cute,' Connie said, sitting down opposite them. 'They both are.' She looked across to Pippa and Olivia.

'I'm so glad you made it to see us before going away.'

'Hey, I wouldn't have missed meeting her for the world.'

'Pippa said you're off to Tanzania?' Sienna asked.

'Yes, for the rest of the year. My aunt lives out there, has her own holiday-property empire, and she's been going on for years about me going back out to visit her but there's never been the chance. I stayed with her for a couple of summers while I was at uni and worked for her, which was pretty cool, but since then real life has got in the way.'

'I can't tell you how jealous I am of you,' Sienna said.

'Sienna's got itchy feet.' Pippa gently adjusted her hold on Olivia until she started sucking again then turned to Sienna. 'Although I don't know what you're complaining about seeing as you're going to be working in Croatia soon.'

'Ah, Tanzania is exotic and I've never been there. That's good enough for me.' Sienna stood up. 'Right, Jacob, little monkey boy, we'd better get home.' She took Jacob from Connie and leant down to kiss Pippa on the cheek. 'See you soon, and good to meet you, Connie. Have a blast in Tanzania. I'll see myself out.'

Pippa watched her best friend until she disappeared inside, shuddering at the thought of how close they'd come to losing their friendship.

'She was the one who didn't want kids?' Connie asked.

'Tell me about it. She seems like she was born to be a

mum, doesn't she?' Olivia finished feeding. Pippa covered herself up and dabbed Olivia's mouth clean with the muslin before popping her on her shoulder and patting her back. 'She's good at everything she puts her mind to but I had no idea she'd take to motherhood as easily as she has.'

'And how are you doing?'

'Tired and sore but she's worth it. How about you?'

'I'm good, I think. I've felt better since filing for divorce. The apartment's been sold so I have no more ties to Felix. I've got money in the bank and I feel like that part of my life is done and dusted. It's not the position I wanted to be in at my age but it's the hand I've been dealt so I'm running with it.'

'Do you want to hold her?' When Connie nodded, Pippa stood up and carefully transferred Olivia from her shoulder to Connie's, tucking the muslin cloth beneath Olivia's mouth. Connie rocked Olivia back and forwards and kissed her on the top of her head.

'It would have been my due date in four days' time,' Connie said, adjusting Olivia on her shoulder and gently rubbing her back. She wiped away a tear. 'The 2nd September.'

'Oh, Connie,' Pippa said, feeling her own tears welling up. 'I'm so sorry.'

'Thank you, but it's okay, I'll get through it. I'm going to be in Tanzania with my aunt, having a fresh start and making the most of life. There are worse places to be in the world. Sunshine, the beach, the ocean and a divorce – that's what I'm looking forward to. Seriously, my aunt's thrown me a lifeline. I don't know how I would have continued here. There are possibilities in Tanzania and for the first time in months I actually feel positive about something.'

'Good, I'm so glad.'

'She had the baby?'

It took Pippa a moment to realise that Connie was talking about Georgie.

'Yes, a girl, at the end of May in a dramatic "need to call the ambulance" style.'

'The baby was okay?'

Pippa nodded. 'Yes, she was fine.' She fiddled with the edge of her skirt and looked at Connie holding her daughter. Life really was cruel to take away a baby Connie wanted so badly and give one to Pippa's sister who would have done anything not to get pregnant. 'The baby's definitely not Felix's. She's the spitting image of Georgie's husband.'

'You know what? I don't care, and I don't think I'd have cared if it had turned out to be his anyway. He keeps trying to tell me that he's sorry, that he loves me, but I don't love him any more. I went through too much heartache while he was off having fun to even begin to forgive him for that. I'm hoping Tanzania will be the physical and emotional distance I need from him.'

Connie left Pippa with tears and a hug and a promise to stay in touch. It was time again for Olivia to feed, so with Clive topping up Pippa's drink and stopping for a quick cuddle with his daughter, Pippa settled back into the wicker chair and helped Olivia to latch on before opening up her laptop and finishing writing her blog post.

*I called this blog The Hopeful Years because that is what these last few years have been – hopeful, while all the time waiting and praying that my dream of having a family would come true. Since writing my first blog post eighteen months ago I've had three rounds of IVF, seven operations and procedures, two miscarriages, made a friend, nearly lost a friend, become an auntie again, a godmother and finally, against all the odds, a mummy. This is what our journey has been all about. Now I can't wait to find out what the next eighteen months will bring.*

Pippa looked up into the leaves of the apple tree where the sunshine glinted and played as the branches moved in the gentle breeze. The past was buried in the soil below the tree. All the hurt, anger, frustration, sadness and bitterness of the last couple of years had been put to rest. Hope had prevailed. She leant forwards and kissed her daughter's head and let her tears drip on to her bare knees and down to the dry earth below.

# ACKNOWLEDGEMENTS

I could never have written this book if my husband and I hadn't undergone four cycles of ICSI at the Bristol Centre for Reproductive Medicine (BCRM). Fertility treatment is a lottery, and along with the skill and expertise of the fertility centre staff, an awful lot of luck is involved. We were one of the lucky ones, but that was after the heartache of three failed cycles. Cycle number four resulted in the birth of our wonderful baby boy, Leo.

I thought about turning my experience of fertility treatment into a memoir, but it felt far too personal to share publicly. Then Pippa popped into my head, followed swiftly by Connie, Georgie and Sienna, and the idea that so many women struggle with both sides of the coin – those longing to have a baby and those who are desperate to not get pregnant. The emotions within *Beneath the Apple Blossom* come from my experience of undergoing fertility treatment – the procedures, the scans and the dreaded two-week wait are true to life, it's just the characters and the situations they find themselves in are fictional.

A lot of people helped me to write this book. My heartfelt thanks go to all the wonderful doctors, nurses, embryologists and front desk staff who work at BCRM for their skill, patience, experience and understanding, for making such a difficult time in our lives manageable and for giving us our much longed for little boy. My acupuncturist Charlotte Brydon-Smith kept me calm and positive, which I have no doubt helped us to eventually gain a positive outcome. My thanks and thoughts go to the brave and supportive women I met online via the fertility centre forum. Not everyone gets lucky. My husband Nik shared the despair and the hope of fertility treatment, and was my rock throughout. My parents supported us in every way they could and I'm beyond happy they were able to share in our delight when Leo was born. My friend Sam was as good a friend as I could have hoped for during a very dark time. Thank you all.

Once *Beneath the Apple Blossom* was written, a lot of people helped see it through to publication. Many thanks go to my honest, insightful and fabulous beta readers: Judith van Dijkhuizen, Donna Witchard and Akeisha from Til' the Last Page Book Blog, along with editor, Helen Baggott, who did an important early edit of the book and gave some great advice. My book editor and proof reader, Alison Jack, did a thorough job and enabled me to put the finishing touches to the manuscript. My talented book designer, Jessica Bell, produced a beautiful cover that outdid my own ideas and expectations. My brother, printmaker and illustrator, Tom Frost, did a cracking job coming up with the logo for Lemon Tree Press.

Lastly, thank you so much Nik for continuing to believe in me. And to Leo, for hanging on in there despite the odds.

# FROM THE AUTHOR

Thank you for taking the time to read *Beneath the Apple Blossom*. If you enjoyed this book, please join my mailing list to be the first to find out about my future book releases. To sign up simply go to www.kate-frost.co.uk, click on 'Fiction Newsletter' and enter your email address. Subscribers not only receive a freebie on sign up, but occasional news about new books and special offers.

If you liked *Beneath the Apple Blossom* please consider leaving a review on Amazon and/or Goodreads, or recommending it to friends. It will be much appreciated! Reader reviews are essential for authors to gain visibility and entice new readers.

You can find out more about me and my writing at www.kate-frost.co.uk, or follow me on Twitter @Kactus77, or on Facebook at www.facebook.com/katefrostauthor.

Lightning Source UK Ltd.
Milton Keynes UK
UKOW01f0449211016

285815UK00002B/1/P